The Politics of the Nazi Past in Germany and Austria

This book argues that Germans and Austrians have dealt with the Nazi past very differently and that these differences have had important consequences for political culture and partisan politics in the two countries. Drawing on different literatures in political science, David Art builds a framework for understanding how public deliberation transforms the political environment in which it occurs. The book analyzes how public debates about the "lessons of history" created a culture of contrition in Germany that prevented a resurgent far right from consolidating itself in German politics after unification. By contrast, public debates in Austria nourished a culture of victimization that provided a hospitable environment for the rise of right-wing populism. The argument is supported by evidence from nearly 200 semistructured interviews and an analysis of the German and Austrian print media over a twenty-year period.

David Art is an assistant professor of political science at the College of the Holy Cross. He teaches courses in European politics, international relations, and globalization. He received his B.A. from Yale University and his Ph.D. from the Massachusetts Institute of Technology. His current research focuses on the development of right-wing populist parties in comparative and historical perspective.

T0381838

The Politics of the Nazi Past in Germany and Austria

DAVID ART

College of the Holy Cross

CAMBRIDGE
UNIVERSITY PRESS

CAMBRIDGE
UNIVERSITY PRESS

32 Avenue of the Americas, New York NY 10013-2473, USA

Cambridge University Press is part of the University of Cambridge.

It furthers the University's mission by disseminating knowledge in the pursuit of education, learning and research at the highest international levels of excellence.

www.cambridge.org
Information on this title: www.cambridge.org/9780521673242

First published 2006

A catalogue record for this publication is available from the British Library

Library of Congress Cataloguing in Publication data

Art, David, 1972–
The politics of the Nazi past in Germany and Austria / David Art.
   p.   cm.
Includes bibliographical references and index.
ISBN 0-521-85683-3 (hardback) – ISBN 0-521-67324-0 (pbk.)
1. Germany – Politics and government.   2. Austria – Politics and government.
3. Political culture – Germany.   4. Political culture – Austria.
5. National socialism – Germany.   6. National socialism – Austria.   I. Title.
JN3971.A58A78   2006
306.2′0943′09051–dc22   2005008713

ISBN 978-0-521-85683-6 Hardback
ISBN 978-0-521-67324-2 Paperback

For Julija

Contents

Preface and Acknowledgments

This book analyzes the influence of the Nazi past on postwar German and Austrian politics. Given the omnipresence of that past in both societies, and given the tomes that have already been written on the subject of historical memory in Germany in particular, this was from the start an audacious enterprise. My interviewees often told me as much, and many friends feared that nothing really new could be written about the subject. Yet from the early stages of my research, I became convinced that the connections between ideas about the Nazi past, political culture, and partisan competition in the two societies had barely been uncovered. Sometimes it is the influence of the 800-pound gorilla in the room that is most difficult to measure. When the gorilla takes the form of an idea, rather than a structural or institutional force, elucidating and measuring its effects become even more difficult. Yet, ideas clearly matter in politics. Shying away from phenomena as significant as interpretations of the rise of Nazism and the Final Solution in the successor societies of the Third Reich was no longer an option once my inquiry began, attractive as it seemed at times.

I never intended to write about public deliberation and debates, much less offer a framework for analyzing the ways in which they can transform politics. Yet, the deeper I delved into ideas about the Nazi past, the clearer it became that the engine of ideational change was elite-led public debates. These public debates occurred in a discontinuous fashion and produced enduring legacies that shaped not only future debates about the Nazi past, but also the political environment more generally. I found intellectual sustenance for this observation from diverse fields in political science, borrowing liberally from studies of issue evolution, media effects, public opinion, deliberative democracy, and historical institutionalism. My hope is that students and scholars working in these fields, whether or not they are intrinsically interested in the Nazi past, may find the approach I have taken useful.

One of my central arguments is that debates about the Nazi past have created very different environments for right-wing political parties and movements in Germany and Austria. I thus offer a political-cultural explanation for the divergent success of the postwar far right in Germany and Austria, one that challenges several of the prevailing theories in the literature. Although I admittedly do not test the hypothesis in this book, I believe that the long-term development of right-wing populist parties is critically influenced by the reaction of political parties, the media, and civil society to them. Despite several recent setbacks in some states (including Austria), their power and influence continue to grow in others. The rise of right-wing populist parties has clearly been one of the most dramatic changes in European politics over the past several decades, and uncovering the elements that help or hinder their development is an important area of research, particularly as European integration, immigration, and globalization raise the types of issues around which the far right appears positioned to mobilize.

It is a pleasure finally to be able to thank all the individuals and organizations that have contributed to this book. Fellowships from the German Academic Exchange Service (DAAD) and from the Program for the Study of Germany at the Minda de Gunzburg Center for European Studies at Harvard University supported two years of field research in Austria and Germany. A grant from the Center of International Studies at MIT allowed me to devote a summer to writing. Professor Karl Kaiser offered institutional support at the German Council on Foreign Relations in Berlin, where Heike Zanzig and Rüdiger Witke were of invaluable help. Gesine Schwann allowed me to participate in conferences at the European University Viadrina and helped me to extend my stay in Germany. In Austria, Anton Pelinka, Ruth Wodak, Heidemarie Uhl, and Walter Manoscheck taught me to navigate the Austrian political scene and provided much hospitality. Nearly two hundred people graciously agreed to be interviewed for this book, and I thank each and every one of them.

Many friends and colleagues commented on this project at various stages. For their helpful suggestions and moral support, I would like to thank Marcos Ancelovici, Steve Ansolabehere, Tim Bale, Adam Berinsky, Dan Carter, Elisabeth Carter, Josh Cohen, Doug Fuller, Kelly Greenhill,

Roger Haydon, Ruud Koopmans, Chappel Lawson, Sarah Lischer, Marc Howard, Dan Metz, Gero Neugebauer, Jessica Piombo, Jeremy Pressman, Jens Rydgren, Steve Van Evera, and Cory Welt. Special thanks go to Danny Breznitz, Dana Brown, Brian Crawford, Sara Jane McCaffrey, Chris Wendt, Amos Zehavi, and Adam Ziegfeld for going far beyond the call of duty and commenting on multiple drafts of this manuscript, and for putting up with me over the years. I thank Lew Bateman at Cambridge for shepherding me through the publication process and the two anonymous reviewers whose helpful suggestions I have done my best to incorporate. I thank the journal *German Politics and Society* for allowing me to reprint materials that first appeared in "The Wild, Wild East," *GP&S* (Winter 2004).

I owe substantial intellectual debts to scholars I studied with at Yale and MIT. Fascinating courses with Alex Wendt and Juan Linz spurred me to apply to graduate school in political science. My dissertation committee at MIT provided more guidance and support than I had any right to expect. Melissa Nobles gave me copious and insightful comments on more drafts than I would care to admit, and discussions with her often prevented me from going astray. Richard Samuels came on board to give this project a burst of enthusiasm and helpful criticism on the structure of the argument. I "recruited" Andrei Markovits from the University of Michigan for the dissertation that led to this book, and his deep knowledge of German and Austrian politics was a critical resource. His warmth, wit, and wisdom at crucial stages of this project were more important than he knows.

My greatest intellectual debt is to Suzanne Berger. It was she who made me enthusiastic about comparative politics in the first place, and her intellectual influence appears in multiple forms throughout this book. Suzanne's inimitable combination of unwavering support and razor-sharp criticism helped me grow as a scholar, and I thank her for all the guidance she has given me over the years.

Families are normally thanked last in books of this sort, not because they are an afterthought but rather because their contributions are often so fundamental to the success of the project and the emotional well-being of the author. Mine is no different and, given its academic bent, has contributed more directly than most to my own intellectual development. My father has set a standard in scholarship and professionalism in the field of international relations that I can aspire to. I can only dream of being as prolific and widely read as my mother, Suzanne, who writes history, or my sister Robyn, who writes poetry. I am grateful to have been raised in a family where learning is a way of life. I am also blessed to have found a new family in Austria that shares similar values and makes fieldwork there a joy.

Finally, no one deserves more thanks than my wife, Julija. She claims to know little about political science, but I turn to her more often than anyone else for ideas, advice, and encouragement. Without her, this book would never have been written and I would not be so happy. I dedicate this work to her as a small token of my gratitude.

The Politics of the Nazi Past in Germany and Austria

I

Introduction

Public deliberation and debate are central to both our normative conceptions and everyday observations about liberal democracies. Politicians,
journalists, scholars, and ordinary citizens in the United States often refer
to the public debate about health care, or gay marriage, or Iraq, or some
other issue of national importance. Concerned individuals also often call
for a public debate about a topic that has either been ignored or considered unproblematic. In some cases, they might have a specific setting in
mind: the floor of the Senate, a town meeting, or perhaps a radio talk
show. But in general, what people mean by a public debate, I suspect,
is something like a national discussion extending beyond any particular
institution or building. Public debates, in this intuitive definition, involve
political elites discussing and contesting basic issues, the media reporting
these fights and taking sides, and the general public coming to regard the
topic of debate as an important national issue.

This book builds on this intuition by analyzing what public debates
are, whom they involve, and why they matter. My central claims are
that public debates produce new ideas, shift the weight of elite opinion,
and change the language elites use to discuss certain political issues. For
analytical clarity, I conceive of this process as a three-step sequence:

- *Step One*: Public debates create and consolidate "frames," which I
  define as an ordered set of messages concerning some aspect of the
  political world. These frames influence political behavior and can also
  become enduring elements of political culture.
- *Step Two*: Public debates produce shifts in elite opinion. They can bring
  the beliefs of political actors closer together or push them further apart.

Although these outcomes are difficult to predict, they matter for future political conflicts and for the formation of mass attitudes.

- *Step Three*: Public debates shift the boundaries of legitimate discursive space in the larger body politic in one of three ways. First, they can create something akin to "political correctness," which defines the realm of acceptable terms and sanctions for those who violate them. Second, public debates can introduce previously taboo subjects into political discourse and extend the limits of acceptable political space. Third, debates can create new "code words" for old ideas. The result of any of these processes is a change in the language that elites, and later ordinary citizens, use to discuss political issues. Changes in discursive space reflect broader ideological shifts in politics and society.

Political elites are the central participants in public debates.[1] I draw upon research in public opinion that explains how elite discourse, and shifts in elite discourse, change mass attitudes.[2] This does not mean, however, that any particular individual, or group of individuals, can manipulate mass attitudes as they wish. Although politicians often spark public debates and hope to profit from them, deliberation often produces outcomes that elites neither intended nor desired. Although mine is largely a top-down version of ideational change, I do argue that public debates can open windows of opportunity for civic activists (still elites, in my definition) to increase their political salience and mobilize portions of civil society. Drawing on work in political communication, I also analyze how the media disseminate and modify elite messages while also injecting their own views into public debates.

My argument is about discontinuous and elite-led political change. It offers a different take on the process of ideational transformation from several existing views in political science. Rather than conceiving of ideas as shifting slowly and gradually, the result of large-scale social processes such as modernization, democratization, or generational change, it focuses on those moments when ideas change rapidly and dramatically. Instead of viewing ideas as preconceived entities waiting for some

---

[1] Following Robert Putnam's definition, I define elites as "those who in any society rank toward the top of the (presumably closely intercorrelated) dimensions of interest, involvement, and influence in politics." Putnam, "Studying Elite Political Culture," *American Political Science Review* 65, no. 3 (September 1971), 651.

[2] John Zaller, *The Nature and Origins of Mass Opinion* (New York: Cambridge University Press, 1992).

powerful carrier to make them salient, I analyze how ideas are created and changed through political battles. Although strategic calculations play a role in this process, deliberation and argument do much of the work. I do not contend that the better argument carries the day; indeed, sometimes ideas that many people find repugnant emerge and attain a broad following during public debates. In other cases, public debates do change the political-moral foundations of political communities in ways that correspond to common conceptions of progress. In either case, public debates set in motion a series of processes that reshape the political environment in which they occur.

There are a limited number of issues that can spark such transformations. Technical policy questions, or other topics that require specialized knowledge, known in the American politics literature as "hard issues," cannot muster the broad participation required for the types of national discussions I have in mind. The universe of cases for public debates is thus restricted to those over foundational issues, such as race, abortion, gender, war, and the like. These issues are often described as "easy," not because they are always pleasant to think about or conceptually simple, but rather because one does not require an extensive background to form opinions about them. Such gut issues have real consequences for the basic ideas and values that guide political communities.[3] The meanings of historical events, particularly traumatic historical events, are such foundational issues.

Debating the Lessons of History

Over the past several decades, "coming to terms with the past" has become a global phenomenon. In advanced industrial societies, the victims of past atrocities have demanded material and symbolic redress from the state. In third-wave democracies, transitions from communism and authoritarianism have involved reckoning with the crimes of the previous regime. In states emerging from ethnic conflict, political elites have established truth commissions to create a public record of atrocities and give victims a forum to tell their stories. International organizations have recently begun to assist developing countries in dealing with their pasts and to identify this reckoning with history as a human rights concern.

---

[3] On hard and easy issues, see Edward G. Carmines and James A. Stimson, "The Two Faces of Issue Voting," *The American Political Science Review* 74, no. 1 (March 1980), 80.

The "politics of the past" has captured the attention of academics and intellectuals. Some view coming to terms with the past simply as a moral imperative, but many others claim that dealing with the past goes beyond settling moral accounts. Carl Nino, for example, argued that deliberation about past atrocities fosters democratic attitudes among citizens in a state transitioning from authoritarian rule.[4] Others view the reconciling of clashing historical narratives as a method of healing rifts in societies plagued by ethnic conflict or of mending fences between adversarial states.[5] Confronting history has also been linked to the deepening of democracy in advanced industrialized countries.[6] There is, in other words, a strong presumption that the way in which a state confronts the past has profound implications for its long-term political development.

This claim, however, rests on scant empirical evidence. Political scientists have only begun to explore how coming to terms with the past matters for later political outcomes.[7] There is currently no vocabulary for analyzing the process of confronting the past, no set of theories or hypotheses to guide inquiry into it, no research program organized around it. As a consequence, we need to ask a number of first-order questions about how ideas about the past, specifically a shameful past, shape the political present. What are the political stakes of coming to terms with the past? Who are the relevant actors in this process? How might such an analysis contribute to enduring concerns for political scientists and for scholars of comparative politics in particular?

I recast coming to terms with the past as a series of punctuated elite-led debates over the lessons of history. Historical interpretations matter because they contain normative and causal claims about politics in general. Political elites try to use the past by framing historical events in ways that justify both their immediate political aims and their worldviews, but history – especially a history burdened by massive violations of human rights – is an unwieldy tool because it invites multiple interpretations. Even in the prototypical case of "radical evil" – the Holocaust – the

---

[4] Carl Nino, *Radical Evil on Trial* (New Haven: Yale University Press, 1998).

[5] See, for example, Stephen Van Evera, "Primed for Peace: Europe After the Cold War," in *The Cold War and After: Prospects for Peace*, eds. Sean M. Lynn-Jones and Steven E. Miller (Cambridge: MIT Press, 1994), 209–211.

[6] W. James Booth, "Communities of Memory: On Identity, Memory, and Debt," *The American Political Science Review* 93, no. 2 (June 1999): 249–263.

[7] Two examples are Nancy Bermeo, "Democracy and the Lessons of Dictatorship," *Comparative Politics* 24, no. 1 (April 1992): 273–291; Samuel P. Huntington, *The Third Wave* (Norman: University of Oklahoma Press, 1991).

"lessons of history" are far from self-evident. Indeed, they are wide open to ideational contestation among political elites seeking a foundation for their policies and ideologies.

The Nazi past is ubiquitous in contemporary German and Austrian politics.[8] Far from fading into history, public debates about the Nazi past have only increased in frequency and intensity. What the legacy of the Holocaust means for politics in the present and future is a question that continues to preoccupy political elites in both states. It is also one that Germans and Austrians have answered very differently over the past two decades, and these differences have had important consequences for political culture and partisan politics.

One consequence is particularly striking: the extent to which right-wing populist parties have established themselves in Austria and Germany over the past two decades. The rise of the far right is, of course, a pan-European phenomenon, and as recent developments in countries like Denmark and Belgium show, a strong indigenous Nazi or fascist movement is not a historical prerequisite for developing a successful right-wing populist party half a century later. But what is nonetheless remarkable about the German and Austrian cases is how divergent the development of the far right in the two surviving successor societies of the Third Reich has been. In terms of the far right's electoral success and integration into the political establishment, Austria and Germany represent opposite ends of the continuum in Western Europe, as Table 1.1 demonstrates.

This divergence is puzzling for many reasons. Germany possessed several of the underlying conditions – such as persistently high unemployment, massive immigration, and popular discontent with the European Union – that right-wing populist parties successfully exploited elsewhere in Western Europe. *Eurobarometer* surveys also regularly show that negative attitudes toward immigration are more widespread in Germany than in practically every other European country. Sixteen straight years of Christian Democratic (CDU) rule (1982–1998), coupled with the massive financial scandal that accompanied the party's fall from power, also would have seemed to augur well for the development of a political party to the right of the Union (the political coalition between the CDU and its Bavarian sister party, the Christian Socialists [CSU]). For these and other reasons, German specialists predicted in the early 1990s that the

---

[8] "Germany" refers here to the Federal Republic of Germany (West Germany) until 1990 and unified Germany thereafter. The German Democratic Republic (GDR), the former East Germany, is not the focus of this book.

TABLE I.I. *The Far Right in Western Europe*

Country	Average Far-Right Vote in National Elections: 1986–2002
Austria	18.0
Switzerland	15.0
Italy	12.4
Norway	12.3
France	11.8
Denmark	8.2
Belgium	7.5
Portugal	7.0
Netherlands	4.6
Sweden	3.0
Germany	1.4
Luxembourg	0.8
United Kingdom	0.2
Greece	0.1

far-right Republikaner Party (REP) would become a permanent presence in the German party system. Why this party failed to do so, and why the far right more generally has failed politically in Germany, is an important and underexplored question.

The success of the Austrian Freedom Party (FPÖ) is also surprising given Austria's strong economic performance over the past two decades. The party engineered its electoral breakthrough in 1986, when the unemployment rate was 3.1 percent, and continued to gain strength over the next thirteen years, when Austria had a lower annual average unemployment rate than any other Western European country except Luxembourg and Switzerland. When the FPÖ won 26.9 percent of the vote in the 1999 national parliamentary elections, the unemployment rate was only 3.9 percent (compared with 8.4 percent in Germany). While immigration was high in Austria, it was slightly less than in Germany and fell off dramatically after 1993. Compared with most other Western European states over the 1980s and 1990s, Austria does appear to have preserved its status as the "island of the blessed," as former Prime Minister Bruno Kreisky once described it. That the FPÖ could do so well under such conditions, and enter a national government with the Austrian People's Party (ÖVP) in 2000, to the consternation of the international community, is remarkable. Whether or not the FPÖ recovers from its electoral implosion in 2002, and whether or not Jörg Haider's newly formed Alliance for Austria's Future (BZÖ) gets off the ground, the populist right has succeeded in radically altering the Austrian party system and will most likely remain an important political force.

To account for the divergent success of the far right in Germany and Austria, I explore the main conventional hypotheses about right-wing populism in advanced industrial societies. Some scholars claim that a postmaterial transformation has led to the rise of right-wing populist parties, and that the variance in their strength depends on their ability to offer a "winning combination" of neoliberalism and xenophobia to a shifting voter base.[9] The German and Austrian cases, I argue, provide only limited support for this theory. The two cases also do not confirm a second group of explanations that focus on immigration and unemployment as the key independent variables. Nor do explanations that focus solely, or mainly, on differences in electoral institutions, such as electoral formulas and district magnitude, provide much analytical leverage. I find some evidence for the hypothesis that established political parties decrease support for right-wing populism by adopting xenophobic discourse and strict policies on immigration. Such cooptation was one factor in the demise of the REPs in Germany. Yet the Austrian case, as well as other cases in Western Europe, suggests that cooptation can also backfire by legitimating right-wing populist parties and increasing their electoral strength.

Using the German and Austrian cases for theory construction, I develop an alternative explanation for the variation in the far right's success. Although postmaterialism, immigration, and European integration have created a host of pressures that favor the far right, these forces in themselves do not translate into electoral success. Like the cooptation hypothesis, I see a large role for other political parties in influencing the fate of right-wing populist parties, but cooptation is not the only possible strategy.

Existing political parties can choose to cooperate with, or try to "tame," the far right and integrate it into the party system. This process often begins at the municipal and state levels, and can result in the formation of coalition governments that include right-wing populist parties at the national level. Although participation in government weakens right-wing populist parties in the short run by eliminating their protest votes, I suggest that cooperation and integration strategies ultimately strengthen them.

---

[9] Herbert Kitschelt, in collaboration with Anthony J. McGann, *The Radical Right in Western Europe* (Ann Arbor: University of Michigan Press, 1995). See also Hans-Georg Betz, *Radical Right-Wing Populism in Western Europe* (New York: St. Martin's Press, 1994).

On the other hand, political parties can choose to combat right-wing populist challengers. The most effective strategy for doing so appears to be a combination of cooptation, confrontation, and marginalization. Established political parties seize on the themes of right-wing populist parties (cooptation) while simultaneously denouncing them as enemies of the system (confrontation) and refusing to cooperate with them, or even speak with them, at any political level (marginalization). By pursuing this strategy, political parties are sometimes forced into unpopular alliances with other parties to avoid cooperation with the far right. In some cases, parties have given up power rather than rely on the support of right-wing populist parties. By denying the far right any hope of participating in coalitions or passing its own legislation, the combat strategy ultimately undermines its electoral appeal.

For the combat strategy to be effective, it must be supported by the national media and by civil society. When the media universally denounce right-wing populist parties and launch campaigns against them, some contumacious voters might be attracted to the far right, but the net result is to weaken public support for it. When members of civil society protest against and stigmatize right-wing populist parties, they create a host of organizational and recruitment problems for such parties. When parts of the national media and civil society are either quiescent or actively supportive of right-wing populist parties, however, this can allow them to overcome their marginalization and attract a wider following.

In short, this book departs from previous studies of right-wing populist parties, and from much of the literature on political parties in general, by focusing on the broader political-cultural environment in which they operate. The emphasis is on the long-term trajectory of parties rather than on the results of any particular election, although I do maintain that the initial reactions of political parties, the media, and groups in civil society to the far right critically influence the latter's development and position in the party system. In this sense, I view party development as path dependent.[10]

How do political parties, the media, and civil society choose between combating and taming right-wing populism? Although strategic considerations can be important for political parties, I argue that reactions to the far right are basically structured by ideas about the legitimacy of right-wing populist movements and perceptions of the threat they pose to the

---

[10] On the path dependence of political parties, see Angelo Panebianco, *Political Parties: Organisation and Power* (Cambridge: Cambridge University Press, 1988).

quality of democracy. These ideas and perceptions, I hypothesize, vary across time and space. In the case of postwar Europe, the fascist era of the interwar years is an important point of reference for contemporary views about the far right.[11]

As noted previously, Germany and Austria have confronted the Nazi past in radically different ways. This was not always the case. In the early postwar period, elites in both states held remarkably similar ideas about the relevance of the Nazi past for contemporary politics. Both saw Nazism as a historical aberration in their nation's histories. Both viewed their own populations as the primary victims of Nazism. Both made only fleeting and vague references to the Holocaust. The political integration of former Nazis proceeded rapidly in both countries, and those who called for critical examinations of the recent past were either isolated or came from the margins of politics and society. Although the extraparliamentary protest movement in Germany challenged this wall of silence in the 1960s, it was only in the 1980s that the Nazi past became a serious political issue in Germany. In Austria, there was no challenge to the idea that Austria was "Hitler's first victim" until the presidential candidacy of Kurt Waldheim evolved into a debate about his, and by extension Austria's, Nazi past. In both states, public debates about the past in the 1980s produced new frames, reshaped elite opinion, and created new discourses about the Nazi era. As we shall see, however, these debates produced radically different outcomes.

This book represents an exercise in theory construction. My arguments about both public debates and the development of right-wing populist parties were arrived at inductively during more than two years of fieldwork in the two countries. I present my theories in abstract, generalizable term so that they may be used, or contested, by scholars working in other areas. I make no claim to have tested them here. For scholars less concerned with social science methodology and more interested in my substantive findings, the theoretical architecture helps to structure what would otherwise be an intricate, unwieldy narrative.

---

[11] It is important to note that I do not view these parties as neofascist, nor do I argue that they share programmatic affinities with National Socialism. Like other far-right parties in Western Europe, such as the National Front in France, the Progress Parties in Denmark and Norway, and the Northern League in Italy, these parties are normally classified as right-wing populist parties. For a further discussion of the differences between neofascist and right-wing populist parties, see Cas Mudde, "The War of Words: Defining the Extreme Right Party Family," *West European Politics* 19, no. 2 (1996): 225–248.

Plan of the Book

Chapter 2 develops a framework for analyzing public debates in advanced industrial societies. I take issue with the concept of "historical memory," and argue that interpretations of historical atrocities contain both normative and causal claims about politics in general. Drawing from work on deliberative democracy, elite discourse, public opinion, media effects, and the policy-making process, I build a theory of public debates as critical junctures in the process of ideational change. I outline the three-step sequence noted previously in greater depth, and finally, I turn to issues of research design and methodology.

Chapter 3 applies my theoretical framework to public debates about the Nazi past in Germany. After sketching the development of elite ideas about Nazism over the first four postwar decades, I analyze the public debate – in fact, a series of public debates – that consumed German politicians, the media, and intellectuals in the mid-1980s. This debate produced two distinct frames linking the Nazi past to contemporary politics. The "normalization" frame, championed by the right, demanded that the Nazi past be allowed to "pass away" in order to allow Germans to develop a healthy national identity. The "contrition" frame, developed and disseminated by the left, countered that memory of, and atonement for, the Nazi past must remain a permanent political duty for all Germans. The only legitimate basis for national identity, in this view, is identification with Germany's democratic institutions and values or "constitutional patriotism." During the second stage of these public debates, the weight of elite opinion converged around the contrition frame and pushed the normalization frame from the political mainstream. The third step was the institutionalization of discursive norms, which I refer to as "political correctness, German style," that demarcate the limits of acceptable interpretations of the Nazi period and sanction those who violate them.

Chapter 4 focuses on Austria and the 1986 debate over Kurt Waldheim. The Austrian right created and disseminated what I term the "new victim" frame, which identified Austria as the victim of international forces seeking to denigrate its history and called on patriotic Austrians to resist this foreign interference. A small group of artists, intellectuals, and left-wing politicians challenged this view and seized upon a version of the German contrition frame. While German elites converged around the contrition discourse, elites in Austria polarized on the issue of the Nazi past. The right used the new victim frame to stoke nationalist sentiment; the left adopted the contrition frame, and began to criticize conservatives for downplaying and trivializing Austria's Nazi past. In Austria, then, the Nazi past became a salient political issue and the subject of many future political battles. Discursive norms were not created, as they were in Germany; instead, the right developed a set of code words that primed anti-Semitic stereotypes and introduced nationalist-chauvinist language into mainstream political discourse.

Chapter 5 shifts back to Germany and explains the failure of the far right to become a permanent force in German politics. Surveying existing explanations for the success and failure of right-wing populist parties, I find that none of them offer an adequate interpretation of the German case. Instead, by utilizing the combat hypothesis sketched previously, I show how it provides the most compelling explanation for why the Republicans, as well as several other far-right movements, failed to consolidate themselves in German politics. Elite norms against right-wing populism, a legacy of public debates about the Nazi past, motivated German political parties, the media, and civil society to take active, and ultimately effective, measures against it.

Chapter 6 analyzes the rise and consolidation of the FPÖ. I demonstrate how the nationalist backlash from the Waldheim debate in 1986 created ideal conditions for the FPÖ's breakthrough in parliamentary elections later that year. Despite occasional statements to the contrary, other political parties tolerated the FPÖ. The party also received strong support from the most powerful paper in Austria, the tabloid *Kronen Zeitung*. Civic groups did not initially protest the FPÖ nearly as actively as their counterparts in Germany, which meant that the FPÖ faced few obstacles to recruitment and organization. Elite ideas about the Nazi past did not prove a handicap, but rather a boon, in the FPÖ's meteoric rise.

Chapter 7 summarizes the key theoretical and empirical arguments of the study. It then reviews some recent changes in German and Austrian political discourse about the Nazi past, particularly the newfound resonance of the German narrative of victimization. I suggest that critical examinations of the fire bombing of German cities or the suffering of German expellees from Eastern Europe (*die Vertriebenen*) do not represent a threat to the hegemony of the contrition discourse. Rather, by raising the theme of German suffering itself, the German left is attempting to wrest the issue of victimization from the German right, thereby robbing it of a tool for stoking nationalist sentiment.

I then turn to the rising tide of far right activity in the former German Democratic Republic (DDR). In the new *länder*, where the lessons of history are different from those in the West, the far right has done remarkably well in recent local and state elections. Even more importantly, right-wing extremist movements have permeated social and political life in many eastern German cities and towns. I show how other political and social actors in the east either tolerated, tacitly supported, or ignored neo-Nazi movements, and how these reactions allowed far-right movements to consolidate and thrive.

The conclusion also uses the shadow cases of Weimar Germany and contemporary France, the Netherlands, and Sweden to demonstrate the portability of my argument about right-wing success and failure. In both Weimar Germany and France, political elites failed to erect a *cordon sanitaire* around incipient right-wing movements, but rather gave them tacit and overt support. Although National Socialism cannot be equated with the French National Front (FN), both right-wing movements profited immensely from the actions of other mainstream political parties, the media, and groups in civil society. In the Netherlands and Sweden, however, political elites combated right-wing populist movements when they first appeared in the 1980s. It is no coincidence that the two countries are home to some of the the least electorally successful right-wing populist parties in Western Europe (see Table 1.1).

This study closes with an appeal to scholars to study other cases of public debates in addition to those concerning the lessons of history. It is my hope that public debates about such foundational issues in the United States and elsewhere can be analyzed using the framework developed in this study. Such deliberative moments – moments when the fundamental values of political communities are intensely contested – represent critical junctures in the process of political change and transform the political environment in which they occur.

2

Public Debates and Political Change

This chapter develops a framework for analyzing public debates in advanced industrial democracies. Although public deliberation is an essential feature of these states, there are certain periods when a society appears to be involved in a "national discussion" – periods when politicians, the media, intellectuals, and civic activists intensely debate a particular set of issues. Some examples in the United States include the health care debate of the early 1990s, the debate about Iraq in 2002, and, potentially, the unfolding debate over gay marriage. To go back further, one might include battles over civil rights, the Equal Rights Amendment, and the Vietnam War as episodes of public debates over foundational issues in American politics.[1] Public debates about such foundational or easy issues are marked by clashes between basic political orientations and values.

Do such public debates matter for political outcomes? Many political scientists argue that they do not. Politics, after all, is all about power and interest; those who possess enough of each determine policy, regardless of

---

[1] On the health care debate, see Jacob S. Hacker, *The Road to Nowhere* (Princeton: Princeton University Press, 1997). The literature on the civil rights debate is massive, but for an analysis of the debate see Edward G. Carmines and James A. Stimson, *Issue Evolution: Race and the Transformation of American Politics* (Princeton: Princeton University Press, 1989). See also Doug McAdam, *Political Process and the Development of Black Insurgency, 1930–1970* (Chicago: University of Chicago Press, 1982). On the debate over the Equal Rights Amendment, see Jane Mansbridge, *Why We Lost the ERA* (Chicago: University of Chicago Press, 1986). On Vietnam, see John R. Zaller, *The Nature and Origins of Mass Opinion* (New York: Cambridge University Press, 1992).

what others have to say.[2] Several central paradigms in political science also assume that the interests of political actors are fixed (or exogenous) and do not change markedly through social interaction.[3] In such accounts, public debates and political discourse have, at best, only a marginal influence on political outcomes.

This book challenges this view. As scholars working in the deliberative democracy paradigm have suggested, deliberation produces changes that are not reducible to power or interest.[4] Drawing on this insight, I conceive of public debates as dynamic political battles with important and enduring legacies. Public debates create new frames for interpreting political issues, change the ideas and interests of political actors, restructure the relationships between them, and redefine the limits of legitimate political space. These changes do not occur because the better argument carries the day, but rather because public debates set in motion a series of processes that reshape the political environment in which they occur.

This chapter analyzes those processes. Before doing so, it defines a public debate and identifies objective measures of its political saliency. It also claims that the relevant participants are political elites rather than ordinary citizens, and that elite messages are both reported and framed by the mass media. In other words, it develops a top-down view of public debate and opinion change, one that is at odds with many normative conceptions of deliberative democracy but is consistent with the dominant paradigms within public opinion and political communications research.

My case studies of public debates are those about past atrocities. The burgeoning literature on coming to terms with the past has raised many of the normative issues in this process but has had much less to say about its political stakes.[5] Although the notion of "historical memory" has gained

[2] Ian Shapiro, "Enough of Deliberation: Politics Is about Interests and Power," in *Deliberative Politics: Essays on Democracy and Disagreement*, ed. Stephen Macedo (New York: Oxford University Press, 1999), 28–38.

[3] The assumption of fixed interest is central to all rationalist theories of politics, from rational choice to Marxism to neorealist theory in international relations.

[4] For introductions to the literature on deliberative democracy, see James Bohman, *Public Deliberation: Pluralism, Complexity and Democracy* (Cambridge: MIT Press, 1996); Jon Elster, ed., *Deliberative Democracy* (New York: Cambridge University Press, 1998).

[5] This study analyzes the empirical issues in coming to terms with the past and does not deal with the moral ones. For those interested in ethical considerations, see Avishai Margalit, *The Ethics of Memory* (Cambridge: Harvard University Press, 2002); Martha Minnow, *Between Vengeance and Forgiveness* (Boston: Beacon Press, 1998); Elazar Barkan, *The Guilt of Nations: Restitution and Negotiating Historical Injustices* (New York: Norton, 2000). For an empirical analysis of coming to terms with the past, see Samuel P. Huntington, *The Third Wave* (Norman: University of Oklahoma Press, 1991).

wide currency within several scholarly fields, it distracts our attention from the contemporary political relevance of historical interpretations. I argue that ideas about the past, particularly about a traumatic past, matter because they constitute both causal and normative claims about politics in general. In debating the lessons of history, political elites are in fact deliberating over the basic ideas and values that should guide the contemporary political community. This is the primary reason that debates about history, like debates about abortion and civil rights, often become so politically salient. In the final section of this chapter, I outline my comparative research design and explain the eclectic qualitative and quantitative methods – interviews, media analysis, content analysis, participant observation, public opinion data – that provide the primary evidence in the empirical chapters. But let us begin with an investigation of coming to terms with the past, both in theoretical terms and in the cases of Germany and Austria.

The Past in the Present

In 1959, the German sociologist Adorno delivered a lecture entitled "What Does It Mean to Come to Terms with the Past?"[6] Since then, politicians, intellectuals, and ordinary citizens in many other societies have asked themselves the same question. Like Germans, they have confronted the legacy of a state massacre – a "large-scale violation of basic human rights to life and liberty by the central state in a systematic and organized fashion."[7] In many third-wave democracies, reckoning with authoritarian or communist pasts has been integral to democratic transitions.[8] In advanced industrial democracies, minorities have demanded symbolic and material redress for past state massacres, like slavery and the annihilation of aboriginal populations.[9] While Adorno implicitly treated dealing with the Nazi past as an exclusively German imperative, it has since emerged as a salient issue in many other countries. The legacy of collaboration has

---

[6] Theodor W. Adorno, "Was beduetet: Aufarbeitung der Vergangenheit," in *Erziehung zur Mündigkeit* (Frankfurt am Main: Suhrkamp, 1970), 10–28.

[7] Mark J. Osiel, "Ever Again: Legal Remembrance of Administrative Massacre," *University of Pennsylvania Law Review* 144 (1995), 463. This is Osiel's definition of "administrative massacre," a term I avoid because it can easily be understood as a euphemism for genocide.

[8] Nancy Bermeo, "Democracy and the Lessons of Dictatorship," *Comparative Politics* 24, no. 1 (April 1992): 273–291.

[9] Melissa Nobles, "Official Apologies: The Politics of Reconciliation in Australia, Canada, and the United States," paper presented at the Comparative Center for Social Analysis, UCLA, 2000.

sparked debate in several Western European states since the late 1960s and has recently become an explosive issue in some Eastern European ones as well.[10] Even Switzerland and Sweden, neutral states during the Second World War, have started to reexamine, and atone for, their complicity in Nazi crimes. In short, dealing with the past has become a political issue in societies across the globe.

Scholars have just begun to analyze how political elites confront state massacres. Those working from a "transitional justice" perspective have assessed how trials, amnesties, truth commissions, apologies, reparations, and other policies are used, or should be used, to promote justice in societies emerging from authoritarian or communist rule.[11] Yet, as many have noted, transitional justice is bound to be imperfect. When democratic consolidation depends on the integration of a large number of former perpetrators, many of whom may still occupy powerful positions in politics and society, dealing with the past is likely to be perfunctory. The legal system in many societies is unable to handle the number of cases resulting from state massacres. The problem of post facto justice renders it difficult to establish individual crimes under criminal regimes. Reparations will never be more than symbolic, and even then they are only exacted through a long and tortuous legal process that often leaves a bitter taste. Given these constraints, many groups focus on a minimum conception of transitional justice that involves publicly examining past atrocities and including them in the national historical narrative.

This minimum requirement, however, is difficult to achieve even under the most auspicious political circumstances. It is difficult to argue that the stability of advanced industrial democracies, as opposed to emerging ones, can be undermined by publicly discussing past atrocities. And since these atrocities occurred decades or even centuries ago, the number of individuals directly involved in them is small or nonexistent. Yet even in advanced industrial democracies, critical examinations of state massacres

---

[10] For the French case, see Henri Rousso, *The Vichy Syndrome* (Cambridge: Harvard University Press, 1991). On cases from both Eastern and Western Europe, see Istvan Deak, Jan Gross, and Tony Judt, eds., *The Politics of Retribution in Europe* (Princeton: Princeton University Press, 2000). See also Jan Müller, ed., *Memory and Power in Postwar Europe* (New York: Cambridge University Press, 2002).

[11] On transitional justice, see Neil Kritz, ed., *Transitional Justice*, 3 vols. (Washington, DC: United States Institute of Peace, 1995); A. James McAdams, ed., *Transitional Justice and the Rule of Law in New Democracies* (Notre Dame, IN: University of Notre Dame Press, 1997); Jon Elster, "Coming to Terms with the Past: A Framework for the Study of Justice in the Transition to Democracy," *Archives of European Sociology* 39, no. 1 (1998): 7–48; Ruti G. Teitel, *Transitional Justice* (New York: Oxford University Press, 2000).

have proceeded slowly and fitfully, and have been marked at every step by resistance from powerful political and social actors. Nowhere has this been more true than in Western European confrontations with the Second World War.

In the decades after the war, Europeans rebuilt their shattered nations in an atmosphere of collective amnesia. In place of critical examinations of the recent past, the majority of politicians, intellectuals, and citizens constructed and accepted what one scholar has termed "founding myths."[12] Each state nourished its own specific myth, but they all shared several common features. By hanging the blame on a foreign power or a small clique of domestic fanatics, they absolved the general population of any complicity in sins of commission or omission during the war. By treating the rise of Nazism, fascism, or wartime collaboration as aberrations in their nations' histories, the purveyors of founding myths sought to restore historical continuity and national traditions. These foundation myths proved to be remarkably enduring, and began to unravel only in the late 1960s as discussions about national guilt became increasingly frequent across Western Europe. These debates led to concrete political outcomes in the 1990s when many states, and groups within states, paid reparations, issued apologies, and otherwise sought to atone for their nation's crimes during the Second World War.

How can we account for this shift from amnesia to critical examination of national crimes? One way of approaching this question is through the study of "historical" or "collective" memory. "Memory" has become a fashionable concept in recent years, and the "memory boom" that began in the humanities in the 1980s has since spread to the social sciences. But despite, or perhaps because of, the vastness of the literature, the study of collective memory remains a "centerless enterprise" fractured by disagreements over basic concepts.[13] Scholars disagree over the precise differences between "history" and "memory." They are conflicted over the proper unit of analysis for the study of memory: individuals, groups, or nations. And while many scholars have analyzed how memories are formed, there has been little attempt to understand how memory shapes social and political life.

---

[12] Tony Judt, "The Past Is Another Country: Myth and Memory in Post-War Europe," *Daedalus* 121, no. 4 (Fall 1992): 83–118.

[13] Jeffrey K. Olick and Joyce Robbins, "Social Memory Studies: From 'Collective Memory' to the Historical Sociology of Mnemonic Practices," *Annual Review of Sociology*, 24 (1998): 105.

Although many political scientists would agree that memory matters, there have been few studies that trace the nexus between ideas about the past and political power.[14] Scholars of international relations and German foreign policy have made the largest contribution to our understanding of how historical ideas shape political outcomes.[15] Comparativists have done much less.[16] One of the principal reasons for this neglect, I suspect, is the murkiness of the concept of memory. What exactly is historical or collective memory? Whose memories count in politics? How can political scientists demonstrate that memory influences political behavior?

Several studies have floundered in trying to answer such questions. The most successful efforts tend to avoid the conceptual minefield and conceive of memory as a set of beliefs about the past, articulated by political elites, that contain causal and normative claims about politics. Andrei Markovits and Simon Reich, for example, see collective memory as the "process through which ideological frameworks are contested and subsequently constructed."[17] Consuelo Cruz views collective memory as central to the construction of a "collective field of imagined possibilities," which she defines as "a restricted array of plausible scenarios of how the world can or cannot be changed and how the future ought to look."[18] In anthropology, Claude Lévi-Strauss developed the notion of *bricolage*, a process by which political elites pick elements from the past in order to mold the future.[19] Richard Samuels has recently used this concept to explain how politicians shaped political development in Italy and Japan.[20] All of these scholars have analyzed how political elites construct and disseminate ideas about history to justify some set of actors, policies, and

---

[14] Jan-Werner Müller, "Introduction," in *Memory and Power in Postwar Europe*, 1.

[15] See, for example, Andrei S. Markovits and Simon Reich, *The German Predicament* (Ithaca: Cornell University Press, 1997); Thomas Berger, *Cultures of Antimilitarism* (Baltimore: Johns Hopkins University Press, 1998); Thomas Banchoff, *The German Problem Transformed* (Ann Arbor: University of Michigan Press, 1999); Peter J. Katzenstein, ed., *Tamed Power: Germany in Europe* (Ithaca: Cornell University Press, 1997).

[16] An important exception is Consuelo Cruz, "Identity and Persuasion: How Nations Remember Their Pasts and Make Their Futures," *World Politics* 52, no. 3 (April 2000): 275–312; See also Peter Katzenstein, *Cultural Norms and National Security: Police and Military in Postwar Japan* (Ithaca: Cornell University Press, 1996). On how breaking with the past was important for the regeneration of Communist parties in Eastern Europe, see Anna M. Grzymala-Busse, *Redeeming the Communist Past* (New York: Cambridge University Press, 2002).

[17] Markovits and Reich, *German Predicament*, 13.

[18] Cruz, "Identity and Persuasion," 276.

[19] Claude Lévi-Strauss, *The Savage Mind* (London: Weidenfeld and Nicolson, 1966).

[20] Richard J. Samuels, *Machiavelli's Children: Leaders and Their Legacies in Italy and Japan* (Ithaca: Cornell University Press, 2003).

large-scale ideologies. The word memory, however, is misleading since the actual recollection of an event is not a requirement for purveying, or believing, historical ideas.

From this perspective, dealing with the past is less about getting the history right, or reconstructing memory, than about defining the basic political ideas and values of *contemporary* political communities. State massacres were the product of political ideas and social visions that, if initially disseminated by fanatical cadres, became deeply embedded in the population. Criminal regimes rested not only on terror, but also on the acquiescence, obedience, and often allegiance of important sectors of society. One task for elites emerging from a state massacre would seem to be the destruction of those ideas that predated, facilitated, and survived the criminal regime. This strategy for dealing with the past, however, is rarely used in the immediate aftermath of transitions. The historical record demonstrates, instead, that most elites have pursued an "institutional" strategy. They have wagered that new institutions would not only prevent the recurrence of atrocities but would also slowly purge their societies of pernicious ideas.[21] This was very much the case in the Federal Republic. The slow but steady growth of democratic attitudes among the population, coupled with West Germany's remarkable political stability, is often taken as evidence that institutional strategies for dealing with the past work.[22]

But West Germany also demonstrates the limits of such strategies. During the 1960s, many West Germans began to call for a "cultural strategy" of dealing with the Nazi past that demanded a critical confrontation with the political ideas that had preceded, flourished under, and survived Nazism. Many attacked institutional strategies as attempts to whitewash the Nazi past and to allow former Nazis to remain in power.[23] They viewed, although they did not always clearly articulate, a critical confrontation with Nazism as a precondition for the deepening of democracy in the Federal Republic. Over the past two decades, groups in other

---

[21] On the difference between institutional and cultural strategies in dealing with the past, see Anne Sa'adah, *Germany's Second Chance: Truth, Justice and Democratization* (Cambridge: Harvard University Press, 1998), 2–5.

[22] Herman Lübbe, "Der Nationalsozialismus im polititischen Bewusstsein der Gegenwart," in *Deutschlands Weg in die Diktatur: Internationale Konferenz zur nationalsozialistischen Machtübernahme im Reichstagsgebäude zu Berlin. Referate und Diskussionen: Ein Protokoll,* ed. Martin Broszat et al. (Berlin: Siedler, 1983).

[23] Ralph Giordano, *Die Zweite Schuld oder Von der Last Deutscher zu sein* (Hamburg: Rausch and Röhring, 1987).

countries that have pressed for critical examination of state massacres have made similar claims about the relationship between dealing with the past and increasing the quality of democracy.[24] The idea is that by drawing lessons from history, societies can both inoculate themselves against pernicious ideas and, in the process, develop liberal democratic values.

But what lessons of history are to be learned from state massacres? One universal slogan that politicians can agree on is "Never again!" In German, this translates as *Nie Wieder*, and politicians of all stripes regularly invoke it when discussing the Nazi past. But what exactly do they mean by it? In one sense, "Never again!" implies a wholesale rejection of the ideas and values that drove societies to commit massive and systematic abuses of human rights. In the case of Nazi Germany, this would appear to be common sense. But even in this most extreme case, the matter is much more complex. If the Nazis created a new ideology, they also constructed it from many preexisting strands of German political thought. To take a well-known example, the Nazis elevated devotion to the German nation to a central political principle. Some politicians thus interpret "Never Again!" as the rejection of any conception of political loyalty based on ethnic or cultural criteria. They view the Nazi past not only as a prohibition against such ideas, but also as an injunction to create a new form of national identity based on a commitment to democratic values. Other politicians who proclaim *Nie Wieder* draw different lessons from the Nazi past. They argue that since Hitler "misused" appeals to the "fatherland" and patriotism, the Nazi past need not rule out the possibility for Germans to identify positively with a shared community of fate. The point is that just what political ideas the Nazi past precludes, and enables, is up for debate. In short, the lessons of history are not self-evident but wide open to ideational contestation.

It is this ideational contestation about the basic, or foundational, political ideas and values of the contemporary political community that is at the heart of the process of coming to terms with the past. At many points over the past six decades in both Germany and Austria, the Nazi past has intruded into the political present and absorbed politicians, members of the media, intellectuals, and civic activists. Historical narratives about the Nazi past have varied widely across time and place, but a general pattern is discernible in each country. In Germany, elites during the first few postwar decades made only fleeting references to the Nazi past, normally describing it as a natural catastrophe that had overcome Germany between 1933 and 1945. During the 1960s, distinctive left and right narratives of the

---

[24] See Carlos Nino, *Radical Evil on Trial* (New Haven: Yale University Press, 1998).

Nazi past developed, and the clash of these historical narratives was especially salient in the 1980s. Since then, German elites across the political spectrum have adopted the contrition narrative – a narrative that identifies atonement for the Holocaust as a central political and moral duty. In Austria, the consensus that Austria was Hitler's first victim prevailed until the mid-1980s. As the victim narrative unraveled, several conflicting narratives of the Nazi past emerged. No new consensus was formed, and multiple narratives of the Nazi past exist in Austria to this day.

The following chapters explain the construction of the first postwar consensus in both Germany and Austria, the erosion of this consensus in each state, the development of the new consensus in Germany, and the multiple narratives in Austria. In other words, they are concerned with the dynamics of ideational change. Although political scientists have recently rediscovered the importance of ideas in political life, the issue of ideational change has been understudied.[25] As one observer suggests, ideational scholars have been so concerned with demonstrating that ideas matter that they have paid little attention to how ideas enter the political arena and change.[26] Before I present my own account of this process, I analyze two general political science paradigms that have been applied to explain the evolution of ideas about the Nazi past in Germany and Austria.

Explaining Ideational Change

The first paradigm identifies generational turnover as the crucial mechanism for ideational change.[27] Scholars working in this paradigm argue that beliefs and attitudes are formed in early adulthood, and that

[25] A recent exception is Jeffrey W. Legro, "The Transformation of Policy Ideas," *American Journal of Political Science* 44, no. 3 (July 2000): 419–432.

[26] Sheri Berman, "Ideas, Norms, and Culture in Political Analysis," *Comparative Politics* 33, no. 2 (January 2001): 233.

[27] Although they are often conflated, there are three distinct models of generational change: the "maturation" model, whereby beliefs change in predictable ways as people age; the "pendulum" model, whereby the members of one generation react to the beliefs of the previous one; and the "experiential" model, whereby the beliefs of members of generations are shaped by critical events. It is the combination of the experiential and pendulum models that is often applied to explain Germany's confrontation with the Nazi past. On these three models, see Richard J. Samuels, ed., *Political Generations and Political Development* (Lexington, MA: Lexington Books, 1977). The experiential model of generations was first developed in Karl Mannheim, "The Problem of Generations," in *From Karl Mannheim*, ed. Kurt H. Wolff, second expanded edition (New Brunswick: Transaction Books, 1993): 351–395. A recent application of the experiential paradigm is Ronald Inglehart, *Modernization and Postmodernization: Cultural, Economic and Political Change in 43 Societies* (Princeton: Princeton University Press, 1997).

generations possess their own belief structures since their members were exposed to the same general socializing influences. Ideational change, defined as change in the distribution of beliefs among a population, occurs as generations die and new ones occupy positions of power. This "experiential" generational paradigm has been widely used to explain how ideas about the Nazi past have changed over time, with the key claim being that generations born after the Second World War are less compromised by their complicity in Nazism and better able to examine it critically.[28]

The generational paradigm grew out of the experiences of the 1960s, when generational conflicts were occurring across all advanced industrial countries. The West German student movement's use of the Nazi past as a weapon against the political establishment would appear to support the argument that the "second generation" – the first generation to be socialized after a formative historical event – will challenge the historical ideas of the "war generation" or the "first generation." But a glance at other democracies shows that the German case is exceptional. In Japan, for example, generational change has done little to stimulate critical examinations of Japanese atrocities in the Second World War.[29] More pertinent for my argument is that generational change in Austria failed to change ideas about the Nazi past. While members of the Austrian "generation of 68" mimicked many of the discourses and practices of their West German counterparts, they never challenged the victim narrative that emerged in the immediate aftermath of the war.[30]

Even if generational change might explain slow shifts in attitudes among the general population, there is still the problem of accounting for the sudden ideational changes that regularly occur in politics. In West Germany, an elite consensus about the Nazi past emerged within several years in the late 1980s, not several decades. Similarly, the victim narrative in Austria lost its hegemonic status quickly in 1986 (during the Waldheim affair) and contending narratives of the Nazi past emerged within several months. Generational arguments cannot account for this type of rapid, discontinuous change.

---

[28] Joyce Mushaben, *From Post-War to Post-Wall Generations* (Boulder: Westview Press, 1998).

[29] On Japan's confrontation with the past, see Carol Gluck, "The Past in the Present," in *Postwar Japan as History*, ed. Andrew Gordon (Berkeley: University of California Press, 1993): 64–95. On the early postwar period, see John Dower, *Embracing Defeat* (New York: Norton, 1999).

[30] Paulus Ebner and Karl Vocelka, *Die Zahme Revolution: '68 und was davon blieb* (Vienna: Überreuter, 1998), 187.

A final problem with the generational argument is that it is impossible to discern the structure of political conflict over the Nazi past using generational categories. The "third generation" – the second generation socialized after the war – has produced the politicians and intellectuals most concerned with promoting apologetic interpretations of the Nazi past. Jörg Haider proclaimed himself the defender of the war generation at the age of thirty-five in 1985; New Right intellectuals in Germany who wanted to rewrite the Nazi past in the early 1990s were mostly in their late twenties and early thirties. Conversely, many politicians from the war generation, such as Willy Brandt and Richard von Weizsäcker, played key roles in constructing and disseminating the contrition narrative. Generational effects explain only a small part of the politics of the Nazi past since neither the war generation nor the third generation constitutes the collective political actor it is often imagined to be.

A second explanation for ideational change conceives of ideas as "hooks" for elite interests and ideational change as the product of shifts in those interests.[31] The notion that elites use or instrumentalize history to achieve specific goals – and that they can "invent traditions" – has strongly influenced how political scientists understand the significance of the past in the present.[32] German and Austrian elites often invoke the Nazi past in parliamentary debates, election campaigns, and other political settings to achieve concrete goals. But what is striking about attempts to instrumentalize the Nazi past in Austria and Germany is the intense reactions they have sparked from rival political parties, the media, and civil society. Attempts at cultural manipulation have repeatedly resulted in public debates that the instrumentalizers did not foresee and have produced a host of unintended consequences.

An example from Germany demonstrates this point. In the early 1980s, Chancellor Helmut Kohl (CDU) pledged to lead a "political-moral turnaround" (*politisch-moralische Wende*) that involved redefining Germany's relationship to the Nazi past. Kohl and other conservative politicians and intellectuals began to emphasize the positive aspects of German history and urged fellow Germans not to view it through the lens of the Holocaust. In other words, Germany should "normalize" its historical consciousness. As I demonstrate in Chapter 3, this turnaround

---

[31] Kenneth A. Shepsle, "Comment," in *Regulatory Politics and the Social Sciences*, ed. Roger Noll (Berkeley: University of California Press, 1985): 231–237.

[32] Eric Hobsbawm and Terence Ranger, eds., *The Invention of Tradition* (New York: Cambridge University Press, 1983).

involved many concrete policies and events – chief among them being the visit by President Ronald Reagan and Kohl to the Bitburg cemetery. Rather than helping the Nazi past to pass away, however, Kohl's initiatives achieved exactly the opposite by turning it into a salient political issue and mobilizing intense opposition to normalization. By the late 1980s, German conservatives had lost their battle to normalize the Nazi past to those who demanded an even more contrite and critical examination of Germany's crimes. Kohl's politicization of history produced a transformation he had neither intended nor desired.

This type of event raises some questions about elite manipulation. Elites do sometimes find wide support for their ideas and play a major role in pushing broader ideational change in the desired direction.[33] Sometimes elites find institutional carriers for their ideas.[34] Sometimes elites find that their ideas have no resonance, drop them for a time, and then advance them during a window of opportunity.[35] These types of scenarios have been well covered in the political science literature. What has received far less attention, however, is the potential for elite discourse to produce reactions from other political parties, from the media, and from civil society. In advanced industrial democracies, elite manipulation can produce unintended consequences and spark a public debate that elites did not necessarily desire or foresee.[36] It is to such public debates that we now turn.

Mediated Elite Debate

Although public debate is central to democratic life, scholars of comparative politics and international relations have rarely treated it as an analytical concept.[37] In democratic theory, however, there has been a recent

<hr/>

[33] See, for example, William Riker, *The Art of Political Manipulation* (New Haven: Yale University Press, 1986).

[34] Peter Hall, ed., *The Political Power of Economic Ideas* (Princeton: Princeton University Press, 1989).

[35] See John Kingdon, *Agendas, Alternatives, and Public Policies* (Boston: Little Brown, 1984).

[36] The ability of elites to brainwash their societies is somewhat greater under authoritarianism, but it can certainly provoke unintended consequences and resistance as well. See, for example, James Scott, *Domination and the Arts of Resistance: Hidden Transcripts* (New Haven: Yale University Press, 1990). See also Lisa Wedeen, *Ambiguities of Domination: Politics, Rhetoric and Symbols in Contemporary Syria* (Chicago: University of Chicago Press, 1999).

[37] An exception is Thomas Risse, "Let's Argue!": Communicative Action in World Politics," *International Organization* 54 (Winter 2000): 1–39.

surge of interest in public deliberation. One key point of contention in this literature is the extent to which deliberation transforms the interests, ideas, and identities of individuals. Some scholars claim that deliberation helps individuals redefine their interests and reach a consensus.[38] Others maintain that while deliberation may not produce consensus on divisive moral issues, it may foster mutual respect among individuals with irreconcilable positions.[39] Disputing such optimistic claims about deliberation, several scholars have argued that debate can exacerbate existing conflicts and create new ones.[40] Still others have argued that the outcome of deliberation depends on the structures of power and institutional configurations in which it occurs, and that actors with enough power can shape deliberation to suit their interests.[41]

This last insight is critical for understanding public deliberation in advanced industrial democracies. Deliberation in these societies is *"mediated*, with professional communicators rather than ordinary citizens talking to each other and to the public through [the] mass media."[42] These professional communicators include politicians, members of organized interest groups, media personalities and journalists, intellectuals, and specialists. Put simply, public deliberation is mediated by political elites. Following Robert Putnam, I define political elites as "those who in any society rank toward the top of the (presumably closely intercorrelated) dimensions of interest, involvement, and influence in politics."[43]

---

[38] John Dryzek, *Deliberative Democracy and Beyond* (New York: Oxford University Press, 2000).

[39] Amy Gutmann and Dennis Thompson, *Democracy and Disagreement* (Cambridge: Harvard University Press, 1996).

[40] Adam Przeworski, "Minimalist Conceptions of Democracy: A Defense," in *Democracy's Value*, ed. Ian Shapiro and Casiano Hacker-Cordon (Cambridge: Cambridge University Press, 1999), 23–55; Cass R. Sunstein, "Deliberative Trouble? Why Groups Go To Extremes," *Yale Law Journal* 110, no. 1 (October 2000): 71–121.

[41] Shapiro, "Enough of Deliberation," 28–38.

[42] Benjamin Page, *Who Deliberates?* (Chicago: University of Chicago Press, 1996), 1 (emphasis in the original).

[43] Robert Putnam, "Studying Elite Political Culture: The Case of 'Ideology,' *American Political Science Review* 65 (September 1971), 651; Putnam draws on Robert Dahl's conception of the political elite as a "small stratum of individuals much more highly involved in political thought, discussion, and action than the rest of the population." See Robert Dahl, *Who Governs?* (New Haven: Yale University Press, 1961), 90. The definition of political elite has not changed fundamentally over the past three decades. John Zaller, for example, largely follows Putnam and Dahl in defining elites as "those on whom we depend, directly or indirectly, for information about the world," who are in turn "persons who devote themselves full time to some aspect of politics or public affairs." Zaller, *Mass Opinion*, 6.

This emphasis on political elites rather than on ordinary citizens marks a departure from most of the literature on deliberative democracy. The implicit model for many theorists in this tradition is the town meeting, where citizens deliberate face-to-face and relative power is not relevant. Mediated deliberation, however, is shaped not only by relative power, but also by political power itself; not only the public good is at stake. The focus on political elites also demands a different conception of the arena for debate from that of deliberative democrats. Many democratic theorists consider "civil society" the forum for deliberation. Seyla Benhabib, for example, argues that "it is through the interlocking net of these multiple forms of associations, networks and organizations that an anonymous 'public conversation' results."[44] Jürgen Habermas, drawing on Hannah Arendt's notion of a free public space distinct from the state and the economy where citizens can deliberate, developed the concept of the "public sphere."[45] For our purposes, the problem with both the civil society and public sphere conceptions of deliberation is that they exclude politicians and state actors – actors who play a crucial role in shaping public debate.

Elite debate profoundly influences mass attitudes. Several important works in American politics have linked shifts in elite discourse to changes in public opinion.[46] Edward Carmines and James Stimson, for example, demonstrate how public opinion responded to changes in elite discourse about race.[47] This shift in mass opinions about race, according to Carmines and Stimson, was not slow and gradual but dramatic and discontinuous, and followed directly from the changing discourse of political elites in the 1960s. As John Zaller notes, "if elite cues can change racial opinions, which appear to be the mostly deeply felt of mass opinions... they can probably affect most other types of opinions as well."[48] Indeed, the central argument of Zaller's book is that public opinion is shaped by political elites who establish the terms of political discourse and frame issues in the mass media.

---

[44] Seyla Benhabib, "Toward a Deliberative Model of Democratic Legitimacy," in *Democracy and Difference*, ed. Seyla Benhabib (Princeton: Princeton University Press, 1996), 75.

[45] For an introduction to Habermas' idea of the public sphere, see Craig Calhoun, ed., *Habermas and the Public Sphere* (Cambridge: MIT Press, 1992).

[46] Shanto Iyengar and Donald Kinder, *News That Matters* (Chicago: University of Chicago Press, 1987). See also David Fan, *Predictions of Public Opinion from the Mass Media* (New York: Greenwood, 1988).

[47] Carmines and Stimson, *Issue Evolution*.

[48] Zaller, *Mass Opinion*, 13.

This focus on elite debate has led us away from deliberative democracy, our initial point of departure, and raises important normative questions about the role of the citizenry in democracy. To what extent do elites control the political preferences of ordinary citizens? To what extent do the media define the boundaries of the political and shape mass opinion? While I cannot deal with these questions here, I would like to emphasize that a central insight of deliberative democratic theory remains critical to this study: deliberation does matter. Public conversation between elites, as between ordinary citizens, is a dynamic process with the potential to transform both the ideas and the interests of the participants. The intense interaction that characterizes public debates produces observable, and important, outcomes. As I will argue, these outcomes can, from a normative perspective, be positive or negative. But at the very least, elite deliberation does have the benefit of exposing the public to a range of opinions and arguments, of rousing some members of the public from their apathy, and of focusing their attention on an issue of national importance.

Public Debates as Events

Elite debate is a permanent feature of everyday democratic politics. Yet there are some periods when elite debate about specific values or policies becomes particularly intense. During such periods, politicians, leaders of organized interest groups, intellectuals, civic activists, and other elites across the political spectrum offer statements about particular issues and react to the statements of others. The national media report these statements and comments on the issue in their opinion pieces. In my conception, a public debate is therefore an episode of concentrated public ideational contestation among political elites reported in the media on a particular subject of some controversy. It is a subset of what several scholars refer to as a "contentious political episode."[49] Before I refine my definition of a public debate, however, let me first outline why scholars should seek to analyze them at all.

---

[49] Doug McAdam, Charles Tilly, and Sidney Tarrow, *Dynamics of Contention* (New York: Cambridge University Press, 2001). The authors define their topic as follows: "The *contentious* politics that concerns us is episodic rather than continuous, occurs in public, involves interaction between makers of claims and others, is recognized by those others as bearing on their interests, and brings in government as a mediator, target, or claimant" (5; emphasis in the original). Although the authors do not refer to public debates as contentious episodes, they do use analogies from public debates to build their conceptual codifications (142).

One reason for studying public debates is that elite actors often articulate and defend their ideas with greater clarity and force during periods of contention than during periods of normal politics. By analyzing public debates, ideational scholars can observe the ideas that elites hold, or at least state publicly, and the range of elite ideas present in political communities. Debates also reveal something about the relative salience and resonance of different political ideas or policies. Since elites often hold multiple ideas and policy alternatives, it is often difficult to assess their relative importance to them when they are not engaged in conflict over them.

My central claim, however, is that public debates do not merely reflect existing ideas, but that the process of debate also changes the ideas of political elites. The process of public debate injects new ideas, and new combinations of ideas, into political discourse. Political entrepreneurs may then use these new ideas for political mobilization. Public debates may lead to the formation of an elite consensus and mark the first step in the institutionalization of political ideas. When public debates involve moral issues, they may create new norms and reshape the political-moral foundations of political communities. Public debates, however, may also produce polarization and new lines of political conflict that can transform the party system.

Before going into further detail, it is important to differentiate my explanation of ideational change from the two paradigms I outlined earlier. First, like the elite manipulation paradigm, I focus on the role of political elites in shaping mass attitudes. Yet, rather than assuming that these attempts are successful, my concept of public debate leaves room for the unintended and unpredictable consequences of elite attempts to impose their ideas on society. Political elites may try to provoke and shape a debate, but often find that they are unable to control the process once it begins. Public debates acquire a certain momentum as statements elicit counterstatements, as the range of elite participants expands, and as new political stakes arise. Public debates, in short, represent contingent political battles.

Second, in contrast to the generational change paradigm, my explanation of ideational change opens up the possibility of sudden and dramatic changes in elite ideas. Ideational change, in this view, is discontinuous rather than continuous.[50] The scientific paradigm for this view is that of

---

[50] For an attempt to explain discontinuous change in collective beliefs, see Legro, "The Transformation of Policy Ideas," 419–432.

"punctuated equilibrium," an idea that the paleobiologists Niles Eldredge and Stephen Jay Gould applied to their own field and that political scientists have since applied to theirs.[51] In his study of America's constitutional development, for example, Bruce Ackerman locates three "constitutional moments" in which extended public deliberation transformed the constitutional order.[52] Scholars of American politics have studied critical realignments that permanently changed the political party landscape.[53] Comparativists working within the historical institutionalist paradigm have analyzed "critical junctures," contingent outcomes of political battles that produce new and enduring institutional configurations.[54] In a similar vein, I conceive of public debates as critical moments that produce enduring changes in elite ideas.

Such public debates can produce sudden and dramatic changes in public opinion as well as in elite ideas. During the health care debate of the early 1990s, for example, public opinion shifted markedly over a relatively short period of time and in line with the debate among political elites.[55] One can find similar trends in the debate over the first Persian Gulf War, as well as that over the Vietnam War.[56] In this view, public opinion, although it is often stable, is also prone to discontinuous change through elite-led public debates.[57]

---

[51] Niles Eldredge and Stephen Jay Gould, "Punctuated Equilibria: An Alternative to Phyletic Gradualism," in *Models in Paleobiology*, ed. Thomas J. M. Schopf (San Francisco: Freeman, 1972), 82–115. For applications to political science, see Frank R. Baumgartner and Bryan D. Jones, *Agendas and Instability in American Politics* (Chicago: University of Chicago Press, 1993); Stephen D. Krasner, "Approaches to the State: Alternative Conceptions and Historical Dynamics," *Comparative Politics* 16, no. 2 (April 1985): 223–246.

[52] Bruce Ackerman, *We the People*: *Foundations* (Cambridge: Belknap Press of Harvard University Press, 1991).

[53] Walter Dean Burnham, *Critical Elections and the Mainsprings of American Politics* (New York: Norton, 1970).

[54] For a recent discussion of critical junctures, see Kathleen Thelen, "Historical Institutionalism in Comparative Politics," *Annual Review of Political Science* 2 (1999): 388–392.

[55] Jeffrey W. Koch, "Political Rhetoric and Political Persuasion: The Changing Structure of Citizens' Preferences on Health Insurance during Policy Debate," *Public Opinion Quarterly* 62, no. 12 (Summer 1998): 209–229. See also Philip H. Pollock III, "Issues, Values and Critical Moments: Did 'Magic' Johnson Transform Public Opinion on AIDS?" *American Journal of Political Science* 38, no. 2 (May 1994): 426–446.

[56] On Vietnam, see John. R. Zaller, "Information, Values, and Opinion," *American Political Science Review* 85, no. 4 (December 1991): 1215–1237.

[57] On the stability of public opinion, see Benjamin I. Page and Robert Y. Shapiro, *The Rational Public* (Chicago: University of Chicago Press, 1992).

Defining a Public Debate

I define a public debate as a set of exchanges among elite political actors
reported in the media. But what differentiates a public debate from the
occasional sparring that occurs between political elites? To add substance
to my intuitive definition of a public debate as a national discussion of
great import among elite political actors, I identify three requirements
that a public debate must meet: *breadth, duration,* and *intensity.*

Beginning with breadth, public debates involve a wide range of elite
actors across the political spectrum. Politicians from different parties and
organized interest groups feel obliged to participate in the debate, and
their silence is publicly noted if they fail to do so. The participants must
include prominent members of the government and political parties and
must not be limited to back-benchers. Positions are not simply stated
once, but are repeated and perhaps modified over the course of public
deliberation. Political elites react to and publicly refer to the statements
of other elites and view themselves as engaged in a debate.

Members of the media are also central participants. The past two
decades of research have discredited the idea that the media exert only
minimal effects and merely reinforce citizens' preexisting views.[58] Drawing on the insights of Walter Lippmann, scholars have demonstrated how
the media influence "the pictures in our heads" that we use to interpret
political and social reality.[59] Three specific forms of media influence have
received particular attention. First, scholars have used experiments to
demonstrate the *agenda-setting* effect of the media, whereby "those problems that receive prominent attention on the national news become the
problems the viewing public regards as the nation's most important."[60]
Second, scholars have found that by elevating some issues over others, the
media *prime* citizens by influencing their evaluative standards for judging
political actors.[61] Third, the media package news in a *frame*, which is often
defined as "a central organizing idea or story line that provides meaning
to an unfolding strip of events, weaving a connection among them."[62]

[58] For classic statements on the "minimal effects" of the media, see Bernard R. Berelson,
Paul Lazarsfeld, and William N. McPhee, *Voting* (Chicago: University of Chicago Press,
1954); Paul F. Lazarsfeld, Bernard Berelson, and Hazel Gaudet, *The People's Choice*, 2nd
ed. (New York: Columbia University Press, 1948).

[59] Walter Lippmann, *Public Opinion* (New York: Macmillan, 1922).

[60] Iyengar and Kinder, *News That Matters*, 16.

[61] Ibid., 63–72.

[62] William A. Gamson and Andre Modigliani, "The Changing Culture of Affirmative
Action," *Research in Political Sociology*, vol. 3, ed. Richard D. Braungart (Greenwich:
JAI Press, 1987), 143.

Although the media often use the frames that political elites construct, they play a key role in choosing which frames to use. The media can also create their own frames.[63]

Agenda-setting, priming, and framing all take place in media coverage. Although television, the most powerful medium, has received the most scholarly attention, these effects are also apparent in the print media. Newspapers and magazines also contribute directly to debate in a way the national television news does not by offering their own opinions in the form of editorials. Newspapers also try to replicate a public debate by publishing different op-eds from "qualified experts." Although the quality press normally tries to present a range of opinions, it structures the debate by choosing which op-eds to print and solicit.[64] The same applies to readers' letters.

Newspapers that do not strive for objectivity at all, of course, may represent only one side of the debate in their editorials, op-eds, readers' letters, and even in their coverage. Such papers, often referred to as "tabloid" papers, often have a significantly higher circulation than quality papers. In Germany, for example, the tabloid *Bild Zeitung* had a circulation of nearly 4.5 million during the mid-1990s, over seven times that of the second leading national newspaper, the *Westdeutscher Zeitung*. This gives *Bild*, and the Springer Press that owns it and other newspapers and television stations, a great deal of political influence. German chancellors, for example, are known to keep in close contact with *Bild*'s editor-in-chief.

The political might of the largest tabloid paper in Austria is even greater than that of its counterpart in Germany. Over 40 percent of Austrians read the *Kronen Zeitung* (*KZ*) daily, giving it the highest circulation rate per capita in Western Europe.[65] In the words of one former Austrian chancellor, "it is impossible to govern without the support of the *Krone*."[66] Despite their power, tabloid papers like the *KZ* and *Bild* are not often the subjects of media analysis. This is a major flaw that this study avoids.

In terms of breadth, a public debate is one that is covered in the major newspapers in the national print media landscape and involves papers

---

[63] Nayda Terkildsen, Frauke I. Schnell, and Cristina Ling, "Interest Groups, the Media, and Policy Debate Formation: An Analysis of Message Structure, Rhetoric, and Source Cues," *Political Communication* 15 (1998): 45–61.

[64] See Page, *Who Deliberates?*, 17–42.

[65] The four other largest papers in Austria, as of 1997, were *Täglich Alles, Kurier, Die Presse*, and *Der Standard*. *Täglich Alles* was driven out of the traditional market by the *Krone* in 2000, although it continued to publish online.

[66] Interview by the author with Armin Thurnher, editor-in-chief of the weekly *Falter*, Vienna, February 5, 2001. Thurnher was referring to former Austrian Chancellor Franz Vranitzky (SPÖ).

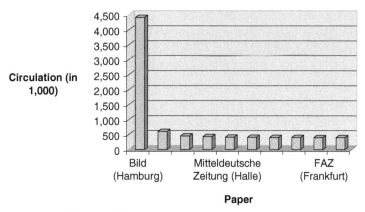

FIGURE 2.1. Top ten German newspapers.

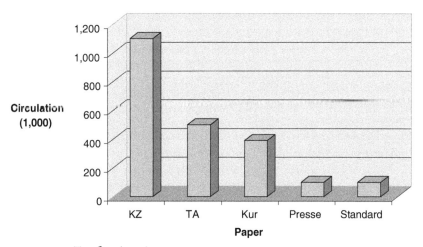

FIGURE 2.2. Top five Austrian newspapers.

with different ideological positions. Debates that appear only in the left-wing or right-wing press do not qualify by my standards. In addition, public debates must appear in tabloid papers as well as in quality papers to ensure that the debate is being disseminated to the wider, less politically sophisticated, audience.

Another feature of public debates is that they move from the political to the intellectual arena. Intellectuals may write articles and op-eds in newspapers and offer other forms of public contribution to the debate. The role and influence of intellectuals differ among societies. In the United States and Britain, for example, intellectuals may speak to limited audiences and seldom appear in the mainstream mass media. In Germany, France, and other European states, however, intellectuals are normally accorded more status and are viewed as important participants in national affairs. As one student of German intellectuals notes:

Only in Germany does one find intellectuals such as Jürgen Habermas occupying the first two pages of a weekly such as *Die Zeit*; only in Germany could a critic literally tearing apart the latest book by Günther Grass make the cover of the country's most important magazine, *Der Spiegel*; only in Germany does one find political scientists regularly publishing popular books on the state of the nation, often with pictures of themselves looking diffident and angst-ridden on the front cover. . . . In short, in Germany, unlike in Britain and the United States, it is almost self-evidently legitimate that men and women who have distinguished themselves in cultural and academic matters should comment on affairs of state.[67]

Public debates must also be reflected in civil society. Individuals may write letters to papers to contribute to public debates or take part in organized discussions. Other forms of civic activism, such as demonstrations or protests, may accompany public debates. As I note later, civic activists may also use public debates as windows of opportunity to mobilize support, gain media attention, and increase their political voice.

In terms of *duration*, episodes of ideational contestation need to last at least a year to meet my definition of a public debate. Temporary blips in the political and media landscapes do not qualify. Public debates, however, may last longer than several years, even becoming permanent features of the political landscape.

Finally, public debates must possess a sufficient *intensity*. Political elites must make frequent contributions to the national discussion, not merely occasional references. A standard proxy for intensity is coverage in the national print media. A crude estimate of intensity is the number of front-page stories over a defined time period. Dividing the total number of stories by time produces a better measure. Totaling the number of column inches of stories over a defined time period, however, provides the most fine-tuned estimate and is the strategy taken in this study. In addition, the number of opinion pieces (editorials, op-eds, readers' letters) over a given time period reflects the importance a newspaper ascribes to a particular issue and provides another proxy for the intensity of public debate.

[67] Jan Müller, *Another Country* (New Haven: Yale University Press, 2000), 14.

Processes and Mechanisms of Public Debates

How do public debates transform the environment in which they occur? Rather than offering hypotheses, I am concerned with the causal mechanisms that link debate to observable changes in politics. This focus on mechanisms, an approach to explanation in the social sciences that dates back to Robert Merton, has recently been championed by several scholars as an alternative to the covering law model.[68] Rather than seeking to construct general laws and models to explain entire categories of events, several scholars have "moved toward the analysis of smaller-scale causal mechanisms that recur in different combinations with different aggregate consequences in varying historical settings."[69]

Following this epistemology, I lay out a three-step sequence to capture the general dynamics of public debates. During the first step, political elites create frames that are disseminated by the mass media. In the second step, elites take positions around these emerging frames and the weight of elite opinion shifts. The two most dramatic outcomes from this shift are elite consensus and elite polarization. The third step in the process of public debate is a shift in political discourse, which reflects deeper ideological changes.[70]

STEP 1. Debates create and consolidate frames. Political science research has largely confirmed sociologist Erving Goffman's insight that the organization of messages affects subsequent thinking.[71] There is significant experimental and empirical evidence that frames, messages that are organized and woven together in a distinct and coherent way, influence political attitudes.[72] Either by stimulating some foundational beliefs

---

[68] Jon Elster, *Nuts and Bolts for the Social Sciences* (Cambridge: Cambridge University Press, 1989); Peter Hedström and Richard Swedberg, eds., *Social Mechanisms: An Analytical Approach to Social Theory* (Cambridge: Cambridge University Press, 1998). On the covering law model, see Carl G. Hempel, *Philosophy of National Science* (Englewood Cliffs: Prentice-Hall, 1966), 51.

[69] McAdam, Tarrow and Tilly, *Dynamics of Contention*, 24. These scholars disagree with Swedberg and Hedström's claim that mechanisms can only be studied on an individual level. Following McAdam et al., I identify both micro- and macro-level mechanisms.

[70] To be sure, actual public debates cannot be divided so neatly into these three steps. Shifts in elite opinion, for example, might produce new frames, as might changes in political discourse. But for the purpose of theory construction, it is useful to divide these processes into distinct stages.

[71] Erving Goffman, *Frame Analysis: An Essay on the Organization of Experience* (New York: Harper & Row, 1974).

[72] See, for example, Thomas E. Nelson, Rosalee A. Clawson, and Zoe M. Oxley, "Media Framing of a Civil Liberties Conflict and Its Effect on Tolerance," *American Political Science Review* 91, no. 3 (September 1997): 567–583; Nayda Terkildsen and Frauke

or by reordering the weight of existing beliefs, frames influence the process of opinion formation. Frames may also outlast the situation of their creation and become a lens for interpreting a range of other political issues. By providing analytical categories, catch phrases, and causal and normative statements about some aspect of the political world, embedded frames structure thinking and influence political behavior. For those uncomfortable with the terminology of frames, one can think of frames as ideas and packages of ideas. These packages are not as encompassing as ideologies, but rather address a single issue or small set of issues about the operation of the political world.[73]

Public debates create and consolidate frames in three ways. First, debates create frames through repetition. Frames coalesce as participants restate their central arguments and become accustomed to presenting issues in certain ways. These frames are repeated by the media and by political elites on both sides of the issue. The top-down diffusion of frames reaches the general population as ordinary citizens begin to use elite frames in their own discussions.[74] Second, debates produce and consolidate frames by condensing information into easily understandable packages. Debaters tend to collapse complex positions into sound bites, slogans, and narratives and to repeat them when pressing their claims and engaging rivals. Third, debates create new frames as political elites package preexisting ideas in new ways. During public debates, elites often draw from existing cultural and ideational resources when making their arguments.

STEP 2. Debates shift the weight of elite opinion. Many debates occur along the fault lines of preexisting political conflicts and do little to change the ideas of the participants. But some public debates *do* transform actors' ideas and interests, or at least how they present those ideas and interests publicly. One possible result of public debates is elite consensus. Liberal thinkers from John Stuart Mill to Jürgen Habermas place great faith in

Schnell, "How Media Frames Move Public Opinion: An Analysis of the Women's Movement," *Political Research Quarterly* 50, no. 4 (December 1997): 879–900; Thomas E. Nelson, Zoe M. Oxley, and Rosalee A. Clawson, "Toward a Psychology of Framing Effects," *Political Behavior* 19, no. 3 (1997): 221–246; Thomas E. Nelson and Donald R. Kinder, "Issue Frames and Group-Centrism in American Public Opinion," *The Journal of Politics* 58, no. 4 (November 1996): 1055–1078; Donald R. Kinder and Lynn M. Sanders, "Mimicking Political Debate with Survey Questions: The Case of White Opinion in Affirmative Action for Blacks," *Social Cognition* 8, no: 1 (1990): 73–103.

[73] For an example of how frames influence policymaking, see Eric Bleich, *Race Politics in Britain and France* (New York: Cambridge University Press, 2003).

[74] William Gamson, *Talking Politics* (New York: Cambridge University Press, 1992).

the power of the better argument to carry the day or of the participants to forge some common ground through deliberation.[75]

One need not share this view of human nature, however, to recognize that public debates can influence how participants articulate their arguments in the future; ideational change can result from recalculation as well as from persuasion. As I noted earlier, public debates are unpredictable affairs that expose the range and resonance of ideas present in political communities. Politicians may gain new information about the political environment from public debates. They may learn, for example, that their positions are less popular among other elite actors than they initially thought or that they leave them open to stinging attacks from opponents. Members of their own party may dissent. The press may pillory them for advancing certain types of arguments. These types of reactions, which politicians may not have foreseen, may cause actors to drop their old ideas in favor of ones closer to those of the other side. Convergence may occur through the new information that public debates provide.

Public debates, however, can also magnify existing cleavages and produce two different types of polarization. First, debates can harden the views of political elites and push them toward more extreme positions. The widening of political elites on a specific idea or issue is one potential outcome of public debates. Second, public debates can turn a formerly latent or nonexistent issue into a salient one that then becomes a point of conflict driving actors further apart in general.[76]

While elite convergence and polarization are the extreme outcomes of public debates, less dramatic shifts in elite opinion are also consequential. It also needs to be stressed that public debates are highly contingent and unpredictable events. Readers hoping for general predictions about the precise outcomes of public debate will thus be disappointed. One can probably identify only in hindsight the factors that pushed one debate toward convergence and another toward polarization. Yet, the outcomes of public debates are nonetheless important for shaping, and therefore analyzing, future political outcomes. In this sense, my argument dovetails

---

[75] This line of argument runs through all of Habermas's work. For Mill's views on debate, see John Stuart Mill, *On Liberty and Other Essays* (New York: Oxford University Press, 1991), 20–61. There is some empirical support for the proposition that deliberation leads to better opinions and to greater respect for opposing points of view. See Vincent Price, Joseph N. Cappella, and Lilach Nir, "Does Disagreement Contribute to More Deliberative Opinion?" *Political Communication* 19 (2002): 95–112.

[76] My thinking on polarization has benefited from conversations with Joshua Cohen.

with historical institutionalism. Scholars working in this paradigm do not provide a general theory of why some institutional configurations are produced at certain historical junctures, but rather claim that these institutions "structure" politics in consistent and predictable ways.[77] In the same vein, I claim that the elite opinion shift resulting from public debates matters for future political outcomes. Elite ideational convergence and polarization are concepts that political scientists should care about.

Elite consensus, for example, can be important for the stability of the political system itself. As David Truman argued over four decades ago, the principal threat to advanced industrial democracies is not the self-seeking behavior of established elites but the demagogue who emerges from political chaos.[78] He argued that elite consensus was necessary to prevent such demagogues from hijacking the state. While Truman was writing in the immediate aftermath of the McCarthy era, the specter of radical populists infiltrating the political system is both an enduring problem and a contemporary threat in Western Europe. Over the past two decades, right-wing populist parties have captured some measure of political power in most Western European states. To foreshadow one of the central arguments of this study, elite consensus is critical to preventing right-wing populist parties from consolidating themselves in contemporary Western Europe.

Conversely, elite polarization creates the opportunity for political entrepreneurs, such as right-wing populists, to exploit political divisions. By provoking the ire of one set of elites, political entrepreneurs – particularly polemical and rhetorically gifted ones – can capture media attention. And since the ideas of political entrepreneurs are not rejected, but either openly or tacitly supported, by another set of elites, these political entrepreneurs are legitimated and possibly viewed as potential partners.

Elite polarization in public debates can also lead to a lasting redefinition of the essential lines of conflict in political communities. As Carmines and Stimson argue, some issues are "capable of altering the political environment in which they originated and evolved."[79] The politics of race in the United States is one example, and the conflict over abortion may

[77] I take this term from Sven Steinmo, Kathleen Thelen, and Frank Longstreth, eds., *Structuring Politics: Historical Institutionalism in Comparative Analysis* (New York: Cambridge University Press, 1992).
[78] David Truman, "The American System in Crisis," *Political Science Quarterly* 74, no. 4 (December 1959): 481–497.
[79] Carmines and Stimson, *Issue Evolution*, 11.

be another.[80] Although such issues are rare, they are important since they produce enduring changes in the partisan political landscape.[81] As Carmines and Stimson note, a necessary ingredient of "issue evolution" is elite contestation, which I have recast as public debate. Indeed, the first step in issue evolution is an elite debate that creates, or magnifies, conflicts over basic ideas or policies.

The outcome of elite public debates is also important for the formation of mass political opinions. Zaller argues that two patterns of elite discourse shape public opinion in distinct ways. When "elites achieve a consensus or near consensus on a value or policy," they produce a "mainstream effect" whereby mass opinions converge on the elite consensus.[82] By contrast, when "elites disagree along partisan or ideological lines," they create a "polarization effect" in mass opinion.[83] The outcomes of elite-led public debates thus have profound and enduring ramifications for mass attitudes.

STEP 3. Debates shift the boundaries of legitimate discursive space. The third step in the sequence of public debates is a change in the language elites and ordinary citizens use to discuss political issues. "Legitimate discursive space" refers to the range of political statements one can make without the fear of sanctions and is thus analogous to the contested concept of "political correctness." Public debates that involve political-moral issues (such as race) help clarify which positions political elites deem legitimate. One possible by-product of debates is a set of discursive norms, which are markers for political ideas that govern future debates and become part of the normative structure of politics and society.

The mechanisms at work in the construction of political correctness are delegitimation and sanctioning. Certain terms, and certain political positions, come to be considered offensive by the majority of the political

[80] Greg D. Adams, "Abortion: Evidence of an Issue Evolution," *American Journal of Political Science* 41, no. 3 (July 1997): 718–737.
[81] To be clear from the outset, I do not claim that ideas about the Nazi past reshaped the party system in Germany and Austria in the same way that the evolution of the issue of race changed the American party system. I do, however, argue that changes in ideas about the Nazi past were consequential for both the German and Austrian party systems in Chapters 5 and 6, respectively.
[82] Zaller, *Mass Opinion*, 97. On the mainstream effect, see ibid., 98–100; For other examples of the mainstream effect, see Dennis Chong, Herbert McClosky, and John Zaller, "Social Learning and the Acquisition of Political Attitudes," in *American Ethos*, eds. Herbert McClosky and John Zaller (Boston: Harvard University Press, 1984); Herbert McClosky and Alida Brill, *Dimensions of Tolerance* (New York: Basic Books, 1983). For an example of a polarizing debate, see Mansbridge, *Why We Lost the ERA*, 1986.
[83] Zaller, *Mass Opinion*, 97. On the polarization effect, see pp. 100–113.

community and are labeled outside the bounds of legitimate discourse. As Stephen Holmes argues, "gag rules" exist in liberal societies to prevent discussion of certain topics.[84] This form of self-sanctioning results in the gradual disappearance of terms from public discourse. Social sanctioning eliminates actors who violate discursive norms from positions of power and in turn reinforces these norms. In American politics, for example, the language of race has changed markedly since the development of the civil rights movement. Rather than describing African Americans by the names that whites have given them, elites in American politics now largely recognize the right of African Americans, and the right of other groups, to be identified by their own terms. Concomitant with this shift has been a radical distancing from the ideas that underpinned racial inequality in general. When Senate Majority Leader Trent Lott challenged this norm by lauding Strom Thurmond in December 2002, Americans observed that political correctness is not confined to the ivory tower but is a powerful political force.

Public debates change not only what one *cannot* say, but also what one *can* say in public settings. They can shift the legitimate discursive space by inviting discussion about subjects that were previously considered taboo. The unfolding debate about gay marriage, for example, has introduced new terms, such as "civil union," into the political debate and challenged the hitherto unproblematic meaning of the term "marriage." While some Americans welcome this debate as a progressive extension of civil rights, others view it as challenging the political-moral foundations of their society. The discussion of taboo issues can thus be a progressive or retrograde development, depending on one's understanding of the issues.

Public debates can also produce changes in the discursive space without altering the political ideas that underlie certain words and phrases. The development of code words – new words for ones that have been delegitimated – is the central mechanism in this process. As some scholars have argued, racist political appeals did not disappear in American politics after the civil rights movement. Rather, politicians (Republicans in particular) discovered a new vocabulary for mobilizing racist sentiment without mentioning race directly.[85] The terms "crime," "welfare," and

[84] Stephen Holmes, *Passions and Constraints: On the Theory of Liberal Democracy* (Chicago: University of Chicago Press, 1995), 202–235.

[85] See, for example, Thomas Byrne Edsall and Mary D. Edsall, *Chain Reaction: The Impact of Race, Rights, and Taxes on American Politics* (New York: Norton, 1991); Tali Mendelberg, *The Race Card: Campaign Strategy, Implicit Messages, and the Norm of Equality* (Princeton: Princeton University Press, 2001).

"reverse discrimination" became the new language of race. Voters who previously spoke of the "negro problem" picked up on these elite cues and integrated these terms into their political discourse.[86]

DEBATES CAN STIMULATE MOVEMENTS IN CIVIL SOCIETY. Up to this point, I have presented a top-down view of public debates. Elite frames shape the ordinary individual's opinions about issues, elite convergence and polarization change mass attitudes, and shifts in elite language are picked up and disseminated by ordinary citizens. Yet under some conditions, the public can come to play an active role in public debate. Since this can occur at any stage of public debates, this process does not fit within the three-step sequence.

Civic activists (also members of the elite, according to my definition) may find that public debates open a window of opportunity for political mobilization among ordinary citizens. Such mobilization may engender informal networks, associations, and new social movements. Public debates may bring diverse groups in civil society together for a common cause. In this sense, public debates can stimulate movements in civil society that survive their founding moments and play important roles in future political conflicts.

The mobilization of civil society – and indeed the growth of civil society – during public debates depend on the presence, capabilities, and skill of political entrepreneurs who are able to exploit such a window of opportunity.[87] But the existence of such a window in turn depends on the "political opportunity structure," which is largely determined by the behavior of politicians and state actors during public debates.[88] When debates erupt and expose the ideational differences among elites, this can help mobilize civic activists who might have previously faced monolithic opposition from the political establishment. Alternatively, when political elites, perhaps for fear of adverse electoral consequences, fail to represent a position in a public debate that commands strong support among some segment of the population, this provides an opportunity for civic movements (as well as for right-wing populists) to champion this position.

---

[86] For a critique of this argument, see Michael G. Hagen, "References to Racial Issues," *Political Behavior* 17, no. 1 (1995): 49–88.

[87] On policy windows, see Kingdon, *Agendas*, 173–204.

[88] See Sidney Tarrow, *Power in Movement* (New York: Cambridge University Press, 1998), 18–20.

Summary

This chapter has developed an argument about discontinuous, contingent, and elite-led political change through the process of public debate. To say that elites lead public debates, however, does not mean that any one individual or elite group can shape debates as they wish. Deliberation matters. Elites in democracies react to, challenge, modify, and adopt the ideas of others as they debate one another through the mass media of communications. Through this process, elites create frames, the weight of elite opinion shifts, and new discourses emerge.

This is a conception of ideational change as a relatively rapid process, occurring within months or years rather than decades. The argument has also implicitly focused on high-volume issues – issues that raise foundational issues about the contemporary political community. Although one could imagine public debates about technical policy issues, often referred to as "hard" issues because they require specialized knowledge in order to understand them, most public debates involve easy issues. These issues are "symbolic rather than technical," "more likely to deal with policy ends than means," and "long on the political agenda."[89] The first section of this chapter made a case for viewing controversies about past atrocities as examples of easy issues. Let us now turn to a research design for understanding how two different societies have debated the lessons of history.

Research Design

This study develops a structured-focused comparison of postwar West Germany (and unified Germany after 1990) and Austria. In terms of culture, partisan political landscape (except for the strength of the far right), electoral institutions, organized interest groups, and the media, it is difficult to find two independent countries that resemble one another so closely. Given that Austria and Germany are the two surviving successor societies of the Third Reich, analyzing them permits us the rare opportunity to observe how the two societies dealt with the same basic historical event.

But have Germans and Austrians really been debating the same history? Was the Nazi period in Germany and Austria similar enough to make

---

[89] Edward G. Carmines and James A. Stimson, "The Two Faces of Issue Voting," *The American Political Science Review* 74, no. 1 (March 1980), 80.

comparison meaningful? Many Austrians would answer no, claiming that the annexation of their state in 1938 (the *Anschluss*) renders their history fundamentally different from Germany's. Underpinning this argument is the conviction that Austrians were, on the whole, less supportive of Nazi ideology and less complicit in its crimes than were Germans.

The historical evidence, however, discredits this view. For one, the roots of both political and religious anti-Semitism in Austria were as deep as, if not deeper than, those in Germany. Turn-of-the-century Vienna under Mayor Karl Lueger, the founder of the Christian Socialist Party (the forerunner of the ÖVP), was in fact the birthplace of political anti-Semitism.[90] During the First Republic (1918–1938), every political party made anti-Semitic appeals to the electorate. The *Anschluss* was also highly popular among Austrian Socialists and, of course, Austrian pan-Germanists. Ordinary Austrians had referred to the First Republic as the "state that no one wanted," and the jubilant crowds that welcomed Hitler throughout Austria testified to the popular support for union with Germany.[91] Immediately after the *Anschluss*, Austrian Nazis and non-Nazis alike began to attack Austrian Jews and organize anti-Jewish boycotts in ways that massively outpaced the Germans. As of May 1939, only 6 percent of Viennese Jews were still employed, while 30 percent of Jews in Berlin had jobs. Hermann Göring held up the Austrians as examples for the Germans to emulate, and the official journal of the SS, *Das Schwarze Corps*, noted the striking pace of "de-Jewification." There was even some concern that the Austrians were moving too rapidly. The Nazis official newspaper, the *Völkischer Beobachter*, noted that "whereas in northern Germany it was the duty of the party to educate the people about the Jewish danger, in Austria the duty of the party was to preserve the purity of the movement by restraining overly exuberant radicalism."[92] Such radicalism was on display during *Reichspogromnacht* (also known as *Kristallnacht* or "night of the broken glass") on November 9–10, 1938. During two days of violence in Vienna, 23 out of 24 synagogues were destroyed, 2,000 apartments were "aryanized," 27 Jews were murdered, 3,700 were sent to Dachau, and several hundred committed suicide.

[90] See Bruce F. Pauley, *Hitler and the Forgotten Nazis: A History of Austrian National Socialism* (Chapel Hill: University of North Carolina Press, 1981).

[91] Evan Burr Bukey, *Hitler's Austria: Popular Sentiment in the Nazi Era* (Chapel Hill: University of North Carolina Press, 2000).

[92] Quoted in Bruce Pauley, "Austria," in *The World Reacts to the Holocaust*, ed. David S. Wyman (Baltimore: Johns Hopkins University Press, 1996), 487.

Austrians also played a central role in Nazi crimes. Although Austrians comprised only 8 percent of the Third Reich's population, over 13 percent of the SS were Austrian. Many of the key figures in the extermination project of the Third Reich (Hitler, Eichmann, Kaltenbrunner, Globocnik, to name a few) were Austrian, as were over 75 percent of commanders and 40 percent of the staff at Nazi death camps. Simon Wiesenthal estimates that Austrians were directly responsible for the deaths of 3 million Jews. As in Germany, the Austrian resistance movement was tiny and the general population stood behind Hitler until the very end of the war. In sum, the view that Austria was the victim of Nazi aggression is a postwar construction, as I explain in Chapter 4, at substantial odds with the historical evidence.

This study does not offer an in-depth analysis of how the East German state, the third successor state of the Third Reich, represented the Nazi period. Very briefly, the communist narrative presented East Germans as heroic antifascists who had liberated themselves from the Nazi capitalists. Like Austrians then, East Germans externalized the Nazi past and assigned their society a historical role that eliminated their complicity in it. But since this study analyzes the role of public debate, the former DDR does not provide a meaningful case for comparison. After 1990, however, the former East Germany does enter the analysis as a part of reunified Germany. It is striking that neo-Nazi violence has been concentrated in the former East Germany, and that far-right movements have become a powerful presence in many Eastern German regions and towns. In the conclusion of this book, I argue that the strength of the far right is in part a legacy of the DDR's externalization of the Nazi past.

Of the many public debates about the Nazi past that occurred in Germany and Austria over the past five decades, why have I chosen to focus only on those since the 1980s? For one, there already exists a rich literature on dealing with the Nazi past (*Aufarbeitung der Vergangenheit*) during the first two postwar decades, especially for the German case.[93] Most of the participants in these debates are also no longer alive, and media analysis alone cannot capture the texture of debates that interviews can. Most importantly, public debates about the Nazi past since the 1980s in both Austria and Germany have been qualitatively different than those that occurred before. As I demonstrate in Chapters 3 and 4, there

---

[93] Two outstanding studies are Jeffrey Herf, *Divided Memory* (Cambridge: Harvard University Press, 1997), and Norbert Frei, *Adenauer's Germany and the Nazi Past* (New York: Columbia University Press, 2002).

has been a massive increase in public attention to the Nazi period since the early 1980s. It was also during this period that a genuine politics of the past emerged, that political actors sought to use history for concrete political goals.

In order to locate German public debates for analysis, I examined the politics section of the *Die Zeit*, Germany's weekly newspaper of record, over a twenty-year period (1980–2000). Using a coding scheme outlined in Appendix A, I counted the total column inches of stories related to the Nazi past published each week. This allowed me to locate the most intense (using column inches per week as a proxy for intensity) and lengthy public debate during that time period. As it turned out, and this should come as no surprise to students of German politics, the most intense public debate occurred in the mid-1980s. Indeed, one continuous public debate involving the fortieth anniversary of the end of the Second World War, the Bitburg ceremony, and the singularity of the Holocaust raged between 1985 and 1987. In Austria, locating the public debate about the Nazi past on which to concentrate was more straightforward. There is a scholarly consensus that the Waldheim affair marked the broadest, most intense, and most sustained debate about Austria's Nazi past.

The public debates of the mid-1980s in each state formed critical junctures in the process of coming to terms with the past. Although they receive the most attention, I also treat several other debates in some detail. To demonstrate the striking differences between German and Austrian debates about the Nazi past, I also analyze the debate that the *Wehrmachtsausstellung* (a traveling exhibit documenting the crimes of the German army during the Second World War) provoked in each state during the late 1990s.

Having chosen public debates based on intensity and length, I then analyze their breadth. I look at the contributions of a wide range of political actors to public debates, keeping the actors consistent across cases. The German and Austrian political, media, and interest group landscapes are similar enough to make this strategy of matched comparisons possible. The Christian Democratic, Social Democratic, and Green parties are of roughly equal size in the two countries. The Austrian national conservative daily (*Die* Presse) is similar to the German *Frankfurter Allgemeine Zeitung*, while the Austrian liberal (in the European sense) daily *Der Standard* is the rough equivalent of the German *Süddeutsche Zeitung*.

The largest papers in each state are national tabloids (*Bild* in Germany and *Krone* in Austria). These tabloids have an enormous influence on public debate, and I focus on them. For several reasons, I have chosen an interpretive rather than a quantitative content-analytic methodology to analyze these tabloids. Content analysis is best when searching for general trends and for discovering subtle biases (or slants) in news coverage. One of the hallmarks of tabloid papers, however, is that they are *all* slanted. Their news stories normally read like editorials, and their editorials are not composed of subtle arguments but unequivocal statements of principle. Content analysis thus has little value added in determining the bias of tabloid papers. In addition, by only using content analysis, the reader would miss the flavor of these texts. Having analyzed over four hundred texts from tabloid papers in each country, I have thus chosen to present samples, in some depth, that I consider representative of the overall line of argument in each paper.

Another important source of information is interviews of political elites. During two years of field work, I conducted 175 interviews with politicians, representatives of organized interest groups, intellectuals, academics, journalists, and civic activists (see Appendix B). For the semistructured interviews with politicians, I used a question set (see Appendixes E and F) that I developed for each country after conducting several pilot interviews. These pilot interviews allowed me to develop a question set that "flowed" and resembled more of a conversation than a question-and-answer session. These interviews lasted between thirty minutes and four hours, and were conducted with local-, state-, and national-level politicians. I attempted to make the number of interviews per party reflect the overall strength of the political party. I also made every effort to include a variety of opinions by asking interviewees to recommend people within their party with different views. This strategy allowed me to include a wide range of opinions in my interviews and reduce the bias toward uniformity.[94]

---

[94] One might contend that German and Austrian elites might not reveal their true opinions about the Nazi past to an American researcher, and that they might express radically different sentiments in their private conversations with friends and colleagues. While this problem is inherent in political interviewing, I do not believe it threatens the internal validity of this study for two reasons. First, and as will become apparent in Chapter 4, Austrian elites offered opinions on the Nazi past during interviews that could be described as controversial and evenly openly revisionist. The fact that German elites were, by and large, less willing to share such opinions – even if they actually held them – is a reflection of the different cultural norms in the two states. The second and related point is that my concern is public discourse, specifically the acceptable boundaries of public discourse. What politicians feel they can say publicly is the object of analysis. It might be that there is a large disjuncture between public statements and private beliefs, but I submit that it would take a major political-cultural shift for individuals, particularly German politicians, to openly challenge the contrition discourse.

I present the results of interviews in two ways. First, I follow the standard method of weaving quotes into the narrative.[95] One problem with this strategy, however, is the tendency to draw broad generalizations from single interviews or isolated quotes. To reduce this bias, I also present the results of my interviews in quantitative form using a coding scheme outlined in Appendixes C and D. Since I asked politicians from parties many of the same questions, I was able to test the hypothesis that there exist strong differences in ideas between political parties within countries.[96] And since I asked several of the same questions in both Germany and Austria, I was also able to test the hypothesis that there were important cross-national differences.

Whereas the first part of the study (Chapters 3 and 4) focuses on ideas as dependent variables, Chapters 5 and 6 treat these ideas as independent variables to explain the divergent fate of right-wing parties since the 1980s: the REPs in Germany and the FPÖ in Austria. Both parties began from minuscule vote totals and support in public opinion surveys and engineered electoral breakthroughs within several years of each other. Both appeared remarkably similar in terms of program, organization, and discourse. Both operated in similar electoral systems and partisan political landscapes. Yet while the FPÖ gained strength throughout the 1990s and captured 26.9 percent of the vote in the 1999 national parliamentary election, the REPs captured less than 2 percent in both the 1994 and 1998 elections and have virtually collapsed. Why, given such similar starting points, were the outcomes so different?

To answer this question, I first consider several alternative hypotheses for the divergent success of the far right in Western Europe, accounts that focus on immigration, unemployment, and electoral rules. Although these explanations certainly capture a part of the story, I argue that each is incomplete without considering the broad and diverse reactions that right-wing populist parties provoked from political parties, organized interest groups, the media, and civil society. These reactions were shaped, I argue, by ideas about the legitimacy of right-wing parties in the surviving successor societies of the Third Reich.

To trace these reactions, I draw on interviews, press releases, party literature, news stories, and secondary literature. I supplement these findings

[95] In the text, the name of the interview subject appears only if he or she gave me explicit permission to use it. Otherwise, only the interview subject's title and party affiliation appear.
[96] This strategy thus represents a cross between in-depth interviews and surveys.

with my own experience witnessing public appearances by right-wing political parties (mostly election rallies) and the reaction they provoked from other political actors. I conducted a dozen such "participant observations" during my fieldwork.

My analysis of the media reaction to right-wing populist parties concentrates on the two tabloid papers. This focus is critical because these papers are targeted at, and read by, the same clientele that right-wing populist parties tend to attract: the average level of education, income, and political sophistication is lower among readers of tabloid papers than among readers of quality newspapers. As I will demonstrate, *Bild* and *Krone* covered the far right in dramatically different ways.[97] In addition to content analysis, I support my argument with open-ended interviews with journalists. As Lawson has argued, journalistic norms play a crucial role in shaping media coverage.[98] My findings also suggest that journalistic norms about the far right shaped media coverage in Germany and Austria.

In order to extend the number of observations, I include many different data points and do not treat the failure or success of the far right as a single case.[99] In Austria, I focus on the FPÖ in different regions and over a twenty-year time period. In Germany, I disaggregate the REPs by looking both at the national organization and at state-level organizations in Berlin, Baden-Württemberg, and Bavaria – the states in which the REPs initially did well in the 1990s and the only ones where they maintained any presence as of 2001–2002. In addition, I trace the rise and fall of several other far-right movements in Germany over the 1990s: the New Right intellectual movement, the attempted Haiderization of the Free Democratic Party (FDP), and the presidential candidacy of the right-wing Stephan Heitmann (CDU). I argue that all of these movements failed for the same reason as the REPs: that institutionalized norms against right-wing political movements offering apologetic readings of the Nazi past trigger powerful reactions from other political parties, the media, and civil society. By extending my argument beyond the failure of the REPs, my argument thus makes broader claims about the

---

[97] It is important to note that I am not equating the political muscle of the *Bild* and the *Krone*. As mentioned earlier, the *Krone* is the more powerful of the two.

[98] Chappell Lawson, *Building the Fourth Estate* (Berkeley: University of California Press, 2002).

[99] Gary King, Robert O. Keohane, and Sidney Verba, *Designing Social Inquiry: Scientific Inference in Qualitative Research* (Princeton: Princeton University Press, 1994), 208–230.

inability of right-wing movements to become permanent forces in German politics.

Using Germany and Austria as cases for theory construction, I develop two general hypotheses about the success and failure of right-wing populist parties.

- Hypothesis one states that when established political parties, the media, and civil society universally and actively coopt, attack, and marginalize right-wing populist parties as soon as they appear, these parties will not be able to consolidate and will dissolve. This is what occurred in Germany, and there is evidence that this dynamic was at work in the Netherlands (1986–2002) and Sweden.
- Hypothesis two states that when established political parties, the media, and civil society attempt to tame right-wing populist parties by cooperating with them or allowing them influence in political office, these parties will not only grow but establish themselves as permanent forces in the party landscape. This is what occurred in Austria, and the evidence suggests that it occurred in France and Italy as well. In East Germany, the far right was able to establish itself as a social presence, if not a political one, in many cities and towns.

To summarize, the central theoretical moves of this chapter are as follows. First, I recast coming to terms with the past as a punctuated series of elite debates over the lessons of history. Second, I developed a framework for analyzing public debates in advanced industrial societies. Third, I foreshadowed my explanation for why right-wing political parties have succeeded in some countries and failed in others. Let us now turn to Germany to see how public debates about the Nazi past have transformed German political culture.

3

The Culture of Contrition

As one longtime observer of Germany writes, "it must be a historically unique phenomenon that a people has decided to commemorate its own crimes."[1] In no other country has the remembrance of a past atrocity become so politically salient, so institutionalized in elite political discourse, so much a part of both popular and political culture. In contemporary Berlin, one can visit the House of the Wannsee Conference, where the Nazi leadership planned the Final Solution; the Topography of Terror that stands on the site of the former Gestapo headquarters and documents the organization's crimes; the Jewish museum that traces the history of German–Jewish relations and the rise of anti-Semitism; and many other monuments and museums dedicated to the victims of Nazism. The gigantic Monument to the Murdered Jews of Europe, Germany's central monument to the Jewish victims of the Holocaust, stands across from the Reichstag. On November 9th, the chancellor, the president, and leading figures from every political party participate in massive demonstrations at the Brandenburg Gate to remember both the victims of the pogroms of 1938 and the contemporary victims of racism. A trip to other major German cities, and even to many small towns, would similarly expose a visitor to Germany's "culture of contrition."[2]

---

[1] Y. Michael Bodeman, "From Jewish Memory to Nationalized Commemoration of Kristall-nacht in Germany," in *Jews, Germans, Memory: Reconstructions of Jewish Life in Germany*, ed. Y. Michael Bodeman (Ann Arbor: University of Michigan Press, 1996), 194.

[2] I borrow this term from Karl Wilds, "Identity Creation and the Culture of Contrition: Recasting 'Normality' in the Berlin Republic," *German Politics* 9, no.1 (April 2000): 83–102.

In the immediate postwar period, however, the seeds of such a culture were hardly detectable. Addressing a crowd in 1946, future chancellor Adenauer (CDU, 1949–1963) demanded that the Western allies "finally" stop punishing the harmless followers of the few Nazi fanatics who had hijacked the German state.[3] Well into the 1950s, nearly half of all Germans believed that "Nazism was a good idea, badly carried out."[4] Rather than remembering the victims of the Holocaust, Germans honored the military and civilian casualties of the Second World War every November on *Volkstrauerstag* (Day of National Mourning). Germans hardly protested as former Nazis were reintegrated into politics and society during the first two postwar decades.

Given such inauspicious beginnings, how did a culture of contrition take root in Germany? The central argument of this chapter is that it was the product – in part the unintended product – of ideological battles between German political elites that emerged during the 1960s and erupted in the mid-1980s. As the first part of this chapter shows, politicians on both the right and the left largely disseminated a narrative of German victimization during the first two postwar decades. In the 1960s, however, the rise of the student movement transformed the past into a salient issue for the New Left, which sought to overturn the political establishment by undermining its foundational narrative and linking it with fascism. The German right responded by denouncing such "false mastering" of the Nazi past that was, in its view, destabilizing German politics. When Helmut Kohl (CDU) tried to free Germans from the burden of the Nazi past in the early 1980s, he unwittingly sparked a series of public debates that dramatically changed elite ideas about the Nazi past and left enduring legacies for German political culture.

This chapter uses the theoretical framework developed in Chapter 2 to analyze this critical juncture in the process of ideational change. Using coverage in the weekly newspaper *Die Zeit* as a proxy for issue saliency, it demonstrates how the year 1985 marked the high point of public debate about the Nazi past. The first step in the debates was the creation and consolidation of frames linking the Nazi past to contemporary politics. Conservatives disseminated the normalization frame, the central claim of which was that the Nazi past should be allowed to pass away. Combating their conservative rivals, members of the German left created the

---

[3] Jeffrey Herf, *Divided Memory* (Cambridge: Harvard University Press, 1997), 223.
[4] Elisabeth Noelle and Erich Peter Neumann, eds., *The Germans: Public Opinion Polls 1947–1966* (Westport: Greenwood Press, 1967), 197.

contrition frame that identified remembrance of Nazism's atrocities as an enduring political duty for all Germans. These debates marked the real beginning of Germany's culture of contrition. After the mid-1980s, monuments to the victims of National Socialism proliferated throughout Germany and critical examinations of the Nazi past became increasingly frequent. The contrition frame also became a central, arguably *the* central, lens for interpreting issues related to national identity and the integration of foreigners.

The second step in the process of debate was elite convergence around the contrition frame. As the German left and the liberal wing of the CDU adopted the contrition frame, conservatives who clung to the normalization frame became increasingly marginalized in public discourse. By 1995, it was clear that even the most conservative political party represented in the Bundestag, the CSU, had adopted the contrition frame.

The third step in the public debate was the institutionalization of linguistic norms that structured discussion about the Nazi past. These norms were supported by sanctioning mechanisms that quickly ended political careers for those who deviated from the key elements of the contrition frame. This ritualized discourse, which I refer to as "political correctness, German style," has become a central feature of unified Germany.

This chapter supports my argument with evidence from over one hundred open and semistructured interviews with German elites and comprehensive analysis of the German print media over a twenty-year period. I analyze the role of the media in agenda-setting and framing, concentrating on the positions taken by Germany's most powerful newspaper – the *Bild*. The Conclusion briefly examines two other explanations for the development of Germany's culture of contrition. Although generational dynamics and international influences were both important factors in Germany's confrontation with the past, neither were as consequential, I contend, as the elite-led public debates of the 1980s. In order to understand the significance of these critical junctures, let us first turn to the climate of historical amnesia that prevailed during the first two postwar decades.

The Adenauer Consensus: 1949–1959

The Basic Law (*Grundgesetz*) of 1949, the constitutional document of the Federal Republic, located the roots of Weimar's collapse in its flawed institutions. The founders of postwar Germany, who were heavily influenced by the Allies, set a 5 percent hurdle for parliamentary representation to prevent the proliferation of small parties that had precluded stable

parliamentary majorities in Weimar. The Basic Law redefined the institution of the presidency as one of symbolic moral authority, removing the
position from electoral influence and stripping it of the emergency powers
that had facilitated Hitler's seizure of power. The Basic Law also created
an organization charged with monitoring and combating political extremism (the *Verfassungschutz*) and outlined procedures for banning political
parties that undermined German democracy. It laid out the institutions of
federalism to prevent the central state from ever again wielding enormous
power. The first section of the Basic Law enumerated the civil and political
rights that Germans were guaranteed, a direct reaction to the Nazi violations of those rights. One of the most liberal constitutional documents
in the world, the Basic Law is widely credited for stabilizing Germany's
postwar democracy and has become a source of pride for many Germans.

Institutional redesign, however, was only one aspect of dealing with the
Nazi past. The record in other areas is mixed. The Nuremberg trials, for
example, demonstrate both the successes and failures of postwar justice.
On the positive side, the trials conducted by the Allied powers between
November 1945 and October 1946 produced a detailed record of the Nazi
regime and its crimes. The trials resulted in some important prosecutions:
ten high-ranking Nazis received death sentences, and three received life
sentences. Nuremberg also established the legal foundations for crimes
against humanity and became the point of reference for future attempts
to prosecute individuals involved in state massacres.

Yet the Nuremberg trials, and the Allied trials that followed them,
touched only the upper echelons of the Nazi regime. As Robert Jackson,
the U.S. Supreme Court Justice who led the American team at Nuremberg, put it, the prosecution concentrated on those "men who knew how
to use lesser folk as tools."[5] Jackson drew a distinction between a criminal
regime, which he sought to prosecute, and an innocent population that
he intended to absolve. He argued that "if the German populace had willingly accepted the Nazi program...no Storm-troopers would have been
needed in the early days of the Party and there would have been no need
for concentration camps or the Gestapo."[6] An editor covering the Nuremberg trials for the Berlin newspaper *Tagesspiegel* quickly recognized how
the prosecution was acquitting the German population: "The murder-
ers are right there in the dock. With every document the prosecution

[5] Quoted in Anne Sa'adah, *Germany's Second Chance: Truth, Justice, and Democratization*
(Cambridge: Harvard University Press, 1998), 155.
[6] Ibid., 155.

produces, another blemish on the soul of the average German disappears, and while the gallery, from Göring to Keitel, looks black as pitch, the average German looks as pure as a romantic full moon over the Heidelberg Castle."[7]

If the trials were a mixed success, denazification is generally agreed to have been a total failure. The enterprise rested on the voluntary participation of Germans who were asked to fill out a questionnaire detailing their level of involvement with Nazism. Less than 1 percent of those who answered were assigned any guilt at all, and countless convinced Nazis represented themselves as mere "fellow travelers" (*Mitläufer*).[8] The onset of the Cold War further undermined denazification, as the Allies became more interested in recruiting anticommunist allies, whatever their past allegiances, than in reshaping West German society.

Yet although denazification generally produced mild rulings, it was bitterly resented by the vast majority of the population.[9] When the Federal Republic was established in 1949, one of the first priorities of Konrad Adenauer's government was to gain amnesties for the "victims" of denazification. With the support of all political parties, Adenauer passed a series of amnesty laws that essentially overturned denazification and led to the reintegration of former Nazis into the professions and the government. In a bold statement of this policy, Adenauer appointed Hans Globke, a former Nazi official who had written commentaries on the Nuremberg race laws, to be his chief of staff in 1949. Adenauer's government also pushed for the release of war criminals. By 1958, only a few war criminals, most of them the original Nuremberg defendants, were still in jail.[10]

Political discourse about the Nazi past reflected these policies of amnesty and integration. Politicians from all political parties, when they spoke about the Nazi past at all, used four general strategies to distance Germans from the crimes of the recent past.[11] First, they placed the entire blame for Nazism's crimes on a small clique of fanatics who had hijacked the German state. In his first postwar political statement, which he gave

[7] Ibid., 157.

[8] The German denazification proceedings have been described as "fellow-traveler factories" by Lutz Niethammer, *Die Mitläuferfabrik: Entnazifierung am Beispiel Bayerns* (Berlin: Dietz Verlag, 1982).

[9] There were over 8 million members of the Nazi Party at the end of the war.

[10] On amnesties and integration, see Norbert Frei, *Adenauer's Germany and the Nazi Past* (New York: Columbia University Press, 2002).

[11] Helmut Dubiel, *Niemand ist frei von der Geschichte: Die nationalsozialistische Herrschaft in den Deutschen Bundestages* (Munich: Carl Hanser Verlag, 1999), 68. Only communist and leftist Social Democrats diverged from this consensus.

as the mayor of Cologne to the British occupying authorities, Konrad Adenauer (CDU) blamed the "indescribable suffering" on the "escapists" who captured power in 1933: "We, you and I, are not the ones [who are] guilty for this suffering. We, you and I, are condemned and impelled, impelled by love of our people, whom we do not want to see completely destroyed, to take upon ourselves this heavy and frightful burden so that at least the worst emergency conditions can be overcome."[12] Adenauer and other politicians routinely portrayed ordinary Germans as misled by Hitler and his inner circle. They used terms like *Hitlerismus, Hitlerregime, Hitlerstaat*, and *Hitlerfaschismus* to link Nazism with Hitler and thereby downplay the extent to which the movement had penetrated every aspect of German politics and society.[13]

Second, and related to the first point, German elites portrayed ordinary Germans as victims. Politicians from all parties stressed that the German population had suffered terribly during the war as well as after it. In the first parliamentary session of the new West German democracy in 1949, the president of the Bundestag, Paul Löbe (Social Democratic Party, SPD), addressed the question of German guilt. Following the common practice of differentiating the Nazi regime from the German people, Löbe noted that German politicians did not "doubt for a minute the incredible amount of guilt that a criminal system placed on the shoulders of our people." But then Löbe shifted his emphasis from German guilt to German suffering: "The critics from outside must not overlook one thing: the German people suffered under a double scourge. It groaned under the footsteps of the German tyrants and under the acts of war and retribution that the foreign powers committed to overcome the Nazi regime."[14]

Third, German politicians used vague, passive constructions when discussing the Nazi past. "Crimes committed in Germany's name" was a common formulation, as was the "unspeakable crimes" of the Nazi regime. In a characteristic remark, Chancellor Ludwig Erhard (1963–1966, CDU) noted that "every generation of our people is deeply affected by the results of the politics carried out in Germany's name between 1933 and 1945."[15]

---

[12] Konrad Adenauer, "Ansprache des Oberbürgermeisters Adenauer vor der von der britischen Militärregierung ernannten Kölner Stadtverordneten-Versammlung," in *Konrad Adenauer: Reden, 1917–1967: Eine Auswahl*, ed. Hans-Peter Schwarz (Stuttgart: Deutsche Verlagsanstalt), 79–81.

[13] Aleida Assmann and Ute Frevert, *Geschichtsvergessenheit, Geschichtsversessenheit* (Stuttgart: Deutsche Verlag, 199), 163.

[14] Quoted in Dubiel, *Niemand*, 39.

[15] Ibid., 98.

Fourth, politicians argued that since the top Nazis were either dead, in jail, or in exile, the legacy of National Socialism posed no danger for the fledgling democracy. Adenauer claimed in 1952 that "after all that happened in the National Socialist period we view it as unworthy and unbelievable that there are still people in Germany who would persecute or despise the Jews because they are Jews."[16] Public opinion polls, however, told a different story. In 1952, 37 percent of Germans agreed with the statement that "it would be better for Germany not to have any Jews in the country," while only 20 percent disagreed.[17]

Adenauer was not unaware of the historical facts or the persistence of anti-Semitic attitudes. He was only too aware of them, and his narrative of the Nazi past reflected his deep pessimism about Germans' political values. Adenauer wagered that the only means of creating a viable democracy was to avoid a critical discussion of the Nazi period.[18] He also wanted to win elections, and his narrative of the Nazi past resonated with most German voters. In 1953, 55 percent of Germans disagreed with the statement that "German soldiers of the last war can be reproached for their conduct in the occupied countries," while only 21 percent answered "in some cases."[19]

Given this public climate and the political costs of critically examining the Nazi past, the Luxembourg Restitution Agreement, which committed West Germany to pay reparations to Israel, must be viewed as a major achievement. Adenauer was the central force behind it, believing that reparations were the price West Germany needed to pay to rejoin the civilized community of states. He faced stiff resistance from his own party and cabinet, and needed the votes of the Social Democrats to pass the reparations bill in the Bundestag.[20] To convince members of his party, Adenauer mixed anti-Semitic stereotypes with appeals to Germany's economic self-interest. "Now as before," Adenauer argued, "the power of the Jews in the economic sphere is extraordinarily strong. This reconciliation . . . with the Jews from the moral and political as well as the economic standpoint is an essential requirement for the Federal Republic."[21] Adenauer also took pains to explain that restitution did not imply that the German population was complicit in the Holocaust. In a parliamentary speech

---

[16] Quoted in Herf, *Divided Memory*, 272.
[17] Noelle and Neumann, *The Germans*, 189.
[18] This is one of Herf's central arguments. See *Divided Memory*, 267–300.
[19] Ibid., 202.
[20] Nearly half of the member's of Adenauer's governing coalition (CDU/CSU–FDP) abstained during the reparations vote.
[21] Quoted in Herf, *Divided Memory*, 286.

supporting reparations, for example, Adenauer stressed that "in an over-whelming majority, the German people abhorred the crimes committed against the Jews and did not participate in them."[22]

During the late 1940s and 1950s, the period known as the "Adenauer restoration," there were several West German politicians who spoke more explicitly about German guilt and the need to remember the Holocaust. President Theodor Heuss (FDP) was the most eloquent spokesman for this position and laid the basis for the contrition discourse.[23] Some leftist members of the SPD, particularly Kurt Schumacher, also argued that the consolidation of German democracy required, rather than precluded, a critical examination of the Nazi past.[24] Like many Social Democrats, Schumacher suffered terribly under the Nazis – he died in 1953 from injuries suffered in the Dachau concentration camp – and possessed moral authority. His party was also less burdened by collaboration with the Nazis than the Christian Democrats or the bourgeois parties and did not face the problem of reintegrating former Nazis. Critically examining the Nazi past thus did not carry the same political costs for Social Democrats as it did for conservatives. But after the elections of 1949, in which the SPD suffered a narrow and completely unexpected loss, SPD politicians spoke less about the Nazi past and the duty to remember. Schumacher supported the reintegration of members of the Waffen-SS into German society and did not oppose the amnesties that these people received. Heuss and Schumacher, to the extent that they called for a critical examination of the past, were also in the minority during the first two postwar decades. As one scholar summarizes: "in the mid-1950s, ascribing the horrors of the Third Reich to Hitler and a small clique of 'major war criminals' was a basic element of public West German awareness. In turn, the West Germans accorded themselves, in their majority, the status of politically 'seduced' individuals, themselves rendered 'martyrs,' in the end, by the war and its consequences."[25]

The Consensus Unravels: 1959–1985

If during the late 1940s and 1950s an elite consensus about the Nazi past prevailed, this consensus unraveled over the course of the next two

---

[22] Ibid., 282.
[23] Ibid., 227–239.
[24] Ibid., 239–261.
[25] Frei, *Adenauer's Germany*, 311.

decades. The left (the Social Democrats) and the New Left (the extraparliamentary movements and, later, the Green Party) pushed for a more critical confrontation with the Nazi past as part of a larger program of democratic renewal. The right viewed this confrontation with unease, fearing that it would undermine the development of a healthy national identity and polarize German politics. Both left and right looked to the Weimar experience to understand the political stakes of the student movement, but drew opposite conclusions from this historical analogy.

Beginning in the late 1950s, a series of events raised the salience of the Nazi past in West German politics. In 1959, the desecration of a newly reopened synagogue in Cologne ignited a wave of neo-Nazi vandalism that drew international media attention. To demonstrate its vigilance in combating right-wing extremism, Adenauer's government commissioned a white paper on neo-Nazi activity. Although the government concluded anti-Semitism was no longer a problem, the neo-Nazi vandalism focused West German politicians and media elites on the enduring legacy of National Socialism. In 1961, the trial of Adolf Eichmann in Jerusalem was widely reported in the German media. The Auschwitz trials from 1963 to 1968, in which SS members who ran the concentration camp were prosecuted, had an even greater impact by making the details of the death camps public knowledge.[26] One result of these trials was heated debates in both 1965 and 1969 in the Bundestag about extending the statute of limitations for crimes committed under the Nazi regime. In both cases, the parliament voted to extend the statute of limitations before finally abolishing it in 1979. Although the trials and parliamentary debates raised the salience of the Nazi past, it was above all the student movement that took hold of the Nazi past as its own political issue and used it to raise questions about the nature of contemporary German democracy.

The Nazi past was an issue for student leaders long before the culmination of the extraparliamentary protest in 1968. The anti-Semitic wave of 1959 inspired a seminar in 1960 at the Free University in Berlin about anti-Semitism in Germany, both during the Nazi era and in the Federal Republic, which several leaders of the student movement attended.[27] The

[26] Andrei S. Markovits and Beth Simone Noveck, "Germany," in *The World Reacts to the Holocaust*, ed. David S. Wyman (Baltimore: Johns Hopkins University Press, 1996), 423.

[27] The following discussion of the student movement draws on an interview with Wolfgang Kraushaar at the Hamburg Institute for Social Research and chief chronicler of the '68 movement, Hamburg, 22 June 2001.

quasi-official organ of the movement, *Argument*, began to print articles about anti-Semitism and the Nazi past in the early 1960s. Students began to research the Nazi pasts of their professors and to make this information public as part of their attack on the academic establishment. At the University of Tübingen, for example, students distributed a picture of a professor in a Nazi uniform. As the student movement developed into a general protest against the political establishment, students also began to "out" politicians with Nazi pasts.[28]

The Nazi past was a useful weapon in the student movement's fundamental critique of West German politics and society. But to see its use of history in purely instrumental terms ignores the relationship between the student movement's reading of the Nazi past and its political ideology. The antiauthoritarian movement, which was the strand of the student movement with the most coherent ideology, takes its name from the Frankfurt School's studies of the authoritarian state and the authoritarian personality.[29] Such works located the roots of Nazism in the personality and family structures that, they claimed, persisted in the Federal Republic. The key question for the antiauthoritarian movement was how to break apart such structures, in particular the internalized need for order that provides a foundation for authoritarian political movements. Communal living, sexual freedom, and other radical lifestyle changes provided a solution. To be sure, young adults in other advanced industrial societies also embraced such practices. But in West Germany, lifestyle changes were explicitly linked to a specific reading of the Nazi past.

The student movement fundamentally altered West German politics as well as West German society.[30] Although the student movement appeared to balkanize after 1968, the veterans of the movement would coalesce in the Green movement in the late 1970s and early 1980s. Antiauthoritarian ideology and a commitment to examining the Nazi past would become central concerns of the Green Party, which entered parliament in 1983. The party in fact defined itself as a political reaction to the Nazi past.[31]

---

[28] Georg Kiesenger (CDU), chancellor from 1966 to 1969, was a member of the Nazi Party and held an important post in Goebbels's propaganda branch. Heinrich Lübke (CDU), president from 1959 to 1964, was criticized for his role in Nazi building projects.

[29] The classic work is Theodor Adorno et al., *The Authoritarian Personality* (New York: Harper, 1950).

[30] These changes were so profound that one prominent German historian refers to them as "the second founding of the Federal Republic." Peter Pulzer, *German Politics 1945–1995* (New York: Oxford University Press, 1995).

[31] See Andrei S. Markovits and Philip S. Gorski, *The German Left: Red, Green and Beyond* (Cambridge: Polity Press, 1993), 18–21; Andrei S. Markovits, "Was ist das 'Deutsche'

As Joschka Fischer, a leading Green politician and the current German foreign minister, once put it: "we became leftists precisely because of German history."[32]

Although members of the student movement transformed the Nazi past into a salient political issue, their narratives of the period bear little resemblance to the contrition frame that would emerge in the 1980s. The students viewed fascism as a product of capitalism that existed in many Western societies. They drew few distinctions between Nazism and what they considered to be its contemporary manifestations, such as the West German or American governments. Like East German communists, the students also largely ignored the Holocaust in their narratives of the Nazi period and adopted hostile positions toward Israel after the 1967 war.[33] Yet for all its lacunae, the student movement's concern with the Nazi past did produce important changes. The New Left's concern with the recent past influenced the Social Democrats, who came to power for the first time in postwar Germany in 1969. When Chancellor Willy Brandt (SPD) challenged Germans to "dare more democracy," he linked an open confrontation with the Nazi past to the further democratization of German society. For Brandt and others, public debates about the basic orienting values of the Federal Republic were essential to the development of a political culture in which argument could flourish without undermining democracy. Such a *Streitkultur* (culture of contention) was something that Weimar had sorely lacked and something that the extraparliamentary protest movement was helping the Federal Republic to develop.[34]

The German right used the Weimar analogy to make the opposite argument about the relationship between extraparliamentary protest and democracy. In a speech in 1969, Chancellor Kurt Georg Kiesinger (1966–1969, CDU) reminded Germans that Weimar "was not destroyed because of the mass unemployment, but rather because of the spiritual and political division of the German people."[35] Kiesinger warned that the violence of leftist groups would push the "startled part" of the population

---

an den Grünen? Vergangenheitsaufarbeitung als Voraussetzung politischer Zukunftsbewältigung," in *Die Grünen: Letzte Wahl?* ed. Otto Kallscheur (Berlin: Rotbuch, 1986), 146–164.

[32] *Die Zeit*, 7 February 1985.

[33] Markovits and Noveck, "Germany," 426–427.

[34] Rob Burns and Wilfried van der Will, *Protest and Democracy in West Germany* (New York: St. Martin's Press, 1988).

[35] Quoted in Dubiel, *Niemand*, 120.

toward right-wing extremism, thereby creating the polarization that had destroyed Weimar.[36]

As the political salience of the Nazi past increased during the 1960s and 1970s, German conservatives began to warn of the dangers of exaggerated remembrance. Chancellor Ludwig Erhard (1963–1966, CDU) argued in 1965 that "we have no need for every endeavor that derives an interminable German sin from the past barbarism and preserves it as a political resource."[37] If conservatives objected to the instrumentalization of history by the left, they also identified a more profound danger for German society in current attempts to come to terms with the Nazi past. The student movement of the 1960s and the terrorism of the 1970s, conservatives argued, were the products of what Alfred Dregger (CDU) termed a "false mastering of the past."[38] In Dregger's view, the anti-authoritarianism of the New Left was a perverted reaction to the Nazi past that was destroying traditional German values:

We who are responsible for the present and future of the Federal Republic of Germany must free ourselves from the shadow of Hitler. Neither the copies of Hitler ... nor the polar opposite of Hitler can be the basis of our actions. ... We must orient ourselves with those basic values that Hitler misused but could not destroy.[39]

For German conservatives, restoring those basic values that Hitler had "misused," such as patriotism and diligence, was a political imperative that found its first coherent expression in Erhard's conception of the integrated society (*formierte Gesellschaft*). Erhard and other conservatives believed that a "healthy national identity" was necessary to check the centrifugal tendencies of modern industrial society. From their point of view, the student movement's rejection of traditional German values was a clear danger to this process. Moreover, their rejection of authority structures was undermining the family – the foundation of society in conservative political thought. As Erhard noted: "The youth have the right to question the generation of their parents. But they also have the duty not to forget the blood, sweat and tears of their mothers and fathers and to protect with their own achievements the gift that fell in their laps."[40]

---

[36] Ibid., 120.
[37] Assmann and Frevert, *Geschichtsvergessenheit*, 59.
[38] Quoted in Dubiel, *Niemand*, 156.
[39] Ibid., 156.
[40] Ibid., 97.

As politicians debated the lessons of Weimar, one central aspect of the Nazi past was left out of the public debate. Despite the trials of the 1960s and the parliamentary debates about the statute of limitations, the Holocaust was not salient in political discourse. The term itself did not appear until the 1970s, and it was not until 1978 that the liberal *Die Zeit* even covered the anniversary of *Pogromnacht*.[41] As noted earlier, German elites rarely referred directly to the Holocaust and almost never went into detail about it. It was also hardly an important issue for the general population. When the American television mini-series *Holocaust* captured the German nation's attention in 1979, the commentary that followed it demonstrated the public's striking lack of knowledge about the Holocaust.[42] In the flurry of special television and radio call-in shows, many Germans displayed a basic unawareness about the major points of the Final Solution. The national print media seized upon the theme and printed scores of articles related to the mini-series, the public reaction to it, and the Holocaust.

Although it was not an elite-led debate, the *Holocaust* phenomenon demonstrates the power of the media to create sudden and dramatic shifts in public opinion. As of 1978, 64 percent agreed with the statement that "one should now draw a line under the Nazi past" and allow the statute of limitations to expire. Only 34 percent believed that "NS crimes should be pursued further." After the airing of *Holocaust* in 1979, however, 50 percent of Germans wanted to pursue Nazi criminals further, while 46 percent wanted to put the past to rest.[43] As of the early 1980s, German public opinion about the Nazi past reflected the polarization among political elites.

Public Debates in the 1980s

The mid-1980s marked a new stage in elite deliberation about the Nazi past. Over the previous four decades, political elites had normally referred to the Nazi past only when events like trials, demands for reparations, and constitutionally mandated debates about the statute of limitations forced

[41] Y. Michael Bodeman, "From Jewish Memory to Nationalized Commemoration of Kristallnacht in Germany," in *Jews, Germans, Memory*, ed. Y. Michael Bodeman (Ann Arbor: University of Michigan Press, 1996), 179–200.

[42] Markovits and Noveck, "Germany," 430.

[43] Joyce Mushaben, *From Post-war to Post-wall Generations* (Boulder: Westview Press, 1998), 58.

them to do so. The New Left was the first political movement to seize on the Nazi past as a political tool. But beginning in the 1970s, conservatives also began to perceive the importance of history for contemporary politics. In order to pave the way for a new conservative program, they sought to make the German past once again usable – a strategy that required both stressing the positive aspects of German history and reducing the political salience of the Nazi past. The series of anniversaries in the 1980s, the most important of which was the fortieth anniversary of the end of the Second World War in Europe, magnified this ideological conflict between right and left.

In 1982, the Christian Democrats regained control of the national government after thirteen years of Social Democratic rule. Chancellor Helmut Kohl (CDU) promised to lead a spiritual-moral turn (*geistige-moralische Wende*) in West German politics and society. He became the primary political carrier for ideas about the German past and German national identity that developed in many conservative think tanks in the 1970s.[44] Echoing Erhard and Dregger, Kohl called for a return to traditional German values and, more than any other German chancellor, sought to use history to engineer this change. Rather than avoiding the Nazi past or discussing it only when necessary, Kohl, who considered himself an amateur historian, confronted German history head-on.

Kohl repeatedly emphasized the positive sides of German history. In his very first speech to the Bundestag as chancellor in 1982, he announced his plans for a museum of West German history in Bonn. This museum, which was later built in Berlin, celebrates the achievements of the Federal Republic. After winning national elections in 1983, Kohl delivered another inaugural speech (*Antrittsrede*) to the Bundestag filled with historical references. He noted that "we Germans must stand by our history with its greatness and its misery, not take anything away, not add anything." Kohl then stressed that German history must become the "spiritual home" for the younger generation and highlighted its positive sides: "We have been left a great cultural inheritance: philosophy, poetry, literature, music. . . . But we were also always and still are a nation of inventors and entrepreneurs, of social reformers and scientists. The nation of Albert Einstein and Max Planck, of Siemens and Daimler, of Zeiss and Röntgen. . . ."[45]

---

[44] Claus Leggewie, *Der Geist Steht Rechts* (Berlin: Rotbuch Verlag, 1987).
[45] Quoted in Dubiel, *Niemand*, 189.

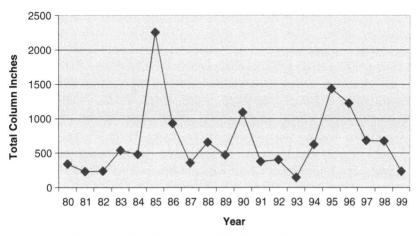

FIGURE 3.1. Coverage of the Nazi past in *Die Zeit*: 1980–1999.

While not ignoring the crimes of Nazism, Kohl sought to distance both himself and contemporary Germans from them. On a trip to Israel in 1984, Kohl noted that he enjoyed the "mercy of late birth (*die Gnade der späten Geburt*)," meaning that he had not been an adult during the Nazi period. Kohl's statement was widely interpreted as a signal that contemporary Germans could no longer be held responsible for the crimes of Nazism. A year later at Bergen-Belsen, Kohl spoke of crimes committed "in the German name," another rhetorical strategy of distancing the German people from the Nazis.

Kohl's statements, as well as those from other conservatives, drew a spirited response from politicians and intellectuals on the left. For nearly three years during the mid-1980s, the right and left in Germany debated the lessons of the Nazi past. Rather than allowing the Nazi past to pass away, Kohl unwittingly sparked a national discussion on it and turned it into a salient political issue.

In Chapter 2, I noted that public debates can be measured in terms of three parameters: intensity, duration, and breadth. To demonstrate the intensity of these debates, I present the results of my content analysis of the weekly paper *Die Zeit* over a twenty-year period in Figure 3.1. Using a coding scheme outlined in the appendixes, I counted the total column inches of stories related to the Nazi past that appeared in the politics section (the front section of *Die Zeit*) each week. This measure is a proxy for both intensity and political saliency. As we can see in Figure 3.1,

1985 witnessed a dramatic increase in the political saliency of the Nazi past.

In terms of breadth, these public debates involved every major political actor, newspaper, and public intellectual in West Germany. Both the chancellor (Kohl) and the president (Richard Von Weizsäcker, CDU) played central roles in them, as did leading politicians from every political party. The unions, churches, and many other interest groups offered their own positions and held their own commemorations. The media covered these debates in great detail, provided a forum for elites to debate one another in print, and injected their own views in opinion pieces. As I will show, they also played a major role in both agenda-setting and framing. Public intellectuals and academics of stature also felt compelled to enter the fray. Although elites played the leading role, ordinary citizens also participated in this national discussion. Many German universities held open lecture series about the meaning of Germany's defeat, as did many local historical organizations.[46]

Step One: Frame Creation

So what were these debates all about? Although there was some dispute over the historical events themselves, they were primarily battles over the proper role of the Nazi past in the political present and future. Two issues became paramount. First, should the Nazi past be allowed to pass away, or should it remain central to the political culture of the Federal Republic? Second, how important was the Nazi past, and the Holocaust in particular, relative to other periods and events in German history? These issues became proxies for positions on German national identity. During the course of the debate, two central frames linking the lessons of the Nazi past to contemporary politics emerged.

The German right (much of the CDU/CSU, the editorial staffs of the *Frankfurter Allgemeine Zeitung* and *Die Welt*, conservative historians like Ernst Nolte and Andreas Hillgruber, and the organization of German expellees) called for Germans to develop a "normal" relationship with their history that would permit a healthy national identity. The normalization frame contains older elements in political discourse about the Nazi past. Like the Adenauer narrative, the crimes of Nazism are attributed to a small clique of fanatics. The years 1933–1945 are treated

---

[46] Jan-Holger Kirsch, *Wir haben aus der Geschichte gelernt* (Cologne: Böhlau Verlag, 1999), 115.

as a natural catastrophe, an aberration in German history, and a period in which almost everyone suffered enormously. The normalization frame also gives pride of place to German suffering, especially to those Germans expelled from Eastern Europe after the war (*Die Vertriebenen*), and views Germans as victims of the Allied powers as well as of the Nazis. Regarding the victims of the Holocaust, the emphasis is on forgiving and forgetting rather than on preserving painful and divisive memories, an argument often supported with reference to Christian values.

The normalization frame also contains several new elements. It calls for reconciliation with the rest of German history to restore a sense of historical continuity that the Nazi past had broken. Advocates search for usable traditions in German history as bases for national pride. The normalization frame does not deny Nazism's crimes, but it downplays them in several ways. It relativizes the Holocaust by arguing that other historical atrocities – such as Stalinism or the bombing of Hiroshima – were of similar magnitude. This move opens up space for the claim that Germany is not fundamentally different from other countries and should be allowed to be normal. Normalization entails "drawing a line" (*Schlusstrich*) under the Nazi past, meaning that the topic no longer needs to be discussed. Focusing on past crimes, in this view, is masochistic and weakens the national identity.

During the course of the public debates, German leftists, and later German centrists, rejected the ideas of the normalization frame and created what I refer to as the contrition frame. This frame contained a set of ideas that were very different from the New Left's narrative of the Nazi past. For one, it placed the Holocaust at the center of German history. Rather than comparing it to other events, such as the wars in Vietnam or Biafra, advocates of the contrition frame viewed the Holocaust as unique. Remembrance of Nazism's crimes and atonement for them were enduring political duties for all Germans. Auschwitz ruled out the normalization of Germany, for the hypernationalism that produced the Final Solution precluded Germans from ever developing a national identity like that of the French, Italians, or Swedes. The only way in which Germans could positively identify with their state was by developing an emotional attachment to their democratic institutions.

The following section takes a closer look at how these two frames coalesced by sketching three debates about particular issues that tied into broader questions about the Nazi past. The first concerned the meaning of May 8, 1945 – the end of the Second World War in Europe. The second revolved around the Bitburg affair, and the third involved the singularity of the Holocaust. These case studies detail how politicians, intellectuals, and the media framed and set the agenda surrounding these political conflicts.

The Meaning of May 8th

The writer Heinrich Böll once claimed that "you will always be able to distinguish Germans by whether they describe May 8th as the 'day of defeat' or the 'day of liberation.'"[47] Those (mostly conservative) Germans who consider May 8th the day of defeat mourn the loss of German sovereignty, the division of the German state, and the capitulation of the German army. Although they condemn National Socialism, they see no reason why Germans should commemorate the culmination of a national tragedy. Furthermore, they point out that defeat in war brought with it tremendous postwar suffering. As the politician Lorenz Niegel (CSU) put it:

> May 8th was and is one of the saddest days in the experience of our nation, a day of profound humiliation. The day of the unconditional surrender of the German army was for millions of German people, who were as innocent as anyone else, who suffered under National Socialist rule, the beginning of imprisonment and internment, of looting and rape, of retribution and expulsion, of hunger and death.[48]

Politicians on the left (Greens, Social Democrats, and most liberals) and leftist intellectuals view May 8th as an unequivocal day of liberation. For them, May 8th marked the end not only of Nazi tyranny but also of the German *Sonderweg*, a term that captures Germany's continual failure to develop viable democratic political institutions since the early nineteenth century. The end of the war brought Western integration, both institutionally through the North Atlantic Treaty Organization (NATO) and the European Economic Community (EEC), and culturally through the embrace of Enlightenment traditions and the rejection of the romantic-nationalist strand in German political thought. Those who describe May 8th as a day of liberation do not mourn the loss of eastern Germany and indeed often regard the concept of the nation-state as retrograde. According to Joschka Fischer, for example, the nation-state is "gone and gambled away by the Germans themselves."[49]

[47] Heinrich Böll, "Briefe an meine Söhne oder: Vier Fahrräder," *Die Zeit*, 3 March 1985.
[48] *Deutsche Tagespost*, 8 May 1985.
[49] Joschka Fischer, "Wir Kinder der Kapitulanten," *Die Zeit*, 3 May 1985.

The weekly *Die Zeit* provided in-depth coverage of the debate over May 8th. It ran a four-month series in its front section titled "Der sperriger Gedenktag" ("The 'Cumbersome' Memorial Day") in which the editors solicited essays from German politicians and intellectuals. The list of participants included some of the most prominent elites in the Federal Republic: Heinrich Böll, Joschka Fischer, Michael Stürmer, Golo Mann, and many others. Also included were essays from foreign experts in German politics, such as Saul Friedländer and Gordon Craig. For readers who did not intend to follow the whole debate, the paper summarized the key arguments of each side in early February.[50]

By placing this four-month series in its front section (politics), *Die Zeit* played an important agenda-setting role in the public debate. It defined May 8th as an important political controversy in late 1984, when an article by Theo Summer titled "Der Griff nach der Vergangenheit" ("The Grasp for the Past") appeared on its front page. As students of the media have argued, leading national papers can often set off a cascade of coverage when "journalists take cues from one another about which events and ideas are newsworthy and how they should be interpreted."[51] This phenomenon has been called "pack journalism" and was at work in Germany in late 1984.[52] Following the *Zeit*'s lead, Germany's other quality newspapers and journals began to discuss the meaning of May 8th. The conservative *Frankfurter Allgemeine Zeitung* and *Die Welt* began their coverage in early January, as did the liberal *Frankfurter Rundschau* and *Süddeutsche Zeitung*. The weekly *Der Spiegel* also began to cover the issue a full four months before the anniversary itself.

In addition to agenda-setting, the media played a central role in framing the debate. While the terms "defeat" and "liberation" had not been prominent in political discourse before 1985, the series in *Die Zeit* was organized around this dichotomy. The titles of the editorials and op-eds in *Die Zeit* and other papers also framed the debate in those terms: "Day of Liberation, Day of Defeat" (*Die Zeit*, April 14), "May 8th: Liberation, New Beginning, or Defeat?" (*Die Welt*, January 8, 1985), "Victory and Defeat" (*Frankfurter Allgemeine Zeitung*, April 20, 1985). Politicians

[50] "Pro und Contra: Feiern zum 8. Mai," *Die Zeit*, 2 February 1985, 67.
[51] Jacob S. Hacker, *The Road to Nowhere* (Princeton: Princeton University Press, 1997), 164.
[52] See Timothy Crouse, *The Boys on the Bus* (New York: Ballentine, 1973); Bernard Roshco, *Newsmaking* (Chicago: University of Chicago Press, 1975).

reacted to such framing by aligning themselves with one term or the other.[53]

The *Bild Zeitung* contributed to these debates through its editorials. As mentioned earlier, *Bild* dominates the German media landscape and claims a readership ten times higher than that of either the conservative *Frankfurter Allgemeine Zeitung* or the liberal *Süddeutsche Zeitung*.[54] *Bild* is a tabloid paper, complete with racy leads, exclamation points, and a daily photo of a topless woman. It also has a clear political slant: conservative with a dash of right-wing populism. At times, it has stirred xenophobic sentiment against immigrants and portrayed asylum seekers as economic refugees who drain the welfare state.[55] During the 1960s, *Bild* and the rest of Axel Springer's media empire battled what they deemed the "chaotic leftists" of the student movement, who in turn denounced Springer as the linchpin of the Federal Republic's fascist political system. On the national question, *Bild* pressed for unification for decades and kept the issue on the political agenda, even when all political parties had all but accepted permanent division. This is one of the five ideological pillars on which the Springer Press is founded and one that editors must agree to support in order to work for it.[56]

But *Bild* possesses another central ideological strain that shapes its position on the Nazi past. The second pillar of the Springer Press is a commitment to reconciliation with the Jewish people. Any editor who works for the Springer Press must sign a contract committing him- or herself to this goal.[57] During his lifetime, Axel Springer (1912–1985) donated large sums to Israel and worked tirelessly for German–Jewish reconciliation. Shimon Peres once stated that "after Adenauer, Axel Springer has contributed

---

[53] Interview with Friedbert Pflüger (MdB–CDU), 27 February 2002, Berlin.

[54] Circulation figures are from *Media Perspektiven Basisdaten, Daten zur Mediensituation in Deutschland 1998.*

[55] See, for example, Christoph Butterwegge, "Ethnisierungsprozesse, Mediendiskurse und politische Rechtstendenzen," in *NS-Vergangenheit, Antisemitismus und Nationalismus in Deutschland*, ed. Christoph Butterwegge (Baden-Baden: Nomos Verlagsgesellschaft, 1997), 172–217.

[56] The five pillars of the Springer Press are as follows: (1) to uphold liberty and law in Germany, a country belonging to the Western family of nations, and to further the unification of Europe; (2) to promote reconciliation of Jews and Germans and support the vital rights of the State of Israel; (3) to support the Transatlantic Alliance and solidarity with the United States of America in the common values of free nations; (4) to reject all forms of political extremism; (5) to uphold the principles of a free social market economy. Taken from the Axel Springer Company (www.asv.de/englisch/unterneh/frame.htm).

[57] Interview with Oliver Michalsky, journalist for the *Berliner Morgenpost* (owned by the Springer Press), Berlin, 21 November 2001.

more than anyone else to the unique, clear, and significant relationship between Germany and Israel." Springer consistently spoke of the need to remember the Holocaust and viewed this as an eternal Germany duty. Upon receiving a Gold Medal from the Israeli Press Club, Springer noted that "there can never be any restitution (*Wiedergutmachung*) in the true sense of the word for the crimes that the Germans committed."[58]

Given Springer's commitment to German–Jewish reconciliation, *Bild* has always played a didactic role in matters relating to the Nazi past. In late January 1985, it printed an editorial urging Germans to celebrate May 8, 1985.[59] The following editorial (translated in its entirety; the bold-face words appear in the original text), printed in March 1985, represents a typical statement of *Bild*'s position:

A small German town and the fear before the visit of an old woman...

The woman is a Jew, and with her would return the memories of an unhappy time.

Hatred of Jews, brown terror, cowardice. The mayor thinks: one shouldn't open new wounds, "there is peace in town."

A deathly peace. It is a disgrace, that many people show no shame fifty years after.

The debate about liberation or defeat leading up to the fortieth anniversary of the end of the Second World War raged from December 1984 to March 1985. It reached a new high point, however, in April 1985 when Kohl and President Ronald Reagan planned for their meeting in Bitburg.[60]

Bitburg

In late 1984, the chancellor invited President Reagan to a memorial service at a cemetery in the small German town of Bitburg to mark the end of the Second World War.[61] It was to be a grand historical gesture that would make three statements. First, since Bitburg was the home of both an American army base and a cemetery in which German soldiers were buried, the reconciliation over the graves was intended to demonstrate the strength of the Atlantic partnership. Second, by honoring Germany's war

---

[58] *Bild*, 31 January 1985.
[59] *Bild*, 28 January 1985.
[60] For an introduction to the Bitburg controversy, see Geoffrey Hartman, ed., *Bitburg in Moral and Political Perspective* (Bloomington: Indiana University Press, 1986).
[61] Kohl at first suggested that the ceremony occur at Dachau. Although Kohl was initially not aware that members of the Waffen-SS were buried in Bitburg, he continued to push Reagan to visit the cemetery after this fact became public.

dead, a common practice between allies, Reagan's visit would demonstrate that Germany had become a normal nation. Third, the reconciliation between two former adversaries would mark the symbolic end of the postwar period. In sum, Bitburg marked the culmination of Kohl's effort to remove the scourge of the Nazi past from contemporary Germany.

But things did not go as planned. As Charles Maier notes, "memory escaped from the control of its normal custodians – politicians who sought to play on it, and academics who lived by analyzing it – and became an unpredictable force as powerful, say, as economic discontent."[62] The Bitburg affair spiraled into the hitherto largest political crisis in both Reagan's and Kohl's governments.

In March, Reagan accepted the invitation to Bitburg and declined to visit a concentration camp on his German visit. The president justified this choice on the grounds that he did not want to stir up unnecessary feelings of guilt among Germans, the majority of whom had been born after the war. This rankled many U.S. senators, who charged Reagan with trying to bury the Holocaust. The affair escalated when it was discovered that members of the Waffen-SS were buried in Bitburg, which spurred massive protests in both the United States and Germany.[63] In the Bundestag, the SPD offered a resolution that "regretted" Reagan's visit, and the Greens proposed a resolution to cancel the Bitburg visit because it honored "a criminal organization – the Waffen SS." Although the CDU/CSU/FDP majority defeated both resolutions, Bitburg was proving to be politically costly. In the United States, fifty-three senators signed an open letter to Reagan urging him to cancel the Bitburg ceremony and to visit a concentration camp instead. Fearing that Reagan might cave in to domestic pressure, Kohl called the president and implored him to go through with the original plans, claiming that the German government would fall if he did not. At the same time, Kohl's team hastily added a visit to the Bergen-Belsen concentration camp to the itinerary. Reagan agreed to visit Bitburg, but provided further controversy when he argued that members of the Waffen-SS were no less victims of Nazism than the racially and politically persecuted.[64]

The Bitburg debate centered on two sets of questions: First, to what extent were German soldiers victims of the Second World War? Second, was it possible and desirable to eliminate the shadows of the Nazi past through a historic gesture of reconciliation? Like the debate over May 8th,

---

[62] Charles Maier, *The Unmasterable Past* (Cambridge: Harvard University Press, 1988), 9.

[63] The Waffen-SS (literally "Armed-SS") was the military wing of the Schutzstaffel (SS).

[64] Maier, *Unmasterable Past*, 9–10.

the Bitburg debate pitted right against left. The conservative dailies (the *Welt* and the *Frankfurter Allgemeine Zeitung*) stood behind the chancellor. A *Frankfurter Allgemeine Zeitung* editorial titled "War Dead" ("Kriegstoten") argued that "those who sort troops into different nations feed the spirit of discord" and recognized German soldiers, including members of the Waffen-SS, as victims of the war.[65] Both papers framed Bitburg as a historical reconciliation between former adversaries. The liberal dailies (*SZ* and *FR*), by contrast, strongly criticized Kohl for failing to distinguish between different sorts of wars. In World War II, in contrast to other wars, "there was only one completely just and one completely reprehensible" side in the conflict.[66] Both papers saw in Bitburg an attempt to "draw a line (*Schlusstrich*) under an incriminating, troublesome piece of history over the graves of German soldiers."[67]

Bild found itself caught between two of its central ideological pillars: commitment to the Western alliance and reconciliation with the Jewish people. Before Reagan finally decided to go through with the visit, *Bild* had urged Kohl to cancel the trip in one of its editorials.[68] But when it became clear that Reagan would visit Bitburg, *Bild* supported the ceremony while trying not to offend German Jews or Israel. As if to emphasize its commitment to fighting anti-Semitism, for example, *Bild* censured a German tabloid (*Quick*) for blaming American Jews for the Bitburg controversy:

Quick is selling the Bitburg discussion with the phrase "The Power of the Jews."

Perhaps they have no idea what they are doing. "The Power of the Jews" – Hitler and Goebbels used this phrase to blame every problem on the Jews.

"The Power of the Jews" – the Nazis used it to foment hate and prepare mass murder.

40 years after, so it is suggested, Reagan dances like a doll to the "Power of the Jews."

This insults the victims of the Holocaust.

Not their power, but their weakness allowed the Jews to die in the gas chambers.[69]

The debates in the editorial pages of German papers mirrored those of politicians. In an open letter published in the *Frankfurter Rundschau* on April 23 and addressed to the fifty-three U.S. senators who had urged Reagan not to go to the cemetary, Alfred Dregger (CDU) warned that

---

[65] *Frankfurter Allgemeine Zeitung*, 26 April 1985.
[66] *Frankfurter Rundschau*, 26 April 1985.
[67] *Frankfurter Rundschau*, 4 April 1985.
[68] *Bild*, 29 April 1985.
[69] *Bild*, 26 April 1985.

canceling the Bitburg visit would be an "insult to his brother," who had been killed in the war. Dregger, who had served on the eastern front, framed his wartime service as a heroic defense against the Red Army. "I ask you," wrote Dregger to the senators, "if you see the German people, who were subjected to 12 years of a brown dictatorship and have stood for 40 years on the side of the West, as an ally or not?"[70] The next day, the *Frankfurter Rundschau* published an open letter to Dregger by Peter Glotz (SPD) titled "Alarming Tones." Glotz accused Dregger of "moral corruption" and asked him if he really wanted to "hide the fact that only a tiny and completely decimated minority were subjugated by Hitler while millions of Germans voted for Hitler and accepted him as the 'Führer' until well into the Second World War?"[71]

Kohl and Reagan ended up visiting the Bitburg cemetery on May 5th. They stood for five minutes in the pouring rain over the graves of German soldiers. Protestors chanted in the background. Although Kohl had delivered a speech at Bergen-Belsen on April 21st, his visit to the concentration camp had done nothing to stem the controversy.

Von Weizsäcker's Speech

It was in this polarized environment that President Richard von Weizsäcker (CDU) delivered an address to the Bundestag on May 8, 1985. Weizsäcker had spent several months preparing this speech, reading the articles from *Die Zeit*'s series on May 8th ("Das sperrigen Gedenktag") and meeting with many different interest groups (Jewish groups, veterans' organizations, the organization for German expellees [BdV]) to discuss the meaning of May 8th.[72] Although a member of the CDU, the president was reportedly "deeply disturbed" by the Bitburg controversy and was ready to recommend that Kohl cancel the Bitburg visit before Kohl released a press statement saying that he was going ahead. Weizsäcker's speech to the Bundestag was both a reaction to Bitburg and a contribution to the debate about May 8th.

In his address, Weizsäcker laid out the central points of what I have termed the contrition frame. Rather than forgetting the Nazi past, von Weizsäcker argued that all Germans, "whether guilty or not, whether

---

[70] "Im Wortlaut: Beleidigung meines Bruders," *Frankfurter Rundschau*, 23 April 1985.
[71] "Im Wortlaut: Erschreckender Tonfall," *Franfurter Rundschau*, 24 April 1985.
[72] Friedbert Pflüger, *Richard von Weizsäcker, Ein Portrait aus der Nähe* (Stuttgart: Deutsche Verlags-Anstalt, 1990), 108.

young or old," had a responsibility to "keep alive the memories of the past."[73] Although Weizsäcker listed German soldiers as victims of the Second World War, he focused on the Jews and on other victim groups (Sinti and Roma, homosexuals, the mentally ill, members of the resistance, communists) whose suffering had never been publicly commemorated by a West German politician. Weizsäcker also argued that Germans were not primarily victims of Nazism, as the Bitburg ceremony had suggested, but complicit in its crimes through acts of commission and omission. He noted that "there were many ways of diverting one's conscience, avoiding responsibility, looking away, keeping silent." Rather than searching for a middle ground between the poles of "liberation" and "defeat," von Weizsäcker described May 8th as an unambiguous day of liberation. In marked contrast to many conservatives, the president suggested that contrition was critical for a healthy national identity – that only by examining past crimes and remembering them could Germans preserve and deepen their democracy. Linking contrition with patriotism and national pride, Weizsäcker identified remembrance as an enduring political duty for Germans of all ages and political orientations.

Weizsäcker's speech represented a turning point in the debate. While the left had been making similar arguments for months, the fact that the German president, and a member of the CDU, had adopted the central ideas of the contrition frame gave contrition bipartisan legitimacy. Social Democratic and Green politicians praised the president's speech, and most German newspapers, including *Bild*, reacted favorably to it and reprinted its crucial sections.

The combination of the May 8th debate, the Bitburg controversy, and Weizsäcker's speech produced a change in the liberal wing of the CDU/CSU. Many Christian Democrats began to express their support for a more critical examination of the Nazi past. Berlin's mayor, Eberhard Diepgen (CDU), for example, announced his project for the Wannsee House several months after Weizsäcker's speech, and one close observer claims that this represented his answer to the Bitburg affair.[74] Politicians both wanted to align themselves with the perceived popular support for contrition and to avoid the appearance of keeping company with the extreme right. For example, Volker Hassemer (CDU), the cultural senator

[73] Richard von Weizsäcker, "Der 8. Mai 1945: 40 Jahre danach," in Richard von Weizsäcker, *Von Deutschland aus: Reden des Bundespräsidenten* (Munich: Deutscher Taschenbuch Verlag, 1987). An English translation can be found in Hartman, *Bitburg*, 262–273.
[74] Interview with Andreas Nachama, director of the Topography of Terror, Berlin, 12 July 2001.

of Berlin, took a contrite position in a statement supporting the initiative for the Topograpy of Terror:

> It is perhaps a question of dignity and self-respect that we do not reject but take over this legacy. No comparisons with the historical atrocities of other nations can help us with this, for we alone are the heirs of this history. One cannot "close the books" on this or put it down under the rubric of a "terrible past."[75]

In Chapter 2, I noted that shifts in mass attitudes follow those in elite discourse. Although there are no public opinion surveys to demonstrate the shift in public opinion before and after the public debates of 1985, the evidence suggests that the German public mirrored the shift in elite discourse toward the contrition frame. After his speech, over 60,000 Germans wrote letters to Weizsäcker, the vast majority of which praised his demonstration of contrition. Heinrich Böll called for the speech to be included in school textbooks, and both the Bavarian and Hessen state governments distributed hundreds of thousands of copies to high school students. In many other states, graduates received a copy of the May 8th speech along with their high school diplomas. The speech soon appeared on records, cassettes, and videotapes, and was republished in countless books and articles. Over two million copies of the May 8th speech have since been published, and it has been translated into more than twenty languages. Now known simply as "the speech," Weizsäcker's May 8th address was rapidly disseminated to the German public and has become one of the central texts in West Germany's political history.

The Historians' Debate

German conservatives did not welcome such developments and vowed to carry on the fight to normalize German history. The key players in this third round of public debates were intellectuals. Michael Stürmer, a conservative historian and political advisor to Kohl, once wrote that "in a country without history, he who fills memory, defines the concepts and interprets the past wins the future."[76] During the early 1980s, several conservative historians, such as Andreas Hillgruber and Ernst Nolte, published works that extracted some usable history – some bases for

---

[75] *Tages-Anzeiger* (Zürich), 17 August 1987.
[76] Michael Stürmer, "Suche nach der verlorenen Erinnerung," *Das Parlament,* 17/24 May 1986.

national pride – from the Second World War.[77] Although similar arguments had been around for some time, they acquired new significance in the wake of the Bitburg affair and the Weizsäcker speech. As *Zeit* editor Gunter Hoffman noted, "it was highly likely that historians like Andreas Hillgruber, Ernst Nolte, Joachim Fest or Michael Stürmer reacted to Weizsäcker's speech, or to the overpowering resonance that Weizsäcker's speech found."[78] The battle over the Nazi past thus moved from the political to the intellectual field and resulted in the so-called Historians' Debate.[79] The debate was largely carried out in the pages of the *Frankfurter Allgemeine Zeitung* and *Die Zeit*, and the chief protagonists were Ernst Nolte and Jürgen Habermas. But as one observer points out, the Historians' Debate enveloped the entire intellectual establishment: "hardly any German periodical with serious pretensions failed to comment on it, and most major West German intellectuals weighed in on one side or the other. No historical controversy in the entire postwar period . . . produced such ferocious polemics."[80]

The Historians' Debate began in June 1986 when Ernst Nolte published an article titled "The Past That Will Not Pass Away" in the *Frankfurter Allgemeine Zeitung*. Nolte lamented that the memory of the Holocaust was being used by unidentified "interests," which had a stake in preserving a "permanent status of [a] select and privileged existence."[81] But it was Nolte's series of provocative questions that sparked the conflict:

Did not the National Socialists, did not Hitler perhaps commit an "Asiatic" deed only because they regarded themselves and those like them as potential or real victims of an "Asiatic" deed? Was not the Gulag Archipelago more original than Auschwitz? Was not the "class murder of the Bolshevists" the logical and factual *prius* of the "racial murder" of the National Socialists?[82]

By suggesting that Nazism was a reaction to Stalinism, Nolte challenged the singularity of the Holocaust. As Charles Maier points out, the

---

[77] Andreas Hillgruber, for example, published a work about the German army's protection of the civilian population from the Russian army at the end of the war. Hillgruber, *Zweierlei Untergang: Die Zerschlagung des deutschen Reiches und das Ende des europäischen Judentums* (Berlin: Siedler, 1986).

[78] *Die Zeit*, 21 October 1988.

[79] There is a large literature on the Historians' Debate. For English introductions to the conflict, see Maier, *The Unmasterable Past*, and Richard J. Evans, *In Hitler's Shadow* (New York: Pantheon, 1989).

[80] Anson Rabinbach, "The Jewish Question in the German Question," *New German Critique* 44 (Winter 1988): 183–184.

[81] Quoted in ibid., 184.

[82] "Vergangenheit, die nicht vergehen will," *Frankfurter Allgemeine Zeitung*, 6 June 1986.

central issue in the Historians' Debate was "whether Nazi crimes were unique, a legacy of evil in a class by themselves, irreparably burdening any concept of German nationhood, or whether they are comparable to other national atrocities, especially Stalinist terror."[83] Several weeks after Nolte's article appeared, *Die Zeit* printed a spirited response by Jürgen Habermas. A philosopher with a longstanding concern for communication in democracies, Habermas believed that the role of intellectuals was to spark public debates and contribute to the process of "democratic will formation."[84] The foremost public intellectual of the liberal left, Habermas "has been known to carefully scan the pages of the *Frankfurter Allgemeine Zeitung* for the first signs of a strengthening of conservative forces eager to re-legitimate nationalism and historicism."[85]

Finding his *casus belli* in Nolte's article, Habermas attacked Nolte and other conservative historians for their "apologetic tendencies."[86] He saw the conservative historians' work as part of a broader neoconservative attempt to legitimate nationalist political ideas by, as he put it, "limiting the damage" of the Nazi past. Habermas argued that such a strategy departed from the fundamental positive achievements of West German democracy: the rejection of romantic nationalist ideas and the adoption of Western liberal ones. He further argued that Auschwitz had forever discredited traditional concepts of national identity in Germany and that the only basis for political loyalty was "constitutional patriotism," whereby citizens identify with their democratic institutions rather than with a shared community of fate.

Intellectual controversies rarely produce clear winners and losers. The German Historians' Debate, however, is an important exception to this rule. The majority of the German media, including *Bild*, and the German historical establishment sided with Habermas's position. Politicians soon followed suit. In 1988, for example, President Von Weizsäcker praised the scholarly debate at the annual meeting of German historians but clearly sided with Habermas.[87] The president emphasized that

[83] Maier, *Unmasterable Past*, 1.
[84] Jürgen Habermas, "Heinrich Heine and the Role of the Intellectual in Germany," in *The New Conservatism: Cultural Criticism and the Historians' Debate*, ed. Shierry Weber Nicholsen (Cambridge: MIT Press, 1989), 71–99.
[85] Jan Müller, *Another Country* (New Haven: Yale University Press, 2000), 91.
[86] "Eine Art Schadensabwicklung. Die apologetischen Tendenzen in der deutschen Zeitgeschichteschreibung," *Die Zeit*, 11 July 1986.
[87] Such close involvement with a historical debate is extraordinary. Could one even imagine an American president (or another American politician) attending the annual convention of the American Historical Association and offering his own views on a scholarly debate?

"Auschwitz remains unique. It was perpetrated by Germans in the name of Germany. This truth is immutable and will never be forgotten."[88] Conservative historian Andreas Hillgruber lauded Weizsäcker's ability to steer between "moral dogmatism" and "moral responsibility" and to highlight the "political responsibility" of remembering the Nazi past.[89] Helmut Kohl, as well as nearly every other important politician, also declared that the Holocaust was a singular event. In the end, Nolte stood virtually alone in his argument that the gulag was more original than Nazism, and that the former had somehow caused the latter. Even the *Frankfurter Allgemeine Zeitung*, Nolte's principal advocate during the debate, admitted defeat. As in the Bitburg affair, the right emerged as the clear loser in the Historians' Debate. While both Kohl and Nolte had, in different ways, wanted to normalize the Nazi past, both ultimately succeeded in making it even more salient in German politics. The unintended outcome of their interventions was a flourishing public discourse about the need to remember, and to atone for, the Holocaust.

Let me summarize the argument to this point. The public debates of the 1980s created two new historical frames: the normalization frame and the contrition frame that were championed by the right and the left, respectively. Although elements of these frames existed before the mid-1980s, it was the process of elite debate that condensed and disseminated them. As I have suggested, political elites began to change their ideas during the debate – the second step in the sequence of public debate – and converge around the contrition frame. The following section documents this shift in elite opinion.

Step Two: The Convergence of Elite Opinion

The fiftieth anniversary of the end of the Second World War in 1995 gave German elites another chance to present their interpretations of the Nazi past. As it was ten years earlier, the anniversary was highly salient politically and in fact represented the second most intense period of discussion about the Nazi past in the twenty-year period analyzed in this study (see Table 1.1). It offered a chance to see if, and how, the debates of the 1980s had changed elite ideas about the Nazi past.

Two central differences between the 1985 and 1995 commemorations stand out. First, in 1995 German elites focused on the Holocaust rather

[88] Quoted in Herf, *Divided Memory*, 359.
[89] Quoted in Pflüger, *Richard von Weizsäcker*, 123.

than on the meaning of 1945 for Germans. On April 27th, Chancellor Kohl, President Roman Herzog (CDU), and Bundestag President Rita Süssmuth (CDU) attended a ceremony at the former concentration camp Bergen-Belsen, where each spoke of the need to remember the Holocaust. In a speech to the Reichstag on May 8th, Herzog warned that focusing on German victimization, as Kohl had done at Bitburg, would "allow the guilt of German political leaders to disappear behind a picture of general ruin." Avoiding abstract formulations such as "crimes committed in the German name," Herzog stated that "the Germans carried out a Holocaust against the innocents of many peoples." When Ignaz Bubis, the leader of Germany's Jewish community, suggested that January 27th, the anniversary of the liberation of Auschwitz, should become a public holiday, Herzog threw his support behind the idea and a majority in the Bundestag voted for it on June 1. On January 20, 1996, Herzog gave an address to the Bundestag before the first "Day of Commemoration for Victims of National Socialism." In contrast to those who claimed that remembering past crimes weakens the national identity, Herzog emphasized that such remembrance is "in our own interest" since "it gives us strength, since it helps us to keep from going astray."[90]

The second difference between 1985 and 1995 was that German elites from all political parties represented in the Bundestag agreed on the need to remember the Holocaust and remain vigilant against those who wanted to forget. Even the head of Germany's most conservative political party, Edmund Stoiber of the CSU, delivered an impassioned speech at Dachau in which he stated that there "is no way a line can be drawn under this darkest chapter of German history." Whereas the debate about the day of liberation or the day of defeat pitted left against right in 1985, politicians from all political orientations referred to May 8th as a day of liberation in 1995.[91] The one protest from the so-called New Right against this consensus, which I detail in Chapter 5, drew a spirited response from the right as well as from the left.

It is important to stress that even the most conservative party represented in the Bundestag, the CSU (the Bavarian counterpart of the CDU), has embraced the contrition discourse. This is a recent development. In the mid-1980s, the CSU's longtime leader, Franz Josef Strauss, denounced efforts to come to terms with the past as masochistic. When the East German prime minister, Erich Honecker, wanted to visit Dachau on an

---

[90] Quoted in Herf, *Divided Memory*, 370.
[91] For more on this point see Kirsch, *Aus der Geschichte*, 151–189.

official visit to Bavaria in 1985, Strauss refused to meet him or even to send a representative.[92] When Edmund Stoiber became head of the CSU in the early 1990s, however, he embraced remembrance. In 1995, he became the first Bavarian chancellor to visit Dachau and has since delivered numerous speeches about the Nazi past. In his addresses, Stoiber always stresses the singularity of the Holocaust and the duty to remember the Nazi past. In 2001, he hosted an exhibition on the Warsaw ghetto uprising in his own Bavarian state chancellory. In the same year, Stoiber also made an official trip to Israel, which was widely interpreted in the German media as a signal that he would seek the German chancellorship in 2002.

The elite consensus around the contrition frame also emerges from seventy-five semistructured interviews with German politicians conducted by the author in 2001–2002. During these interviews, politicians from all political parties and different levels of government were asked the same set of questions about the Nazi past. They were asked, for example, whether they viewed May 8th as a liberation or a defeat, whether they believed the Holocaust was singular or not, and how they understood the meaning of the term normalization. I coded these interviews using a procedure outlined in the appendixes and assigned each interview a value on a composite "contrition index" (also outlined in the appendixes). The higher the value, the more contrite were the respondent's attitudes toward the Nazi past. Negative scores on the contrition index indicate that the respondent tended toward the normalization frame. A score of zero indicates that the respondent adhered to the major points of the contrition frame.

The results of this coding procedure are presented in Figure 3.2. Each point on the graph represents the composite score of at least one politician. Moving from left to right, the lines on the x axis represent the (PDS) (1), Greens (2), SPD (3), FDP (4), and CDU/CSU (5). As we can see, the vast majority of interviews with German politicians (sixty-seven out of seventy-five, or 89 percent) produced contrition scores of 0 or above. Although the negative scores were concentrated in the CDU/CSU, it is important to note that the majority of CDU politicians produced positive contrition scores and that the average score for the CDU/CSU was +1.3. The figure also indicates that contrition scores were positively correlated with leftist political ideology. The average contrition scores were 1.3 for the CDU, 2.2 for the FDP, 3.7 for the SPD, and 5.0 for both the Greens and the PDS.

---

[92] Interview with Barbara Distel, director of the Dachau Memorial, Dachau, 25 April 2002.

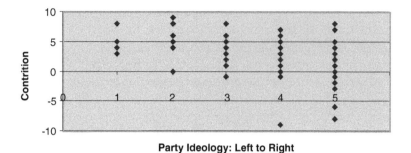

FIGURE 3.2. Contrition and party: Germany.

The results of depth interviews also suggest that the issues that were hotly debated in the 1980s are no longer disputed. The term "*Niederlage*" ("defeat") has virtually disappeared as a description for May 8th among German politicians; it was not mentioned in a single interview. Seventy-eight percent of the interviewees referred to May 8th as a day of liberation, while only 22 percent referred to it as something else. Similarly, there is now a broad consensus on the singularity of the Holocaust. Eighty-one percent of respondents described the Holocaust as singular, while only 12 percent said it was comparable to other tragedies (7 percent did not know).

The debate about the Holocaust Monument in Berlin also demonstrates that remembrance of the Nazi past as such no longer divides right and left. During this national discussion, which spanned nearly a decade, the question was not about whether memory of the Holocaust should be a central part of German political culture (it already was), but rather what form that memory should take.[93] In this debate, one could be against the Holocaust Monument while still taking a strong position on remembrance. Many Green and Social Democratic politicians opposed the monument because it was explicitly for the Jews and thus was not devoted to other victims, such as the Sinti, Roma, homosexuals, the handicapped and mentally ill, and Wehrmacht deserters. Politicians from all parties also argued that the monument was not an "authentic site," like the concentration camps or the Wannsee House, and was therefore too artificial and abstract. Many therefore demanded that the money be used to maintain the numerous existing memory sites or to sponsor other Holocaust education projects.

---

[93] For an anthology of these debates, see Michael Jeismann, ed., *Mahnmal Mitte* (Cologne: Dumont, 1999).

One politician demanded that the money be used to ensure that every German student could take a guided tour of a concentration camp. Others politicians opposed the monument on aesthetic grounds. During an interview with a CSU politician, for example, the interviewee told me that he was very unhappy with the outcome of the monument debate. I asked him why, expecting him to offer an argument about German masochism. His response, however, was that he had "hoped for more trees."

What explains this elite convergence around the contrition discourse? More specifically, what explains the shift in conservative thinking away from the ideas of the Bitburg visit and the Historians' Debate and toward those of Weizsäcker's May 8th speech? As I noted in Chapter 2, my framework for analyzing public debates does not offer general predictions about the outcome of public debates. These political conflicts are contingent, and the factors that push elites toward consensus or polarization can only be identified post hoc. In the German case, three factors were important for elite convergence.

First, the conservative drive to normalize the Nazi past lost strength when the liberal wing of the CDU/CSU adopted the contrition frame of the left. This turned contrition into a bipartisan issue, and meant that conservatives who called for normalization could only count on support from the extreme right wing of the Union and extreme-right political parties. The fear of being placed in the far-right corner led many Union politicians to jettison the normalization frame. Second, and a point I develop further in Chapter 5, the rise of right-wing populist parties that offered apologetic interpretations of the Nazi past put pressure on the CDU/CSU. Although the CDU/CSU coopted many issues from the far right, the Union increasingly used their contrite narrative of the Nazi past to differentiate themselves from right-wing populist parties. Third, the dominance of the *Bild* pushed German conservatives toward the contrition discourse.[94] The Springer–Israel connection is common knowledge among German politicians, and the *Bild* threw its weight behind the key principles of the contrition frame during the 1980s. The paper both commented on and contributed to Weiszäcker's popularity among the general population, thereby insulating the president from conservative critics. As the political salience of the Nazi past increased after 1985, politicians became much less willing to make controversial statements about the Nazi past for fear that they might be harshly criticized in the *Bild*.

---

[94] This point emerged during many in-depth interviews with Christian Democratic politicians.

Indeed, the political costs of challenging the contrition discourse rose markedly during the 1980s. Bitburg had demonstrated that forced normalization produced political controversy. At one point, Kohl feared that his government might collapse under its weight. The formula that Weizsäcker provided, however, brought both domestic and international accolades and quickly emerged as the only legitimate means for German elites to discuss the Nazi past.

Step 3: Shifting Discursive Space and Political Correctness, German Style

The public debates of the 1980s changed the boundaries of the legitimate discursive space in Germany and produced what I term "political correctness, German style." The appearance of a ritualized language for publicly discussing the Nazi past marked the third and final step in the process of public debate.[95] This was not only a result of normative change, but also a product of sanctioning mechanisms that eliminated individuals who challenged the contrition frame – or gave the appearance of challenging it – from political life. The dramatic fall of one prominent politician was enough to make other elites extremely wary of deviating from the central ideas of the contrition frame.

On November 10, 1988, Phillip Jenninger (CDU), president of the Bundestag, delivered a speech to parliament marking the fiftieth anniversary of *Pogromnacht*. His intention was to give an address similar to Weizsäcker's, but things went badly from the beginning. Speaking in a monotone, Jenninger tried to re-create the mindset of ordinary Germans who had participated in the pogroms by asking a series of rhetorical questions. "Did not Hitler turn into reality," asked Jenninger, "what William II had only promised, namely to lead the Germans to wonderful times?" He asked whether the Jews "had occupied a role...that they did not deserve?" and "had they not deserved to be put in their place?" Finally, he asked, "did not the propaganda – excluding the wild and unrealistic exaggerations – conform to one's own speculations and convictions in important ways?"[96] These questions were meant to be rhetorical and expose the perverse ideas of ordinary Germans, but a combination of poor oratorical

---

[95] See Jeffrey K. Olick and Daniel Levy, "Collective Memory and Cultural Constraint: Holocaust Myth and Rationality in German Politics," *American Sociological Review* 62, no. 6 (December 1997): 921–935.

[96] Extracts from Jenninger's speech can be found in Dubiel, *Niemand*, 215–218.

skills and sloppy speechwriting gave the impression that Jenninger was making excuses for the perpetrators. Social Democratic and Green politicians left the chamber in protest midway through the address.

In retrospect, it is clear that Jenninger was indicting Germans for looking the other way during what is often considered the first step of the Final Solution. But his speech broke from the contrition discourse by focusing on the motivations of ordinary Germans rather than remembering the victims. SPD leader Hans Jochen Vogel criticized the speech, as did Count Otto Lambsdorff, the leader of the German liberals (FDP), who called it "a partial justification" of *Pogromnacht*. Jenninger's allies also distanced themselves from him. Theo Waigel (CSU) warned that the speech would have "consequences." The commentary in the normally government-friendly *Bild* was also harsh. "It was not what he said that was the real scandal," wrote Gerhard Mumme in the editorial "Cold Words," "but what he failed to say . . . for the victims of the Holocaust he found no words of shock, of regret, of sympathy, or of horror."[97] Under pressure from Kohl and members of his own party, Jenninger resigned the next day.

Several days later, in a speech to the World Jewish Congress in New York, Kohl made sure to emphasize the singularity of the Holocaust and to distance himself from any attempts at normalization. Several days before, the chancellor had spoken to members of the Jewish community in Frankfurt am Main. During his contrite remarks, Kohl noted that he "was aware that your trust is easily shattered: by the presence of the eternal yesterday and sometimes also by the thoughtlessness of the well-meaning."[98] Perhaps this last phrase was a reference to Bitburg and his own earlier flirtations with normalization. In any event, there would be no other Bitburgs during the rest of Kohl's tenure. The chancellor was now an outspoken supporter of the Holocaust monument and of contrition.

The shift in Kohl's discourse reflects that of German politicians in general. Since the May 8th speech, politicians of all political orientations have tried to imitate Weizsäcker's address when referring to the Nazi past. This had led to a certain "ritualization" of public discourse and the development of a three-part "liturgy" of the Nazi past: (1) the Holocaust was a unique event (therefore not comparable with other atrocities; (2) the critical examination of the Holocaust is a permanent responsibility for all Germans; and, following from the second point, (3) there

[97] *Bild*, 11 November 1988.
[98] Quoted in Herf, *Divided Memory*, 361.

can be no forgetting and no drawing a line (*Schlusstrich*) under the Nazi past. Nearly every political speech on the Holocaust since the late 1980s contains these three elements, and a speechwriter for a prominent conservative politician confirms that they are necessary ingredients in public addresses concerning the Nazi past.[99] One can thus speak of a political correctness in Germany, which applies to no other sphere of discourse as much as it does to the Nazi past. As I show in Chapter 5, Jenninger was the first of several German politicians whose careers were effectively ended by violating the culture of contrition.

Evidence from semistructured interviews demonstrates the existence of discursive norms concerning the Nazi past. German politicians, for example, are often unwilling to use the phrase "mastering the past" (*Vergangenheitsbewältigung*), which had been widely used and was unproblematic until at least the mid-1980s. When asked to describe what mastering the past meant, the majority of respondents immediately distanced themselves from the term, arguing that the word mastering implied drawing a line under the Nazi past. Politicians also recognize that singularity has become an element of political correctness. As one conservative politician put it: "of course, as a German politician you have to say that the Holocaust was singular." The legacy of the Historians' Debate has thus reached far beyond academic circles and changed the discourse of political elites.

Many German politicians have also redefined the term normality. In interviews, only a small minority continued to use the term as a synonym for lessening the burden of the Nazi past. Many respondents denied that Germany could ever be normal and emphasized that the Nazi past would remain a salient political issue for future generations. One of the most interesting trends was the recasting of normality as remembrance rather than forgetting. As one politician put it: "it is normal that memory is a part of our political culture... and that November 9th [the anniversary of *Pogromnacht*] marks an important date in our calendars. So long as this is normal, I have no problem with the term."

Although German politicians from every political party (except the extreme right) are aware of political correctness and follow its dictates, German conservatives appear especially sensitive to it. During interviews with the author, many Union politicians felt that they, as conservatives, were held to a different standard, and that they must appear to be especially committed to memory of the Nazi past. As one prominent CDU

---

[99] Interview with a speechwriter for a prominent conservative politician, Munich, 23 April 2002.

politician put it, conservatives must "quasi-overreact" to "the shadows of the Nazi past."[100]

Germany's Culture of Contrition

In Chapter 2, I claimed that frames that are repeated, consolidated, and disseminated through public debates can become enduring elements of political culture and shape interpretations of other political issues. The following section demonstrates how the contrition frame became the bedrock of Germany's culture of contrition. Three particular aspects of this culture are explored. First, using monuments and memorials to the victims of National Socialism as an indicator for contrition, I show how Germans' willingness to expose the crimes of Nazism in public spaces increased dramatically after the debates of the mid-1980s. Second, I analyze how the German political establishment and the public participated in two debates – the Goldhagen debate and the debate about the exhibit "Crimes of the German Army" – that extended the circle of complicity in Nazism's crimes far beyond the circle of top Nazis. Third, I claim that the contrition frame still strongly influences the way political elites conceive of national identity and the integration of foreigners. Two case studies of the so-called *Leitkulturdebate* ("Leading Culture Debate") of 2000 and the *Stolzdebate* ("Pride Debate") of 2001 demonstrate how frames formed during the public debates of the 1980s influenced debates about other political issues that occurred nearly two decades later.

Monuments and Memorials

The contrition discourse has literally changed the face of Germany.[101] Before the mid-1980s, most monuments and memorials in the Federal Republic were dedicated to German soldiers killed in the two world wars, testaments to the German narrative of victimization I detailed previously. As of 1980, there were only six state-supported monuments and museums dedicated to other victims of National Socialism. Since the mid-1980s, however, there has been nearly a tenfold increase in the number of such monuments. Moreover, there has been a proliferation of smaller

---

[100] Interview with Günther Nooke (CDU–MdB), 9 April 2002.
[101] There is a massive literature on monuments and memorials in Germany. For an introduction, see James E. Young, *The Texture of Memory: Holocaust Memorials and Meaning* (New Haven: Yale University Press, 1993).

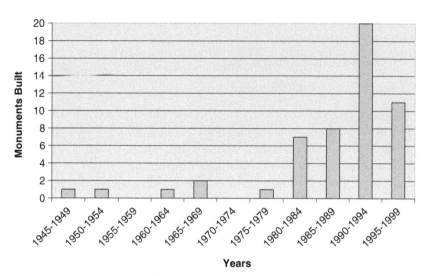

FIGURE 3.3. Monuments built: 1945–1999.

monuments (those not supported by the federal government) to the victims of National Socialism on the community and state levels since the 1980s.[102] Figure 3.3 shows the dramatic rise in official monuments in Germany.

This sharp increase reflects two important developments in the politics of monuments and memorials. First, there has been an increase in demand for memory sites. Although citizens' initiatives have been the major claimants, individual politicians and political parties have demanded monuments as well. Second, there has been a decrease in political opposition to such monuments. Initiatives that stood little chance of getting through local, state, or national legislatures in the 1970s found a much more receptive environment in the 1980s and 1990s. Moreover, the German media as a whole have generally supported the creation of monuments to the victims of National Socialism, and few politicians are willing to come out as opponents of memorials in principle.

Nowhere is the "memory boom" more apparent than in Berlin. Before the 1980s, a visitor in West Berlin would have had a difficult time finding traces of the Nazi past in the former capital of the Third Reich. Since

---

[102] One specialist estimates that there are 600 of these monuments. See Norbert Kampe, "Nationale Identität durch Erinnerungstätten und Mahnmale?", paper presented to the German Studies Association, September 27, 1997, 2.

the Bitburg debate, however, politicians and citizens have remade Berlin into something akin to a gigantic museum and memorial to the Nazi past. In 1986, Berlin's mayor, Eberhard Diepgen (CDU), decided to turn the Wannsee House, the site of the Wannsee Conference where the details of the Final Solution were discussed, into a permanent museum and center for political education. The *Topographie des Terrors* (Topography of Terror), which lies on the former headquarters of the Gestapo and contains a permanent exhibit explaining the instruments of Nazi repression and torture, opened in 1987. The movement for a monument to the murdered Jews of Europe began after the Historians' Debate, and a gigantic monument is currently being built in the center of Berlin. Although not a museum about the Holocaust, the long-awaited Jewish Museum opened its doors in 2001. In addition to these memory sites, numerous smaller museums and memorials have sprung up in Germany's capital city.

Widening the Sphere of Complicity

A second pillar of the culture of contrition is a critical examination of the role German society played in the Holocaust. Since Weizsäcker and other politicians admitted that many Germans, not just Hitler and fanatical Nazis, had committed sins of commission and omission, German and foreign academics have explored the complicity of major social groups, such as the army, academia, industry, the churches, the medical profession, and many others, in Nazism's crimes. Two examples from the mid-1990s demonstrate the enormous public interest and approval that such examinations generate in Germany.

In 1996, Daniel Jonah Goldhagen's book *Hitler's Willing Executioners* sparked an intense debate about "ordinary Germans and the Holocaust."[103] Goldhagen's thesis was simple and bold: neither Nazi ideology nor coercion forced Germans to kill Jews; rather, a longstanding "eliminationist" anti-Semitism unique to Germany was the central force behind the Holocaust. To support this argument, Goldhagen focused on members of reserve police battalions, which he claimed represented a sample of ordinary Germans that willingly and joyfully murdered Jews in Nazi-occupied Poland. A best-seller in the United States, *Hitler's Willing Executioners* drew enthusiastic reviews from the American media. Its reception among academics, however, was mixed. Many historians

---

[103] The quotes are the caption to the book. Daniel Goldhagen, *Hitler's Willing Executioners* (New York: Knopf, 1996).

criticized the book for its supposedly selective use of evidence, oversim-
plification, and exaggerated claims to originality.[104]

Germany's academic establishment was even harsher. Beginning in
April 1996, German dailies ranging from the conservative *Frankfurter
Allgemeine Zeitung* to the left-liberal *Tageszeitung* printed responses to
the (not-yet-available) German translation of *Hitler's Willing Executioners*, and the reading public was exposed to seven months of critique from
German historians. Most of these historians were liberal and had built
their careers investigating the crimes of the Third Reich.[105] "Simply a
bad book." concluded Eberhärd Jackel, who had sided with Habermas
in the Historians' Debate.[106] Hans Mommsen, who was completing a
project on slave labor at Volkswagon, deemed it "behind the current state
of research in many ways."[107] The weekly *Die Zeit* offered the most in-
depth coverage of the Goldhagen controversy, publishing a ten-part series
and printing a long response by Goldhagen to his critics.

The Goldhagen debate in Germany, however, shifted dramatically after
the German edition appeared in August and the author came for a book
tour. The reaction from ordinary Germans was unexpectedly massive and
positive. As one of Goldhagen's critics admitted, "it is unprecedented that
a historical work and its author should attract such great attention."[108]
For fifteen straight weeks, *Hitler's willige Vollstrecker* occupied either first
or second place on the best-seller list. It was the tenth best-selling book of
1996 and the eighth of 1997.[109] During his book tour, Goldhagen spoke
to sold-out audiences, numbering in the thousands, throughout Germany
and did a blitz of radio and television interviews. Many ordinary Germans
agreed with Goldhagen's indictment of their parents and grandparents.

The tone of the German media changed in response to what Josef Joffe
of the *Süddeutsche Zeitung* termed the "Goldhagen Phenomenon."[110]
Joffe wrote that "it is reassuring that today's ordinary Germans neither repressed nor reacted defensively to" Golhagen's argument.[111] Volker
Ulrich of *Die Zeit* noted that "the book tour turned into a triumphant

---

[104] See, for example, Robert R. Shandley, ed., *Unwilling Germans? The Goldhagen Debate*
(Minneapolis: University of Minnesota Press, 1998).
[105] Conservative historians, perhaps remembering the Historians' Debate, mainly stayed
out of the Goldhagen debate.
[106] Eberhard Jäckel, "Einfach ein schlechtes Buch," *Die Zeit*, 17 May 1996.
[107] Hans Mommsen, "Schuld der Gleichgültigen," *Süddeutsche Zeitung*, 20/21 July 1996.
[108] Nobert Frei, quoted in *Die Zeit*, 13 September 1996.
[109] Martin Kött, *Goldhagen in der Qualitätspresse* (Konstanz: UKV Medien, 1999), 19.
[110] *Süddeutsche Zeitung*, 11 September 1996.
[111] Ibid.

march," and interpreted this as a sign of a "new sensibility" toward the Holocaust.[112] Even Franz Schirmacher, editor of the conservative *Frankfurter Allgemeine Zeitung*, did not criticize the popular reception to Goldhagen and viewed is as proof that the Germans were not trying to escape their history.[113] In its year-end wrap-up, *Die Zeit* termed the "open-mindedness that Goldhagen encountered in the land of the perpetrators" one of the "most gratifying events of the year."[114] Similarly, Joffe noted in his last column of 1996 that "ordinary Germans should be a little bit proud" of their reaction to a book that erased the distinction between Germans and Nazis.

Gaining pride by examining national crimes: this was the message that Weizsäcker had offered and the Goldhagen affair had confirmed. Germans not only bought Goldhagen's book and tickets to his book tour, but honored him as well. The *Journal for German and International Politics* (*Blätter für deutsche und Internationale Politik*) presented Goldhagen with the prestigious Democracy Prize. In the words of the journals' editors, this award, which recognized service to German democracy, "needed to be deserved," and had not been granted since 1990, when it was given to the former citizens' movement of East Germany.[115] None other than Jürgen Habermas presented Goldhagen with the award.[116] Quoting the prize trustees, Habermas noted that Goldhagen's book had increased Germans' "sensibility for what constitutes the background and the limit of a German 'normalization.'"[117]

The national debate over the exhibition "Verbrechen der Wehrmacht" ("Crimes of the German Army") followed on the heels of the Goldhagen controversy.[118] The exhibition had actually been created in 1995 by the

---

[112] Volker Ullrich, "Daniel J. Goldhagen in Deutschland: Die Buchtournee wurde zum Triumpzug," *Die Zeit*, 13 September 1996.
[113] *Frankfurter Allgemeine Zeitung*, 13 September 1996.
[114] Jahreskronik, *Die Zeit*, 3 January 1997.
[115] Atina Grossman, "The 'Goldhagen Effect:' Memory, Repetition, and Responsibility in the New Germany," in *The Goldhagen Effect*, ed. Geoff Eley (Ann Arbor: University of Michigan Press, 2000), 118.
[116] Geoff Eley, "Ordinary Germans, Nazism, and Judeocide," in *The Goldhagen Effect*, 29–30.
[117] Ibid., 30.
[118] For contributions to, and analyses of, this debate, see Hamburger Institute für Sozialforschung, ed., *Eine Ausstellung und ihre Folgen* (Hamburg: HIS Verlag, 1999); Heribert Prantl, ed., *Wehrmachtsverbrechen: Eine deutsche Kontroverse* (Hamburg: Hoffmann and Campe Verlag, 1997); Hans-Günther Thiele, ed., *Die Wehrmachtsausstellung: Dokumentation Einer Kontroverse* (Bremen: Temmen, 1999); Landeshauptstadt München, ed., *Bilanz Einer Ausstellung* (Munich: Droemersche Verlag, 1998).

Hamburg Institute for Social Research (HIS) to commemorate the fiftieth anniversary of the end of the Second World War. Its central purpose was to undermine the "myth of the clean army" (*Mythos der sauberen Wehrmacht*) that, despite several decades of academic scholarship on the crimes of the German army, remained firmly anchored in German political culture. Politicians since Adenauer had praised members of the Wehrmacht as brave soldiers whom Hitler had misused, and the army was even considered an institution of "inner emigration" where a soldier could defend his country while opposing Nazi ideology and steering clear of Nazism's crimes. The photos and documents that comprised the *Wehrmachtsausstellung* (German army exhibit) challenged this conventional view by demonstrating that the Wehrmacht had been an integral part of the Final Solution and had committed war crimes on a massive scale.

Like *Hitler's Willing Executioners*, the *Wehrmachtsausstellung* broadened the circle of complicity and attracted enormous attention. Between 1995 and 1999, nearly 800,000 people visited the exhibit as it traveled to thirty-three cities, making it "*the* contemporary history exhibition in the Federal Republic: the most visited and the longest lasting."[119] But unlike the Goldhagen affair, the debate surrounding the exhibit became entwined with partisan politics that, in a repeat of previous debates, pitted conservatives against liberals. While the FDP, SPD, and Greens universally supported the exhibit, the CDU/CSU's close links with the Bundeswehr and with veterans' groups made the party highly sensitive to complaints from former soldiers, who argued that the exhibit constituted a historically false and undifferentiated condemnation of the Wehrmacht.

The debate can be divided into three stages.[120] During the first stage (1995–1996), the CDU/CSU was relatively quiet and generally supportive of the exhibit. Defense Minister Völker Ruhe (CDU) stated that "The *Wehrmacht* was as an organization of the Third Reich...involved in the crimes of National Socialism."[121] The second stage began when the exhibit moved to Munich and Peter Gauweiler, a maverick member of the CSU known for his populist tactics, mounted an unsuccessful campaign to block it. Gauweiler succeeded in rallying the CSU's conservative clientele, who saw the exhibit as a blanket condemnation of the German army. But Gauweiler's polemics provoked a strong counter reaction and

---

[119] Hannes Heer, "The Difficulty of Ending a War," *History Workshop Journal* 46 (Fall 1998), 188 (emphasis in the original).

[120] The following draws on an interview with Hannes Heer, the organizer of the *Wehrmachtsausstellung*, Hamburg, 22 June 2001.

[121] Quoted in Michael Klunt, *Geschichtspolitik* (Cologne: Papyrossa, 2000), 48.

turned the exhibit into a popular attraction. People waited for three to four hours to see it, and debated the issue passionately as they did so. The neo-Nazi National Democratic Party (NPD) organized a demonstration against the exhibit, which prompted the unions, Greens, SPD, and other groups to organize a counterdemonstration. The events in Munich drew national and international attention and turned the exhibit into a pressing political issue.

Although it could play little tangible role in the conflict, the German Bundestag took the extraordinary step of devoting two parliamentary sessions to debating the merits of the *Wehrmachtsausstellung*. Politicians from every party except the CDU/CSU supported the exhibit, and representatives from all five parties made a concerted effort to come to a common resolution about it. In the end, the CDU/CSU would not accept any text that stated that the Wehrmacht as an organization was involved in the Final Solution. The final resolution, passed by the CDU/CSU-FDP majority, noted that while parts of the Wehrmacht had been involved in the shooting of prisoners of war, massacres in occupied territories, and the killing of Jews, the majority of Wehrmacht soldiers were not involved in such crimes.

Yet the Wehrmacht debate did in fact produce a change within the conservative camp. After the parliamentary debate, many local and state CDU politicians began to support the exhibition. This trend began in Münster and continued in Aachen and several other cities. In the state of Lower Saxony, the CDU joined the SPD and the Greens in a common resolution supporting the exhibit. The *Frankfurter Allgemeine Zeitung*, which had strongly opposed the exhibit, also changed its tone. On September 1, 1999, the former editor of the arts pages (Feuilleton), Ulrich Raulff, wrote a column praising the exhibit as the most successful of its type and crediting it with a paradigm change in public views of the Wehrmacht. When a new, corrected version of the exhibit opened in 2000, there were no protests from conservatives.[122]

One final debate about complicity deserves mention. Since the early 1990s, many of German industries' household names – such as Volkswagon, Daimler, Bertelsman, Deutsche Bank, and numerous others – have faced legal challenges from former slave laborers and other victims of National Socialism. Although some firms fought these challenges to the bitter end, others commissioned historians to investigate their companies'

---

[122] It turned out that some of the photographs used in the exhibit had been falsely labeled in the Soviet archives. The HIS corrected the exhibit, and it reopened in 2001.

role in Nazi crimes.[123] In 2000, the Bundestag voted into law the "Reparations for Slave Labor Act" that committed the German government and German industry and finance to pay reparations to slave laborers.[124] This law and the debate that produced it opened yet another sphere of inquiry for contemporary Germans: the role of German economic actors in the Holocaust.

National Identity and the Integration of Foreigners

The contrition frame has not only shaped views about the Nazi past, but also debates about national indentity. Before the 1990s, the West German left had failed to stake out a position on the national question. The dominant voices were those of leftists such as Günther Grass and Joschka Fischer, who argued Auschwitz ruled out German unification, and this extreme position explains the left's ambivalent reaction to the fall of the Berlin Wall. After unification, however, the German left needed some paradigm for discussing national identity. They turned to the notion of constitutional patriotism that Habermas had disseminated and championed as an option for the left during the Historians' Debate.

Constitutional patriotism is often criticized, usually by conservatives, for being too abstract to create the emotional attachments required for a feeling of community. Yet interviews with German politicians indicate that many, especially those on the left, have embraced the concept. One FDP politician described himself as a "downright (*ausgesprochene*)" constitutional patriot and indicated the copy of the Basic Law that he and many other FDP politicians keep on their desk. Over half of the respondents (54 percent) identified themselves either as constitutional patriots or "partial constitutional patriots," meaning that they also identified with something other than Germany's democratic political institutions. Although several Christian Democrats described themselves as constitutional patriots, most believed that the concept did not provide enough of an emotional attachment for group identity.

The so-called Pride Debate (*Stolz Debate*) of March 2001 demonstrates the importance of constitutional patriotism for the German left. The debate began when the general secretary of the CDU, Laurenz Meyer,

[123] Volkswagon, for example, commissioned Hans Mommsen to write a history of slave labor in their factories during the Nazi era. Hans Mommsen and Manfred Grieger, *Das Volkswagenwerk und seine Arbeiter im Dritten Reich* (Berlin: Econ, 1996).
[124] On reparations, see Matthias Arning, *Späte Abrechnung* (Frankfurt am Main: Fischer, 2001); Ulrike Winkler, ed., *Stiften Gehen* (Cologne: PapyRossa, 2000).

stated that "he was proud to be a German." Although similar statements
are unproblematic in other national contexts, and indeed are expected of
most politicians, the phrase has been hijacked by the German far right
over the past decade, and few mainstream politicians dare use it. React-
ing to Meyer's statement, the minister of the environment, Jürgen Trittin
(Greens), criticized Meyer for possessing the "mentality of a skinhead."
The CDU charged Trittin with "instrumentalizing" right-wing extremism,
called for his dismissal, and claimed that they intended to begin a debate
about German patriotism "without nationalist tones."[125]

Not wanting to cede the Pride Debate to the right, politicians on the left
reacted by championing constitutional patriotism; they proclaimed their
pride in Germany's democratic political culture and Germany's commitment to remembrance. President Johannes Rau (SPD) immediately distanced himself from Meyer's statement, noting that one can only be proud
of something that one had achieved. Rau did say that "he was proud of
what we have built in Germany" and was "happy to be a German."[126]
Chancellor Gerhard Schröder noted that he was "proud of the democratic culture" Germans had built.[127] The editor-in chief of the liberal
Süddeutsche Zeitung, Heribert Prant, wrote: "In Germany democracy
has developed, the Germans have regained their unity, and they are trying
to discard authoritarian traditions – one can be proud of that and it is
with this type of pride that a democrat should take on the blood-and-earth
(*Blut-und-Boden*) pride of right-wing radicals."[128] Similarly, the editor-in
chief of *Die Zeit*, Josef Joffe, wrote:

When a German wants to be proud of this country, he need not fish in the brown
[right-wing] soup – not in resentment against others, not in murmurs about nation
and fatherland. He can refer to the fact that a democracy, which in many ways
is more liberal than in France or Britain, has taken root in soil contaminated
with authoritarianism and totalitarianism. The past? Even after 56 years it has
not been disposed of; remembrance and responsibility have become principles of
state.[129]

The German public appears to support this understanding of patriotism, suggesting that constitutional patriotism has become, at least for
many Germans, a reality. During the Pride Debate, a poll by the radio

---

[125] *Süddeutsche Zeitung*, 17 March 2001.
[126] *Frankfurter Allgemeine Zeitung*, 21 March 2001.
[127] *Süddeutsche Zeitung*, 20 March 2001.
[128] *Süddeutsche Zeitung*, 20 March 2001.
[129] *Die Zeit*, 15 March 2001.

station N24 found that 61 percent of Germans agreed with Rau's statement that "one can only be proud of something that one has achieved," while only 26 percent disagreed.[130] Nearly half of those who supported the CDU/CSU agreed with Rau, signaling that their potential new theme did not really resonate with their voter base.

Moreover, many CDU politicians appeared uncomfortable with the nationalist tones the debate was producing. One noted in an interview with the author that Christian Democrats could not broach the subject of pride, since it was so deeply associated with the extreme right.[131] Another stated that "although he was conservative," saying that "he was proud to be a German" was "too strong" for him.[132] Only 4 percent of German politicians who answered the question supported the slogan "I am proud to be a German." Twice as many, however, answered that they "were proud to be a European," and nearly 30 percent said that they were proud of Germany's democracy and culture of memory. Forty-three percent claimed that they were not proud to be German, for the concept of national pride had no meaning for them.

The Pride Debate was similar to another debate over what should constitute the "leading culture" (*Leitkultur*) in Germany. The background for the debate was the historic decision by the CDU/CSU in September 2000 to accept, after decades of stating the opposite, that Germany was a "land of immigration." The apparent condition for this new openness to foreigners, however, was that they conform to what Friedrich Merz (CDU) called a German "leading culture" (*Leitkultur*). Merz's term produced immediate reactions from the German left, which claimed that any attempt to impose German culture on others had been discredited by the Nazi past. Many members of the CDU also expressed discomfort and downright confusion with the term. Many wondered exactly what Merz meant by German *Leitkultur*: Schiller and Goethe? Bratwurst and beer? In interviews, over 90 percent of German politicians distanced themselves from Merz's phrase. The public outcry was also so negative that the CDU, after several weeks of trying, stopped defending the term and dropped it from its position paper on immigration.

Four years later, however, *Leitkultur* reemerged in conservative political discourse following the brutal murder of the Dutch filmmaker Theo van Gogh, who had made films highly critical of Muslims, by

---

[130] Agence France Presse, 23 March 2001.
[131] Interview with MdB, CDU, Berlin, 2 February 2002.
[132] Interview with MdA–BW, CDU, Stuttgart, 17 April 2002.

an Islamic extremist. Political elites across Western Europe argued that multiculturalism had failed and demanded a greater degree of integration from their Muslim populations. The CSU, in particular, resuscitated the *Leitkultur* concept. Many members of the CDU like Wolfgang Schäuble, however, refused to adopt the term, as did Chancellor Schröder, who spoke instead of the need for *Integrationsbereitschaft* (willingness to integrate) on the part of both Muslims and Germans.[133]

Whether or not the term sticks the second time around, the debate over *Leitkultur*, like that over German pride, demonstrates that conceptions of national identity are still viewed through the contrition frame. This frame also shapes debates about a range of other political issues, such as euthanasia, the projection of German military power, and genetic engineering. Ideas about the Nazi past have, in others words, become a principal lens through which German elites perceive and react to a gamut of contemporary political issues.

Has the elite culture of contrition become a mass-level phenomenon? As I noted earlier, ordinary Germans were highly receptive to Weizsäcker's speech, Goldhagen's book, and the *Wehrmachtsausstellung*. While these examples suggest that segments of German society have embraced the contrition frame, we have not yet examined mass attitudes toward the Nazi past or tested the proposition that such attitudes reflect patterns in elite discourse.

Unfortunately, the dearth of longitudinal public opinion surveys makes it difficult to draw clear conclusions. There are no surveys that have asked the same battery of questions at regular intervals over a period of twenty years or longer. Since responses to questions about the Nazi past are highly sensitive to question-wording, it would be misleading to draw conclusions about attitudinal change using different surveys at different periods.[134]

The limited evidence that we do have, however, is at least consistent with the hypothesis that mass attitudes respond to shifts in elite discourse. Over the course of the 1990s, German public opinion appears to have mirrored the growing insistence of German elites to critically examine the Nazi past. Although there was little change in the school curriculum between 1994 and 2001, ordinary Germans' expectations about the necessary amount of knowledge about the Nazi past changed. Whereas in 1994, 42 percent considered the treatment of Hitler in school to be too

---

[133] *Der Spiegal* 48, 2004.
[134] On this point, see Eric Langenbacher, "Memory Regimes in Contemporary Germany," (Ph.D. diss., Georgetown University, 2002), 141–164.

thin, by 2001, 57 percent believed that children learn too little about the Nazi past in school.[135]

There is also evidence that the singularity thesis has become widely accepted by the German public. Since there are no survey data on this issue prior to the 1990s, it is impossible to analyze changes over time.[136] But given the dominance of the victimization frame in German political discourse prior to the 1980s, however, it is reasonable to assume that many Germans, perhaps a majority, would not have drawn any distinctions between the suffering of the German population and the suffering of Jews during the Second World War. By the 1990s, a majority of Germans seemed to have absorbed the result of the Historians' Debate. According to a poll conducted by the Emnid Institute for *Der Spiegel* in 1995, 36 percent agreed with the statement that "the expulsion of the Germans in eastern Europe was as great a crime against humanity as the Holocaust of the Jews." Twenty-seven percent disagreed with the statement, while 35 percent argued that the crimes cannot be compared.[137] Seven years later, a FORSA (Society for Social Research and Statistical Analyses [Gesellschaft für Sozial for Schung und Statistiche Analysen]) poll designed by Eric Langenbacher produced similar results. Respondents were asked to choose between the following two statements; first, "suffering and death are suffering and death. All were victims of the dictatorial and criminal Nazi regime and are comparable"; second, "a basic difference exists between the experiences of Jews and Germans. They cannot be compared." While 31.2 percent chose the first answer, 59.8 percent chose the second, supporting the hypothesis that the German public has absorbed the noncomparability thesis of the German elite.[138]

Conclusion

By placing domestic politics at the center of Germany's confrontation with the Nazi past, this chapter has deviated from two competing accounts. First, it has made little mention of the generational changes that several

---

[135] *Der Spiegel* 38, 1994; *Der Spiegel* 19, 2001.
[136] The fact that the singularity issue was not addressed in public opinion data is telling in itself.
[137] *Der Spiegel* 19, 1995.
[138] See Eric Langenbacher, "Memory Regimes and Support for Democracy in Contemporary Germany," paper prepared for the American Political Science Association's annual meeting, Philadelphia, August 29–September 1, 2003, 19.

scholars have deemed critical to coming to terms with the Nazi past.[139] Second, it has largely ignored the international environment that shaped German postwar domestic politics and, as some scholars have argued, pushed German elites toward contrition.[140]

Beginning with generational change, it is certainly true that generational conflict was an important component in the tumult of the 1960s. The generation that came of age during the "economic miracle" period did question their parents about their actions under Nazis. The antiauthoritarian New Left that coalesced in the Green Party has also played a leading role over the past two decades in political conflicts over reparations, monuments, and other facets of coming to terms with the past. But as I noted earlier, contemporary Green attitudes toward the Nazi past bear little resemblance to those that prevailed among the New Left in 1968. The student movement viewed Nazism through a Marxist lens and considered it a manifestation of the fascism present in most modern industrial societies. The racist ideology that formed the core of Nazism was largely ignored, as was the Holocaust itself. In addition, the anti-Semitism that characterized some strands of the New Left precluded a critical examination of the Nazi past. If the 1960s paved the way for a more critical examination of the Holocaust, genuine contrition did not emerge until the mid-1980s.

The contrition frame was also introduced into political discourse by a politician from the war generation – the generation most hostile to the process of coming to terms with the past. Weizsäcker's statements carried so much weight precisely because he had been a member of the Hitler Youth, fought on the eastern front, and defended his father at Nuremberg. He was, in other words, not vulnerable to the common charge that "you were not there; you cannot understand." It is reasonable to doubt that a member of the second or third generation could have been as powerful a carrier of the contrition narrative.

The culture of contrition also did not evolve slowly, as a generational account predicts, but suddenly and dramatically. The middle to late 1980s witnessed a flurry of monument building, the publication of scores of popular and academic books on the Holocaust, and a rapid rise in other observable measures of public interest in remembering the Nazi past. It was the elite-led public debates that sparked these shifts.

---

[139] See, for example, Mushaben, *From Post-War to Post-Wall Generations.*
[140] Making this argument is Jenny Lind, "Sorry States: Apologies and International Politics" (Ph.D. diss., Massachusetts Institute of Technology, 2004).

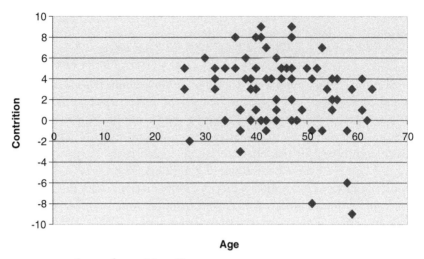

FIGURE 3.4. Age and contrition: Germany.

The notion that age influences attitudes toward the Nazi past, an observable implication of the generational explanation, is also not confirmed by evidence from semi-structured interviews with German politicians. As Figure 3.4 makes clear (each point represents the composite contrition score of an interview), there is only a weak correlation between age and scores on the contrition index.

The results of the FORSA study designed by Langenbacher are also not consistent with the hypothesis that members of different generations hold different attitudes toward the Nazi past. For example, 30.0 percent of respondents aged 14–25 agreed with the statement that "all were victims of the dictatorial and criminal Nazi regime and are comparable." For cohorts aged 26–40 and 41–60, the percentages were 31.1 percent and 31.8 percent, respectively. Responses to other questions similarly failed to produce significant differences among generations, leading Langenbacher to conclude that cohort differences are a weak predictor of attitudes toward the Nazi past.[141]

A second explanation for German contrition focuses on the constraints of the postwar international environment. Some scholars, for example, have argued that the United States compelled Germans to confront the Nazi period. The mechanisms in this Allied reeducation campaign include denazification, school reform, and the banning of political parties, as well

[141] Langenbacher, "Memory Regimes," 17.

as the myriad pressures exerted by the occupying powers. In this account, German elites had little room to maneuver and were essentially forced into paying reparations and demonstrating contrition. Such behavior is often identified as the price Germans had to pay to enter the NATO alliance. When the Berlin Wall fell forty years later, the argument might continue, Germans were once again compelled to signal their benign intentions to their wary European neighbors through acts of contrition.

This chapter has taken a far less constraining view of the international environment. If the United States did seek to reshape German society immediately after the war, it largely abandoned this goal with the onset of the Cold War. Although much has been made of US officials forcing German civilians to visit concentration camps in 1945, the Nuremberg trials sent a very different signal: punishment for the big fish and absolution for everyone else. As the historian Michael Wolffson argues, there is little evidence that the United States pressured Adenauer into paying reparations to Israel.[142] In general, one can argue that the West played a limited role in German contrition. Recall that it was U.S. President Reagan who described Waffen-SS soldiers as victims of Nazism. During the 1990s, the fear among Western leaders was not that Germany did not demonstrate enough contrition, but that its overabundance prevented Germany from pulling its weight internationally.[143]

This is not to say that German elites did not often claim that the international community demanded contrition from Germany. Adenauer used the argument to push through the unpopular reparations to Israel in 1952, and CDU/CSU politicians still use it to justify their support for monuments, reparations, and other acts of remembrance to skeptical constituencies within their party.[144] As one conservative politician told me: "if we don't remember our history, the international community (*Das Ausland*) will remind us of it." The threat of international sanction, however, has always been more imagined that real. Most importantly, the invocation of *Das Ausland* has been a remarkably effective means of legitimating the domestically generated culture of contrition and defending it from its critics.

The culture of contrition has become a central element of contemporary German political culture – a defining feature of the new "Berlin Republic."

---

[142] Michael Wolffson, *Eternal Guilt?* (New York: Columbia University Press, 1993), 13–21.
[143] On this point, see Andrei S. Markovits and Simon Reich, *The German Predicament* (Ithaca: Cornell University Press, 1997), 78.
[144] Helmut Kohl, for example, used this argument in support of the Holocaust Monument.

The public debates of the 1980s produced the contrition frame that provided its foundation, the elite consensus that gave it broad currency, and the discursive norms that reinforced it. In Chapter 5, I document the multiple challenges to the culture of contrition that emerged in the late 1980s and early 1990s. I argue that not only did political and social actors ward off the threat, but that the confrontation with the far right strengthened the culture of contrition even further. But before following this story, let us turn to Austria and how Austrian elites represented and debated their Nazi past from 1945 to the end of the 1980s. Like their German counterparts, if to a much greater degree, Austrian elites portrayed their state and nation as victims of Nazism in the immediate postwar period. When this consensus broke down in the mid-1980s, however, Austrian elites reacted in ways that would produce something very different from Germany's culture of contrition.

4

The Victim Culture

Sixty years after the end of the Second World War, the Nazi past has become a salient and divisive issue in Austrian politics. In May 2002, political parties debated the meaning of May 8th and proponents of diverging historical interpretations clashed in the streets of Vienna. Several weeks earlier, members of the Austrian People's Party (ÖVP) and the Austrian Freedom Party (FPÖ) had condemned the revised edition of the *Wehrmachtsausstellung*, while Green and Social Democratic (SPÖ) politicians delivered opening speeches praising it. In November 2000, Chancellor Wolfgang Schüssel (ÖVP) and the head of the Green Party, Alexander Van der Bellen, publicly sparred over whether Austria was primarily a victim, as Schüssel claimed, or a perpetrator during the Second World War. Since the formation of the ÖVP-FPÖ coalition in February 2000, the battle lines in these and other historical debates have been clearly drawn, pitting the right (the FPÖ, the ÖVP, and the conservative press) against the left (the Greens, the SPÖ, and the liberal press), and members of all parties regularly accuse their opponents of using history for partisan political gain.

The current polarization of Austrian historical consciousness is surprising given the elite consensus, which held for over four decades, that Austria was Hitler's first victim. To paraphrase an old joke, "the Austrians succeeded in convincing themselves and the world that Beethoven was an Austrian and Hitler was a German." The Holocaust was Germany's problem. As the first section of this chapter demonstrates, not a single important actor in Austrian politics or society challenged this victim narrative for four decades.

Why, then, has the Nazi past become a partisan political issue? Why do historical controversies that have been largely settled in Germany persist in Austria? The central argument of this chapter is that the current polarization is a legacy of a political conflict that shattered the elite consensus and transformed the Nazi past into a salient political issue. In 1986, the controversy over the wartime biography of Kurt Waldheim, the ÖVP's presidential candidate, sparked a transformative public debate about Austria's Nazi past. The second section of this chapter analyzes this debate in detail, noting how it marked an unprecedented national discussion about the Nazi past in terms of intensity, duration, and breadth. The Waldheim debate not only transformed elite ideas about Austria's complicity in Nazism's crimes but also reshaped partisan politics and political culture. It marked the beginning of the end of Austria's consociational democracy and foreshadowed the realignment of Austrian politics into the two political camps that now compete for political power.

The first step in the Waldheim debate was the construction of two distinct frames linking the Nazi past to the political present. The right adopted a defensive posture during the Waldheim debate and disseminated what I call the "new victim frame." Christian Democratic politicians, the conservative press, and the powerful *Kronen Zeitung* presented Austria as the victim of international forces seeking to denigrate its history. They linked foreign Jews with a "campaign" against Waldheim and exhorted the Austrian population to resist this challenge. The new victim frame resonated with the Austrian public – Waldheim won the election handily – and became an integral part of the ÖVP's political arsenal.

As the Austrian right championed the victim frame, members of Austrian civil society mobilized against what they considered a reversion to national chauvinism and anti-Semitism. A small number of artists, intellectuals, civic activists, and leftist (mostly Green) politicians began to demand that Austrian elites and citizens critically examine the Nazi past and recognize Austria's complicity in Nazism's crimes. They created and disseminated an Austrian version of the German contrition frame. Through protest activities, informal meetings, and, later, formal organizations, this left-liberal milieu coalesced into the movement for the "other Austria," which it defined as the part of Austrian society that took responsibility for the Nazi past. This civic movement emerged as one of the most important voices against historical apologia and right-wing populism.

The formation of the other Austria foreshadowed the second stage of the Waldheim debate: the polarization of elite opinion. Although it took several years to do so, the SPÖ eventually joined the Greens in adopting the contrition frame. This magnified the growing ideological divide between left and right. Using material from semistructured interviews, this chapter documents this elite polarization. While German elites generally agree on the singularity of the Holocaust and the designation of May 8th as a day of liberation, Austrian elites are split on these points. Moreover, there is no consensus on whether Austria was a victim or a perpetrator in the Second World War. Fewer than half of all Austrian politicians scored o or above on the contrition index, and contrition is much more highly correlated with political party in Austria than it is in Germany.

The transformation of the Austrian political discourse marked the third stage of the Waldheim debate. The "Waldheim camp" (meaning Waldheim's defenders) developed a number of code words meant to activate anti-Semitic attitudes without referring to Jews directly. By publicly using chauvinist language and anti-Semitic stereotypes, Christian Democratic politicians shifted the bounds of the legitimate discursive space and rendered ideas previously associated with the extreme right acceptable (or *salonfähig*, to use the German expression). The sanctioning mechanisms that have nearly eliminated apologetic narratives of the Nazi past in Germany do not exist in Austria, and politicians are therefore free to adopt revisionist positions without risking their careers. The discourse of the ÖVP during the Waldheim debate legitimated, and indeed mainstreamed, extreme-right political ideas and paved the way for the rise of Jörg Haider.

In sum, the Waldheim debate transformed the political environment in which it occurred. Especially since the *Wende* (or "turn") of February 2000, when the ÖVP formed a national coalition government with the FPÖ, the politics of the past has become a central issue dividing right and left and has redefined the nature of political cleavages. In this sense, the Nazi past represents a case of issue evolution. Before examining why the Waldheim debate in Austria unfolded in dramatically different ways from similar debates in Germany, let us turn to the elite consensus that prevailed for the first four postwar decades.

Hitler's First Victim: 1945–1986

It is difficult to imagine a better advertisement for Austria than *The Sound of Music*. This Hollywood film showcases Austria's twin treasures – its landscape and its music – and broke all box office records in the United States in 1961. The story of the Von Trapp family's escape from the

Nazis also paints a sympathetic picture of Austria's incorporation in the Third Reich. Nazism appears as a German import, the only Austrian Nazi featured in the story (Rolf, the boyfriend of Admiral Von Trapp's eldest daughter) is a misguided youth, and the Von Trapps receive critical help from Austrian nuns during their escape. During the filming of the movie in the city of Salzburg, however, the American producers needed to indicate the arrival of Nazism in Austria and sought permission to put Nazi flags on the Residenzplatz (one of Salzburg's main squares) during shooting. "No, no, you cannot do this," replied local politicians, "because the people of Salzburg never belonged to the Nazi Party." The American producers then threatened to use actual newsreels from 1938 showing Hitler's enthusiastic reception in Salzburg instead. The politicians granted permission to fly the Nazi flags on the condition that the producers would not attempt to portray the cheering crowds of 1938.[1]

The view of Austria's Nazi past that Salzburg's politicians sought to defend has become known as the "victim narrative" and contains two central claims. First, the Austrian state was Hitler's first victim. The state ceased to exist when it was annexed against its will in 1938 and did not reappear as a legal entity until the Declaration of Independence of 1945. Second, the vast majority of Austrians were victims of Nazism, an ideology they rejected and resisted. In a radio address of 1949, the Socialist politician Rosa Jochmann, who had spent several years in a concentration camp, summarized this interpretation: "We were all victims of Fascism. The soldier who experienced war in its most terrible form on the front was a victim. The population in the homeland that waited in horror for the bomb sirens to flee to their shelters . . . was a victim. Those who had to leave their homeland and suffer the sad fate of the emigrant were victims. And finally, we who were handed over to the prisons and concentration camps of the SS were victims."[2] Between 1945 and 1986, this interpretation of Austria's Nazi past was accepted and disseminated by every significant actor in Austrian politics and society.

The victim narrative was not invented by Austrian elites but emerged as the unintended consequence of the Allies' wartime policy. In 1943, the United States, Great Britain, and the Soviet Union met in Moscow and released a document known as the Moscow Declaration. Although

[1] Jacqueline Vansant, "'Harry Lime und Maria von Trapp treffen sich am Stammtisch': Die Entnazifizierung Österreichs in amerikanischen Filmen," in *The Sound of Austria*, ed. John Bunzl (Vienna: Braumüller, 1995), 172.
[2] Quoted in Brigitte Bailer, "Alle Waren Opfer," in *Österreich in ersten Jahrzehnt der Zweiten Republik*, ed. Wolfgang Kos and Georg Rigele (Vienna: Inventur, 1996), 185.

Austria was a small topic on the Allies' agenda, their statements about it would have enormous implications for the country. The Allies wrote that "Austria, the first free country to fall victim to Hitlerite aggression, shall be liberated from German domination." This was intended to assure Austrians that they would be treated fairly after the war and prevent them from holding out until the bitter end for fear of retribution. But the Allies did not let Austria completely off the hook. A second passage in the Moscow Declaration stated that "Austria is reminded, however, that she has a responsibility for participation in the war on the side of Hitlerite Germany and that in the final settlement, account will inevitably be taken of her contribution to her liberation." This second passage was intended to bolster the tiny Austrian Resistance, but it never produced the desired effect.

After the war, Austrian politicians seized on the first passage of the Moscow Declaration and buried the second. In the Declaration of Independence of April 27, 1945, the "Hitler's first victim" passage is prominent. The second passage concerning responsibility, however, is hidden at the end and referred to as a "postscript" (*Nachsatz*), a term that did not appear in the Moscow Declaration.[3] On the eve of the signing of the Austrian State Treaty in 1955, which restored fully Austria's sovereignty, Foreign Minister Leopold Figl (ÖVP) fought to delete the second passage of the Moscow Declaration from the treaty's preamble. He argued that it was unfair to burden Austria with guilt about its past just as it was regaining its sovereignty.[4] Figl convinced the four powers and succeeded in removing the phrase "Austria has a certain responsibility" for the Nazi war from the State Treaty, thereby expunging the second passage of the Moscow Declaration from the Austrian Second Republic's founding political document.[5]

The victim narrative was literally woven into the Austrian state symbol: the unchained eagle on the Second Republic's flag represents Austria's "foreign occupation" between 1938 and 1945.[6] The Austrian government also commissioned the Red-White-Red book (the pattern of colors of the

---

[3] Anton Pelinka, *Austria: Out of the Shadow of the Past* (Boulder: Westview Press, 1998), 16.

[4] Hella Pick, *Guilty Victim: Austria from the Holocaust to Haider* (New York: I. B. Tauris, 2000), 31.

[5] Gerhard Stourzh, *Kleine Geschichte des österreichischen Staatsvertrages* (Graz: Styria Verlag, 1975).

[6] Heidemarie Uhl, "Das 'erste Opfer,'" *Österreichische Zeitschrift für Politikwissenschaft* 30 (2001), 21.

Austrian flag) in 1946 that used "official sources" to show that Austrians were the victims of Hitler and that "despite the terror, the ideas of National Socialism were only supported by a small minority."[7] It rested on the premise that "anybody who knows anything about Austrians understands and accepts that Prussianism, militarism, and Nazism are basically as alien to Austrians as to any other people in Europe."[8]

Austrian politicians from all three camps disseminated the victim narrative in election campaigns, political journals, and other arenas. The future foreign minister and chancellor, Leopold Figl, used an opening ceremony for a monument to the Red Army's fallen soldiers in Vienna on August 19, 1945, to underscore that Austrians were also victims of Nazism: "The Austrian people languished for seven years under Hitler's barbarism. The Austrian people were subjugated and oppressed for seven years . . . brutal terror and violence forced people into blind submission."[9] In the first edition of the *Österreichische Monatshefte*, the theoretical organ of the ÖVP, the author protested against the assertion "that the majority of Austrians ever favored National Socialism," adding that "there is no idea or movement more antithetical to the innermost Austrian essence than National Socialism."[10] Socialist politicians invoked the victim narrative and distanced Austrians from Nazism as fervently as their Christian Democratic counterparts. Theodor Körner (SPÖ), the mayor of Vienna, wrote in the *Arbeiter Zeitung*, the SPÖ's official paper, that "Vienna has never witnessed anti-Semitic outrages of the kind found in other countries . . . for the Viennese is a cosmopolitan and thus from the word go not an anti-Semite."[11]

Why Austrian politicians would choose to represent their state and nation as the victims of Nazism is not surprising. There was little political incentive to critically examine Austrian history from 1938 to 1945, and the Moscow Declaration provided Austrian elites with a convenient means of avoiding moral responsibility for Nazism's crimes. But the victim narrative would come to assume such importance in Austrian politics not simply

---

[7] Quoted in Albert Sternfeld, *Betrifft: Österreich* (Vienna: Böhlau, 2001), 56.

[8] Quoted in Pelinka, *Austria*, 17.

[9] Uhl, "Das 'erste Opfer,'" 20.

[10] Carl Hollenberg, 'Wir und der National Sozialismus,' *Österreichische Monatshefte* (November 1945), 10; quoted in Walter Manoscheck, "How the Austrian People's Party Dealt with the Holocaust, Anti-Semitism and National Socialism after 1945," in *Austro-Corporatism: Past, Present, Future* (New Brunswick: Transaction Publishers, 1996), 319.

[11] Richard Mitten, "The Social Democratic 'memoire volontaire' and Coming to Terms with the Legacy of National Socialism in Austria," in *Austro-Corporatism: Past, Present, Future*, 346.

because it allowed Austrians to forget the past, but also because it served four crucial political functions.

First, the victim narrative helped smooth two principal tensions between the SPÖ and the ÖVP and served as the ideational basis for Austria's consociational democracy. The two parties had fought one another during the civil war of 1934, hardly a hospitable background for a coalition government. Elements of the two parties had also supported the *Anschluss* and collaborated with the Nazis, and were afraid that this could be used against them. The victim narrative helped to bury the memory of the civil war as politicians from both camps found common ground in their suffering as political prisoners. They claimed that living next to one another in concentration camps had forged a spirit of cooperation and willingness to forget their past conflicts and named this new ethos the "spirit of the concentration camp street" (*Der Geist der Lagerstrasse*). In addition, not speaking about the failures of the other camp between 1938 and 1945 was important in establishing mutual trust. "Each side," writes one Austrian political scientist, "had taken the other hostage: If you [the ÖVP] dare speak about Renner or other aspects of social democratic weakness [the SPÖ reasoned], we will expose the truth about the bishops and other leaders of the Catholic camp."[12]

Second, the victim narrative helped construct a new Austrian national identity. The consensus was that the lack of a specific Austrian identity had doomed the First Republic (1918–1938) and facilitated the *Anschluss*, and that the stability of the Second Republic depended on Austrians developing an emotional attachment to their state. Since Austrians had long identified themselves as Germans, and had received eight years of Nazi propaganda that strengthened this sentiment, the principal problem in constructing an Austrian nation was disentangling it from the German one.[13] By classifying Germans as perpetrators and Austrians as victims, political and intellectual elites found a compelling means of doing so. This dialectical opposition became the basis for the construction of an Austrian national identity immediately after the war, a deliberate political and intellectual effort that involved movement on several fronts. A separate Austrian history was discovered, written, and disseminated, the primary goal of which was to show that Austrians had long possessed a national identity and had not considered themselves German. Historians

---

[12] Pelinka, *Austria*, 17–18. Karl Renner, the leader of the SPÖ and the first postwar Austrian chancellor, had supported the *Anschluss*. The Austrian Catholic Church had collaborated with the Nazis.

[13] On the development (or nondevelopment) of Austrian national identity, see Barbara Jelavich, *Modern Austria* (New York: Cambridge University Press, 1994).

argued that Austrians were a mixture of different peoples and thus were racially distinct from Germans. Catholicism was used to differentiate Austrians from the predominantly Protestant Germans, and Austrian scholars argued that a people need not possess a unique language to qualify as a nation.[14]

Third, the victim myth solved the problem of reparations.[15] The first chancellor of postwar Austria, Karl Renner (SPÖ), argued that Austria should not be forced to pay reparations since "we have been punished enough by living for seven years under Hitler's regime, and do not deserve an extra punishment."[16] In 1953, Chancellor Julian Raab (ÖVP) told members of the Jewish Claims Committee that "the Austrian government regrets that it was persecuted after the occupation and that it was not possible to protect its citizens from the rush of the overpowering occupiers.... What followed was similar, in effect, to a natural catastrophe. Austria was not, by herself, in the position to repair the damage caused in these years."[17] When Nahum Goldmann, the founder of the World Jewish Congress and leader of the Jewish Claims Committee, visited Austria later that year, Raab told him that "Jews and Austrians are both victims of Nazism," to which Goldmann replied: "yes, Herr Chancellor, that is why I have come to ask you how much money the Jews owe the Austrians."[18]

Politicians had in fact been secretly discussing the restitution issue for years. The discovery and publication of Austrian cabinet meetings demonstrate that anti-Semitism and historical apologia were prevalent among Austria's political elite.[19] Vice Chancellor Adolf Schärf, for instance,

---

[14] Werner Suppanz, *Österreichische Gesichtsbilder* (Vienna: Böhlau, 1998).

[15] In fact, in Austrian political discourse of the late 1940s, the term "reparations" was used primarily in connection with former Nazis who had lost their jobs and pensions during denazification, not in connection with Jews. In a cabinet meeting in May 1945, Karl Renner underscored this position: "It would be entirely incomprehensible if every small Jewish businessman or peddlar were compensated for his loss, but that there would be no legal remedy for the losses of an entire class and a movement to which 46 percent of the population had belonged, which had the accumulated results of their diligent savings and organizational work simply taken away without punishment and [without] compensation." Quoted in Mitten, "The Social Democratic 'memoire volontaire," 347.

[16] Robert Knight, "Besiegt oder Befreit?" in *Die Bevormundete Nation*, ed. Günter Bischof and Josef Leidenfrost (Innsbruck: Haymon Verlag, 1988), 84.

[17] Bailer, "Alle Waren Opfer," 184.

[18] Luc Rosenweig and Bernard Cohen, *Waldheim* (New York: Adama Books, 1987), 106.

[19] Robert Knight, "*Ich bin dafür, die Sache in die Länge zu ziehen*": *die Wortprotokolle der österreichischen Bundesregierung von 1945 bis 1952 über die Entschädigung der Juden* (Frankfurt am Main: Athenäum, 1988).

stated in 1952 that he was "certain that the number of Austrian Jews who died was relatively small" since "most had escaped across the border."[20] Minister of the Interior Oskar Helmer (SPÖ) warned his colleagues in 1952 that he detected "Jewish expansion all around, notably among doctors and in the trading sector in Vienna."[21] He noted that "the Nazis lost everything in 1945 and some of their academics have been forced to become laborers. We are no longer living in 1945. The English are now engaged in Palestine; the Americans have not implemented their promises [to the Jews]."[22] The best way of dealing with the reparations issue, according to Helmar, was to "drag the matter out." He argued that "even the Jews themselves will understand... the issue, since they themselves are aware of the antagonism that they arouse among many people."[23] The Austrian government largely followed Helmar's recommendation to drag the matter out, and only agreed in 1962, after nine years of negotiations, to pay a modicum of reparations to the Jewish Claims Committee. Whereas the West German government paid $822 million to Jewish survivors, not counting the $52 billion it had given to Israel by the 1990s, the Austrian government gave only $22 million plus 10 percent for administrative costs.[24]

Fourth, the victim narrative helped to justify the massive reintegration of former Nazis into Austrian politics and society. In marked contrast to their policy in Germany, the Allies put the three antifascist parties in Austria (the SPÖ, the ÖVP, and the Communist KPÖ that played little role after 1947) in charge of denazification.[25] The three parties formed "special commissions" to decide who had been a "big Nazi" and who had been a *Mitläufer* – a "fellow traveler." This established a certain pattern whereby former Nazis sought the protection of a particular party and the parties developed their own clientele of former Nazis. All three parties ignored the Austrian roots of Nazism and treated National Socialism as an organizational phenomenon in order to attract the *Mitläufer* to their camp.[26]

[20] Ibid., 239. Of the 190,000 Jews living in Austria in the early 1930s, 65,000 died in the Holocaust.
[21] Ibid., 206.
[22] Ibid., 206–207.
[23] Ibid., 199.
[24] Bruce Pauley, "Austria," in *The World Reacts to the Holocaust*, ed. David S. Wyman (Baltimore: Johns Hopkins University Press, 1996), 496.
[25] Dieter Stiefel, *Entnazifizierung in Österreich* (Vienna: Europa Verlag, 1981).
[26] Pelinka, *Austria*, 18–19.

In 1947, a general amnesty was passed for most of those who had been affected by denazification. Two years later, nearly 500,000 former Nazis regained the franchise. The reentrance of this voting bloc led to the formation of the League of Independents (Verband der Unabhängigen, VdU), the forerunner of the FPÖ (founded in 1956). The VdU leadership presented the party as the reemergence of the national-liberal camp, but its base was dominated by former Nazis.[27] The ÖVP strongly opposed the legalization of the VdU and lobbied the Allied powers to ban the party, fearing that it would cut into its bourgeois voter base. The SPÖ, making a similar calculation, supported the formation of the VdU. In the event, the Allies permitted the establishment of the VdU, which fielded candidates for the 1949 national parliamentary elections. The ÖVP tried to reach a deal with several former Nazis still banned from political activity. In a secret meeting with former SS and SA leaders in Oberweis, for example, future Chancellor Julius Raab (ÖVP) promised to give these incriminated ex-Nazis the power to name the twenty-five ÖVP candidates for secure seats in the national election if they helped deliver the votes of recently enfranchised former Nazis. Raab also promised the former SS and SA leaders that they would determine the governor of the state of Styria, which was safely under the ÖVP's control.[28] For its part, the SPÖ surpassed the ÖVP in bringing former Nazis into the party. As a party of workers, the SPÖ lacked educated party members and was all too ready to integrate educated former Nazis and those with special skills.

During the 1949 election campaign, both the SPÖ and the ÖVP presented former Nazis as well-meaning, if misguided, patriots who had suffered enough for their political mistakes.[29] Politicians also relentlessly courted former soldiers, many of whom could vote for the first time in 1949, in campaign speeches, such as the following from future Chancellor Alfons Gorbach (ÖVP):

Nowhere, during the events of the recent past, was there so much genuine decency, so much selfless performance of duty as there was among the soldiers of this war.... The emigrant gentlemen [this is a coded reference to the Jews forced to flee Austria] can spread all the moralistic poison they want: those individuals out on the battlefield who withstood the severest test of their manhood knew better

[27] Sixty percent of the VdU were former Nazis. For more on the VdU, see Max Riedelsperger, *The Lingering Shadow of Nazism* (Boulder: Eastern European Quarterly, 1978).
[28] Ibid., 64.
[29] Pelinka, *Austria*, 19.

what decency is than those who scampered to safety overseas at the first sign of trouble.... I say that the emigrants have no right to an opinion in the question of the National Socialists.[30]

Although Austria, unlike Germany, assumed no responsibilities for the crimes of National Socialism, political elites in the two societies discussed the Nazi past in strikingly similar ways during the first two postwar decades. In both states, politicians represented the population as victims of circumstance and emphasized their suffering, rather than that of the Jews, Slavs, and other victims of Nazism.

The comparison to this point should not blind us to the differences between Germany and Austria in the immediate postwar period. The most important difference for our purposes is the fact that Germany was more fundamentally reshaped through Allied policies than Austria. The Austrians, after all, had their own government as of 1945, and this in part explains their latitude in dealing with the remnants of National Socialism. German elites, particularly before 1949, had little such room for maneuver. But as I noted earlier, Allied efforts to reshape German ideas about the Nazi past were neither very comprehensive nor successful. It is thus difficult to claim that Allied policies pushed Germany and Autria on different trajectories in dealing with the past. And as I have argued, the similarities in both elite and mass opinion in the immediate postwar period regarding the Nazi past in the two societies are more significant than the differences.

It was during the 1960s that German and Austrian confrontations with the Nazi past began to diverge. Earlier, I noted that the student movement in Germany used the Nazi past as a weapon against the political establishment. This confrontation with the Nazi past in Germany in the 1960s was not merely a product of generational change but was sparked by several political events – the most critical being the wave of neo-Nazi violence in 1959. In Austria, there was also a specific event that had the potential to spark an intense public debate about the Nazi past: the "Borodajkewycz affair."[31]

Taras Borodajkewycz, an Austrian of Polish ancestry, was a professor in the history of trade at the Hochschule für Welthandel (now the

[30] Quoted in Manfried Rauchensteiner, *Die Zwei: Die Grosse Koalition in Österreich 1945 bis 1955* (Vienna: Bundesverlag, 1979), 134–135.
[31] For a detailed analysis of this affair, see Andrei S. Markovits, "The Austrian Student Right: A Study in Political Continuity" (Ph.D. diss., Columbia University, 1975), 348–364.

Wirtschaftsuniversität-University of Economics) in Vienna. He joined the Nazi Party in 1934 and described March 8, 1938, the day of *Anschluss*, as the greatest day in his life. An unrepentant Nazi, Borodajkewycz received his university post after the war and continued to spread anti-Semitic ideas in the 1950s and 1960s. In lectures, for example, he referred to Karl Marx as "the Jew Marx" and demanded that his students do so as well.[32] He once devoted an entire two-hour lecture to the question of whether or not Hitler had had Jewish blood, concluding that he had not.[33] Borodajkewycz's tirades did not reach beyond his students until two members of the Socialist Student Party (VSStÖ), Heinz Fischer and Ferdinand Lacina, took notes during Borodajkewycz's lectures and published them in the SPÖ's *Arbeiter Zeitung* in the early 1960s.[34] The affair reached a larger public in 1965 when the VSStÖ called a press conference to demand that Borodajkewycz be forced into retirement. Borodajkewycz attended the press conference and used the same anti-Semitic language that he had in lectures.[35] Many of his students were present and cheered him on.[36]

The press conference sparked a series of student demonstrations on March 29, 1965, in which members of the VSStÖ clashed with members of the RFS (the student organization of the FPÖ), who defended Borodajkewycz and held signs reading "Long Live Auschwitz." A concentration camp survivor demonstrating with the VSStÖ was struck and killed by Günter Kumel, a former boxer and member of the RFS. Kumel was sentenced to a mere ten months in prison and was not expelled from the Austrian university system. This mild ruling could have provoked strong protest and energized an autonomous student movement.[37] But not only did the VSStÖ fail to use the Borodajkewycz affair to its advantage, the RFS was able to increase its share of the vote in the next university elections.[38] The SPÖ was never happy about the behavior of the VSStÖ in the Borodajkewycz affair, fearing that it would adversely affect the party in upcoming elections, and gave the socialist students little support.[39]

[32] Borodajkewycz used the same construct when referring to any other historical figures who were Jewish.

[33] Interview with Ferdinand Lacina, Vienna, 27 November 2000.

[34] Heinz Fischer later wrote a book about the Borodajkewycz affair: *Einer in Vordergrund: Taras Borodajkewycz* (Vienna: 1966).

[35] Interview with Lacina.

[36] Paulus Ebner and Karl Vocelka, *Die Zahme Revolution: '68 und was davon blieb* (Vienna: Überreuter, 1998), 61.

[37] Ibid., 62.

[38] Interview with Lacina. See also Ebner and Vocelka, *Die Zahme Revolution*, 63.

[39] Interview with Lacina.

The Borodajkewycz affair thus failed to stimulate either a left-wing student movement or a far-reaching public debate about the recent Austrian past. Tellingly, not even Borodajkewycz's opponents challenged the victim narrative. Although a student movement in Austria did develop and mimicked many of the discourses and practices of its German counterpart, it never used the Nazi past as a weapon against the political establishment, as the German 68ers had done.[40] The Austrian student movement was only able to muster "A Tame Revolution" (*Eine Zahme Revolution*) with few real consequences for Austrian politics.

One reason that the SPÖ disapproved of the VSStÖ's actions against Borodajkewycz was that it was wooing the FPÖ. The pivotal figure in the reconciliation of the Social Democrats and the extreme right was Bruno Kreisky. As he was a Jew who fled Austria in 1938 and spent the war in Sweden, it might appear odd that Kreisky would want to improve relations with the party of former Nazis. But Kreisky observed in exile how the Swedish Social Democrats had been able to split the bourgeois parties and thereby create a Social Democratic hegemony. By strengthening the FPÖ at the ÖVP's cost, Kreisky sought to secure permanent absolute majorities for the SPÖ.[41] To this end, the SPÖ made substantial contributions to the FPÖ's election campaign fund in 1963.[42] Kreisky also cultivated personal ties with the FPÖ leadership, particularly with Friedrich Peter, as early as 1959.[43]

In April 1970, Kreisky led the SPÖ to its first postwar victory in the national parliamentary elections. Since the SPÖ had failed to gain an absolute majority, Kreisky's minority government was dependent on the toleration of the FPÖ, with which Kreisky had cut a secret deal that ensured the FPÖ's parliamentary representation. In what was widely interpreted as a tribute to the FPÖ, Kreisky appointed four former members of the Nazi Party to his eleven-member cabinet. While Kreisky's cabinet provoked little immediate reaction inside Austria, the German weekly *Der Spiegel* published a story about one of Kreisky's appointees, Karl Öllinger, who had served in the Waffen-SS and been involved in massacres on the eastern front.[44] Although Öllinger then resigned, Kreisky appointed another former Nazi in his place.

---

[40] Ebner and Vocelka, *Die Zahme Revolution*, 187.

[41] Andrei S. Markovits and Anson Rabinbach, "The Dark Side of Austrian Social Democracy," *Dissent* (Summer: 2000), 117.

[42] Pick, *Guilty Victim*, 105.

[43] Anton Pelinka, *Die Kleine Koalition* (Vienna: Böhlau, 1993), 18.

[44] Pick, *Guilty Victim*, 106.

The affair escalated when Simon Wiesenthal, an Austrian concentration camp survivor who hunted down Adolf Eichmann and other Nazi
fugitives, released documents detailing the Nazi pasts of Kreisky's cabinet appointments. Kreisky responded with a series of scathing attacks
on Wiesenthal. In an interview with the Dutch daily *Vrij Nederland*,
for example, Kreisky accused Wiesenthal of being a "Jewish fascist"
and a "reactionary man."[45] Kreisky found unanimous support from his
party and from the Austrian press.[46] The *Kurier* criticized Wiesenthal for
"making no distinctions between criminals and ordinary members of the
NSDAP."[47] The *Kronen Zeitung* accused Wiesenthal of orchestrating a
"manhunt" (*Menschenjagd*) and fomenting anti-Semitism.[48]

Even those papers that traditionally supported the ÖVP supported
Kreisky. This is doubly surprising, since the ÖVP could have conceivably tried to use the event to weaken Kreisky and since Simon Wiesenthal
himself was close to the ÖVP. Yet the ÖVP-friendly *Die Presse* accused
Wiesenthal of launching a "witch hunt" reminiscent of the McCarthy era,
and argued that joining Nazi organizations were political mistakes that
did not disqualify one from holding a cabinet position in the Austrian
government.[49] Even the ÖVP's official newspaper, the *Südost Tagespost*,
criticized Wiesenthal's so-called witch hunt and praised Kreisky's cabinet
choices as an act of reconciliation.[50]

A second, and even bitterer, confrontation between Kreisky and
Wiesenthal erupted in October 1975. During a press conference, Wiesenthal announced that Friedrich Peter, the leader of the FPÖ, had been a
member of the First SS-Infantry Brigade that had massacred Jews, Sinti,
and Roma, and other civilians in the Soviet Union. Peter acknowledged
having been a member of the brigade but denied having any knowledge of
war crimes. Kreisky sprang to Peter's defense and charged that Wiesenthal
had conspired with the Gestapo during the Second World War and was
currently using "Mafia methods."[51] The chancellor argued for reconciliation, claiming that most of those who had turned to the Nazis had been

---

[45] Quoted in Heinz Wasserman, *"Zuviel Vergangenheit tut nicht gut!"*: *Nationalsozialismus im Spiegel der Tagespresse der Zweiten Republik* (Vienna: Studien Verlag, 2000),
75.

[46] Ibid., 89–129.

[47] *Kurier*, 12 June 1970.

[48] *Neue Kronen Zeitung*, 15 June 1970.

[49] *Die Presse*, 2 June 1970.

[50] Wasserman, *"Zuviel Vergangenheit,"* 107–109.

[51] Pick, *Guilty Victim*, 107.

victims of the political situation.[52] Once again, the Austrian press rallied around Kreisky, as did Austrian public opinion. Fifty-nine percent of Austrians agreed with the statement that "Wiesenthal's goal is to see as many Nazis as possible convicted, regardless of whether they are guilty or not," while only 24 percent disagreed.[53]

While many Austrian politicians claimed that the political success of a Jew (the years 1970–1983 are referred to as the "Kreisky Era" and Kreisky himself as the "Sun King") proved that Austrians had mastered the past, Kreisky was never interested in a critical examination of the Nazi period and did much to prevent it. Most Austrians held similar views. As of 1985, 57 percent of Austrians were in favor of no longer speaking about "acts committed during the Second World War," and only 27 percent wanted to "keep alive the memory of the period."[54] The Waldheim debate that erupted one year later was thus an unwelcome development for most Austrians.

The Waldheim Debate

Kurt Waldheim, secretary general of the United Nations from 1971 to 1981, was the only active Austrian politician besides Kreisky with an international reputation. After an unsuccessful bid for a third term at the UN, both the SPÖ and the ÖVP tried to claim Waldheim as their presidential candidate for the 1986 elections. Although the presidency is largely a ceremonial post in Austria, it is nonetheless an important prize for each party, and both the SPÖ and the ÖVP believed that Waldheim was unbeatable. Waldheim eventually sided with the ÖVP, and the SPÖ, after pondering supporting Waldheim as well, decided to field its own candidate, Kurt Steyrer.[55]

For many years, rumors had circulated about Waldheim's wartime past. In 1980, Congressman Stephen Solarz from New York wrote a letter to Waldheim asking him about it. Waldheim replied that he was injured in 1941 and spent the bulk of the war in Austria completing his dissertation in law. He further claimed that he returned to the front only at the very end of the war and denied ever having belonged to any Nazi organizations.[56]

[52] Ibid., 108.
[53] Wasserman, *"Zuviel Vergangenheit,"* 82.
[54] Ibid., 133.
[55] Richard Mitten, *The Politics of Anti-Semitic Prejudice: The Waldheim Phenomenon in Austria* (Boulder: Westview Press, 1992), 43.
[56] Wasserman, *"Zuviel Vergangenheit,"* 171.

In October 1985, a reporter from Germany's *Stern* magazine challenged Waldheim's account of his wartime past and alleged that Waldheim had been a member of the Nazi Student Union (NSDStB). The Austrian weekly *Profil* researched this charge and initially found no support for it.[57] But on March 3, 1986, the magazine published an article with supporting documentary evidence that Waldheim had been a member of the NSDStB and a member of the SA. *Profil* thus claimed that Waldheim had made "incomplete, inexact, and sometimes also false" statements about his past.

The day after the publication of the *Profil* article, the World Jewish Congress (WJC) held a press conference. Like *Profil*, the WJC claimed that Waldheim had entered the SA in 1938 and, despite his repeated denials, had joined the NSDStB on April 1, 1938, three weeks after the *Anschluss*. The WJC also went beyond *Profil*'s accusations and charged that Waldheim had not spent the majority of the war in Vienna writing his dissertation, but had served from 1941 to 1943 in the Balkans under the command of General Alexander Löhr, who had been hanged in Yugoslavia in 1947 for war crimes.[58] The WJC declared that Waldheim had received a medal from Croatia's Ustasa regime (a Nazi puppet state) for "service under enemy fire" in July 1942, which proved that Waldheim had returned to the Yugoslav front by March 1942. (Questions were also raised about Waldheim's role in the deportation of Jews from Salonika in northern Greece.) In sum, the WJC charged that Waldheim had been a Nazi, and that he had lied about his Nazi past and his wartime record.[59] On the same day as the WJC's press conference, the *New York Times* published a story by John Tagliabue, who had also been researching Waldheim's past, which made similar allegations and supported them with files.[60]

The affair surrounding Waldheim's past dominated the first and second rounds of the Austrian presidential campaigns and will be examined in greater detail later. Waldheim came within 1 percent of capturing the 50 percent necessary to win the elections outright in the first round of April 1986. And in the second round in late May, Waldheim not only won but also posted the best showing ever for a nonincumbent (53.9 percent). Although Waldheim thus emerged victorious within Austria, the affair

---

[57] Mitten, *Anti-Semitic Prejudice*, 48.

[58] Löhr was responsible for the deportation of 42,000 Jews from Saloniki, Greece, between March and May 1943.

[59] Ruth Wodak et al., *"Wir sind alle unschuldige Täter!"* (Frankfurt am Main: Suhrkamp, 1990), 74.

[60] John Tagliabue, "Files Show Kurt Waldheim Served under War Criminal," *New York Times*, 4 March 1986.

had damaged his international reputation beyond repair. He made few foreign visits during his six-year tenure, mostly to Arab countries. On April 27, 1987, the U.S. government placed Waldheim on a watch list, which prohibited him from entering the United States as a private citizen. The Austrian government then appointed an international commission of historians to investigate Waldheim's past, hoping that it would clear his name and remove him from the watch list. Although the final report, published on February 8, 1988, stopped short of accusing Waldheim of war crimes, it stated that Waldheim had "tried to let his miliary past pass into oblivion, and as soon as that was no longer possible, to make it appear less harmful." Although Waldheim had claimed he had no knowledge of the deportations in Salonika, the historians wrote "even if Waldheim was absent during certain periods from Salonika, he must undoubtedly have noticed that a fourth of this city's population [the Jews]...had suddenly disappeared." It concluded that Waldheim, far from being the junior desk officer he had claimed to be, "had been exceptionally well informed" and "had been involved in the process of knowledge and action."[61] The report thus confirmed the initial allegations that *Profil*, the WJC, and the *New York Times* had made. In an address to the nation, Waldheim sought to make the best of the report, claiming that it showed that he had not been a war criminal.[62] Despite his international isolation, Waldheim considered running for a second presidential term in 1992, and was only persuaded not to run by his friends and advisors.[63]

The debate about Waldheim's past has been well covered elsewhere, and the precise evidence that the participants used to make their claims lies outside the bounds of this study.[64] More important for our purposes is how the debate about Waldheim's Nazi past rapidly turned into a debate about *Austria's* Nazi past. From the very beginning, Waldheim and his supporters claimed that the "campaign" against him was in fact directed at the entire war generation. During an election rally, Waldheim argued that the campaign "was not about the fate of Kurt Waldheim, but rather

---

[61] The Waldeim Report, international commission of historians designated to establish the military service of Lt/1st Lt. Kurt Waldheim, submitted to Chancellor Vranitzky, 8 February, 1988. Quoted in Pick, *Guilty Victim*, 162.

[62] See Bernhard Heindl, *"Wir Österreicher sind ein anständiges Volk"* (Linz: Sandkorn, 1991), 24.

[63] Interview with Thomas Chorherr, editor-in-chief of *Die Presse* (1976–1995), Vienna, 5 February 2001.

[64] For a detailed account of the debate about Waldheim the individual, see Mitten, *Anti-Semitic Prejudice.*

that one wants to denigrate an entire generation of respectable people and make them into war criminals."[65] The campaign against Waldheim was also framed as an attack on Austria as a whole. Alois Mock, the leader of the ÖVP, claimed that "these attacks against Kurt Waldheim... have appeared as attacks against Austria and our history. We must be aware of this. One wanted to strike Waldheim, and one struck Austria and her history."[66] Those who criticized Waldheim also agreed with Mock's assessment. Edgar Bronfman, the president of the WJC, argued:

> The issue is not Kurt Waldheim. He is a mirror of Austria. His lies are of secondary importance. The real issue is that Austria has lied for decades about its own involvement in the atrocities Mr. Waldheim was involved in: deportations, reprisal murders and others too painful to think about.[67]

Although there had been debates involving the Nazi past before, the Waldheim affair marked the most intense and sustained public debate about the topic. Politicians at every level participated actively in it, as did ordinary citizens, who wrote thousands of letters to newspapers and made hundreds of calls to radio stations.[68] The debate dominated the national print media for over three months. Between March 3 and June 30, 1986, the *Presse* published 188 texts on the Waldheim affair and the *Krone* 173.[69]

The public debate did not dissipate after Waldheim won the election but remained a politically salient issue thereafter. The powerful *Krone* played a central role in keeping the Waldheim affair in the political spotlight. In 1987, the *Krone* printed ninety-three reports on the Waldheim affair, meaning that *Krone* readers were exposed to the Waldheim affair once every four days. The *Krone* also published seventy-two editorials and sixty-one readers' letters. Of these editorials, forty-four were written by Richard Nimmerichter (Staberl), by far the most widely read columnist in Austria at the time.

For the most part, Austria's system of consociational democracy had hitherto prevented partisan differences from erupting into public conflicts. The leaders of Austria's four social partners (the ÖVP, the business associations connected with the ÖVP, the SPÖ, and the labor federation ÖGB) normally made critical political and economic decisions behind

---

[65] *Die Welt*, 3 May 1986.
[66] Quoted in Heindl, *"Wir Österreicher,"* 190.
[67] *New York Times*, 16 February, 1988. Quoted in Heindl, *"Wir Österreicher,"* 163.
[68] Interview with Hans Rauscher, Vienna, 5 February 2001.
[69] Wodak et al., *"Unschuldige Täter,"* 121.

closed doors before publicly announcing their agreements. This pattern of consensual politics made Austria, as Kreisky once put it, an "island of the blessed" and the envy of other European states plagued by political and social conflict. The Waldheim affair, however, marked the first major dent in Austrian consociationalism as the conflict over Waldheim's Nazi past became a topic for public debate among political parties, organized interest groups, the media, and activists from Austria's nascent civil society.

The pro-Waldheim camp consisted of the traditional conservative base: the ÖVP, the ÖVP's official newspapers, church organizations, and all other organized interest groups connected with the ÖVP. The FPÖ also supported Waldheim, even though it was in a coalition government with the SPÖ. The national daily *Die Presse*, the regional *Kleine Zeitung*, and many other Austrian dailies took Waldheim's side in the conflict.

Most importantly, so did the powerful tabloid *Kronen Zeitung*, which acted as a sort of "self-appointed pro-Waldheim hit squad."[70] As noted in Chapter 2, the *Krone* (as it is referred to colloquially) dominates the Austrian media landscape. In terms of readership per capita, the *Krone* is the most widely read paper in the advanced industrialized world. Over 40 percent of Austrians read it, a figure that dwarfs the 10 percent national readership that the *Bild* claims. Many Austrians claim that the *Krone*'s owner, Hans Dichand, who at eighty-five continues to check every issue before publication, is the most powerful man in Austria. Chancellor Franz Vranitzky once noted that "it was impossible to govern Austria without the support of the *Krone*."[71]

Like the *Bild*, the *Krone* concentrates on human-interest stories but also has a clear right-wing populist political slant. Its articles read like editorials, and its editorials are short and clear enough that even the most impatient reader can get through them. The *Krone* employs a large team of columnists, the most influential of who was Richard Nimmerichter, known by his pen name, Staberl. From the early 1970s until his retirement in 2001, Nimmerichter's columns appeared *every day* except Tuesday, when enthusiastic readers' letters addressed to Staberl were published instead. Although little is known of Nimmerichter's past – he almost never grants interviews – it is likely that he served in the Second World War. In any event, Nimmerichter consistently defended the war generation throughout his career and disseminated apologetic narratives of the

[70] Mitten, *Anti-Semitic Prejudice*, 199.
[71] Interview with Armin Thurnher, editor-in-chief of *Falter*, Vienna, 5 February 2001.

Nazi past. Many have accused him, and the *Kronen Zeitung* in general, of fomenting racism, sexism, and anti-Semitism.

The anti-Waldheim forces were considerably less powerful than the Waldheim camp. The small Green Party, which only entered parliament in November 1986, criticized Waldheim but did not receive much notice. Of the print media, the *Salzburger Nachrichten* argued that Waldheim's lies about his wartime past, but not that past itself, disqualified him from holding public office. The leftist *Kurier* took the same position. The weekly *Profil*, which first broke the story, was the fiercest opponent of Waldheim in the Austrian press landscape. Yet, as I will explain, the most vocal and committed protest against Waldheim and the view of the Nazi past he stood for emerged from outside of the political and media establishments.

The SPÖ took an ambiguous position during the Waldheim debate. Most members of the party did not criticize Waldheim's past and in fact argued that it should not be an issue in the campaign. Although some members of the party pushed for a more open confrontation with the Nazi past, many others defended the victim narrative or argued that the past should be allowed to pass away. It would be several years before the SPÖ advocated a more critical confrontation with Austrian history.

Step One: Frame Creation

The Christian Democrats and the New Victim Frame During the Waldheim debate, the pro-Waldheim camp created and disseminated a new victim frame linking the Nazi past to contemporary politics. The key elements of this frame were that (1) Waldheim, and by extension Austria, were the victims of a smear campaign by an international Jewish lobby; (2) it was the patriotic duty of all Austrians to repel this attack and elect Waldheim; and (3) Austrians had behaved decently during the Second World War and had no need to confront their past. The new victim frame consisted of older repertoires in Austrian political culture, such as the theme of victimization and anti-Semitic stereotypes. But the appeal to Austrian nationalism in the face of international criticism was a novel element, and Waldheim's election showed that it was a winning one. As the Nazi past emerged as a central political issue in the decades following the Waldheim affair, conservatives sought to score political points in these battles by turning the defense of Austria's past into an issue of patriotism. Three brief case studies – the conflict over the monument to the "Victims of War

and Fascism," the play *Heldenplatz*, and the *Wehrmachtsausstellung* –
demonstrate the enormous resistance that Austrian Christian Democrats,
in marked contrast to their German counterparts, mounted against efforts
to come to terms with the Nazi past.

The new victim frame emerged in the opening days of the Waldheim
affair. In his first televised reaction to the allegations, Waldheim spoke of
"the greatest slander campaign in the republic since 1945."[72] *Die Presse*
wrote as early as March 5, two days after the publication of the initial *Profil* article, of a campaign against Kurt Waldheim.[73] The *Kronen Zeitung*'s
columnist Peter Gnam titled his March 7th article "The Campaign."
Thus, from the very first days of the Waldheim affair, the Waldheim camp
alleged that there was an international campaign to discredit an Austrian
presidential candidate. The existence of such an international campaign
quickly became a fixed element in political discourse, and one that even
Waldheim's critics accepted.[74]

The Waldheim camp also shaped the debate from the outset by denying
that Waldheim was a war criminal. This was a charge that neither the
WJC nor the *New York Times* ever made. Yet, like the existence of an
international campaign, the notion that the WJC and the *New York Times*
had charged Waldheim with war crimes became a fixed point of reference
and was not questioned even by the anti-Waldheim camp.[75] It proved to
be a highly effective tactic, for by showing that the alleged allegations of
war crimes were without merit, the Waldheim camp was able to discredit
the critical examination of Waldheim's past in general.

Having established the existence of a coordinated campaign against
Waldheim, members of the Waldheim camp then sought to uncover who
was behind it. Although the SPÖ was their initial suspect, their focus
quickly shifted first to the WJC and then to Jews in general. In an interview
with the *Kurier*, Waldheim claimed:

Certain Jewish circles (not all) always try to damage Austria's international
reputation.... I regret all this, since one should not thereby awake anti-Semitic
feelings.... We Austrians are a respectable people! I will do everything, despite
these hateful accusations, to calm our people.... I am not considering giving these
people [the members of certain Jewish circles] the satisfaction of determining who
the next president of Austria will be.[76]

[72] Wodak et al., *"Unschuldige Täter,"* 205.
[73] *Die Presse*, 5 March 1986.
[74] Mitten, *Anti-Semitic Prejudice*, 200.
[75] Ibid., 209.
[76] *Kurier*, 24 March 1986.

The Waldheim camp consistently portrayed the WJC as dishonorable and irrational and speculated about its motives for launching the attack.[77] One theory was that the WJC was exacting retribution for Waldheim's friendliness to Arab states as UN secretary general. After being placed on the watch list, Waldheim charged that "this lobby that exists on the east coast of the United States is enormously brutal and insensitive and has only one desire: to extract revenge – revenge for my service as General Secretary of the United Nations, where I objectively represented the interests of the entire population of the world."[78] Another of Waldheim's theories was that the WJC was seeking revenge because Austria had not paid reparations to Israel.[79] A third theory was that Jews in general were so traumatized by the Holocaust that they were prone to behave irrationally. "One should say in these Jewish functionaries' favor," wrote a columnist from the *Kleine Zeitung*, "that we are dealing with people who, like so many other Jews, have been psychically severely damaged."[80] In a speech, Waldheim borrowed from this argument and implied that the Jews, although they had suffered a great deal, did not, like Austrians, possess the virtue of tolerance.

The Jewish people have suffered more than many other people on this earth. I am moved by this suffering. But other peoples, such as the Austrians, have also brought their suffering – not only their guilt into the common history of mankind. I respectfully cite a sentence by the Jewish writer and theologian Elie Wiesel, who wrote: "suffering as such does not confer any sort of privilege. It depends on what one makes from one's suffering." The whole world can see what Austria has made out of her suffering: a tremendous work of reconstruction in the spirit of tolerance and reconciliation.[81]

The Waldheim camp ascribed enormous power to an international Jewish lobby. Playing on entrenched stereotypes about Jewish control of the media, the *Krone* columnist Viktor Reimann frequently referred to the "World Jewish Congress and its minions in the mass media."[82] The term *Ostküste* (east coast) was used as a code word for the concentration of Jewish political and media power, and members of the Waldheim camp often suggested that the *Ostküste* controlled the U.S. government. This international Jewish lobby, with its center in the United States, was

[77] Wodak et al., *"Unschuldige Täter,"* 100.
[78] Quoted in Heindl, *"Wir Österreicher,"* 113.
[79] *Wochenpresse,* 7 November 1986.
[80] *Kleine Zeitung,* 27 March 1986.
[81] *Wiener Zeitung,* 21 May 1986.
[82] See, for example, his article in the *Kronen Zeitung,* 3 May 1986.

identified with *Das Ausland*, a term that translates poorly as the world outside of Austria.

Waldheim and his defenders claimed that while they themselves were not anti-Semitic, the smear campaign against Waldheim was provoking a new wave of anti-Semitism in Austria. In a front-page editorial in *Die Presse*, the columnist Ilse Leitenberger claimed that the WJC "never misses a chance to profit from a dark past" and "carries a veritable quantum of guilt that a new anti-Semitism can no longer be denied."[83] The liberal Catholic paper *Die Furche*, which had consistently distanced itself from anti-Semitism, carried an editorial arguing that "our Jewish friends must see the writing on the wall. What is happening these days begets new evil, where only reconciliation can heal. Whoever fears what is most frightful deep down in the Austrian soul, should not rouse it with wild actions."[84]

In addition to charging the WJC with reviving anti-Semitism, many of Waldheim's supporters accused them of behaving like Nazis.[85] For example, a columnist in the official ÖVP newspaper, the *Neues Volksblatt*, wrote that "the authors of this trash can campaign against Kurt Waldheim could have been taught by Joseph Goebbels. He is known for his recipe: One makes slanderous assertions and supports them with documents which raise suspicion but prove nothing."[86] Richard Nimmerichter wrote that the WJC was taking over "the barbarous principle of *Sippenhaftung*" (loosely translated as "collective punishment" or "guilt by association") from the Nazis in claiming that contemporary Austrians possessed collective guilt for Nazism's crimes, an allegation that the WJC never made.[87]

The Waldheim camp promoted an apologetic view of the Nazi past. In his statements and speeches, Waldheim consistently spoke of himself before the victims of National Socialism. Only once did he ever mention a common responsibility for Nazism's crimes.[88] When asked in a press conference as president "who had fulfilled their duty, the enemies of the Nazi regime or its assistants in the *Wehrmacht*?" Waldheim answered, "both."[89] In an election brochure sent to every Austrian household

---

[83] *Die Presse*, 25 March 1986.
[84] *Die Furche*, 28 March 1986. Quoted in Mitten, *Anti-Semitic Prejudice*, 219.
[85] Wodak refers to this as the "victim-perpetrator reversal." Wodak et al., *"Unschuldige Täter."*
[86] *Neues Volksblatt*, 12 April 1986.
[87] *Kronen Zeitung*, 1 March 1987.
[88] Heindl, *"Wir Österreicher,"* 76.
[89] Ibid., 81.

(3.6 million copies), Waldheim wrote: "I didn't do anything different in the war than a hundred thousand Austrians – I fulfilled my duty as a soldier."[90]

Waldheim and his supporters thus saw little need for examining Austria's wartime history. In an interview with the German magazine *Der Spiegel*, Waldheim argued that "forty-one years after the end of the war enough is enough."[91] *Profil* quoted him as exhorting people to "finally stop muckraking in the past" and "making people appear bad." Alois Mock (ÖVP) argued that "we must stop this hunting around in the past, otherwise it's questionable if we can concentrate on the future."[92] Waldheim's supporters were also confident that Austria had mastered the Nazi past. According to Ludwig Steiner, the ÖVP's foreign policy speaker, "we Austrians have mastered the past and can easily compare ourselves with other states. Austria does not need any tutoring in history."[93] Other Waldheim supporters dismissed the idea of dealing with the past altogether. For Thomas Chorherr, editor-in-chief of *Die Presse*, the process of historical self-reflection was forced on Austrians by *Das Ausland* and served no useful purpose.[94]

The *Kronen Zeitung*'s framing of the Waldheim affair mirrored that of the ÖVP and the *Presse*. Its stories, editorials, and readers' letters tirelessly and unanimously defended Waldheim and attacked his, and Austria's, critics. The paper played a key agenda-setting role by keeping the Waldheim affair front-page news long after the presidential campaign. "It is now in," wrote star *Krone* columnist Richard Nimmerichter in April 1987, "to see Austria as a veritable bulwark of Nazism. Indeed many people behave as if Hitler came to power in Austria and then with his Austrian Nazi troops occupied Germany and then Europe."[95] Nimmerichter alone wrote forty-four columns about the Waldheim debate in 1987 – the year after the high water mark of the debate – each of which painted the campaign as either malign or ridiculous. In Chapter 2, I noted that the frames are created through the process of repetition and condensation. Each of Nimmerichter's, and other *Krone* writers', short columns condensed the new victim discourse into its vital elements and repeated them ad nauseum. Any regular *Krone* reader would have been heavily exposed to

---

[90] Ibid., 69.
[91] *Der Spiegal*, 14 April 1986.
[92] Heindl, "*Wir Österreicher,*" 145–146.
[93] Ibid., 146.
[94] Interview with Chorherr, Vienna, 5 February 2001.
[95] *Krone Zeitung*, 16 April 1987.

the new victim frame, and the *Krone* became the key actor disseminating this frame to the general Austrian population.

If Waldheim's wartime biography at first appeared a hindrance to his presidential campaign, the Austrian right turned the defense of Austrian history into a winning issue. For the first time in the postwar era, a national election campaign was organized around appeals to Austrian nationalism. Election posters appeared throughout Austria carrying a picture of Waldheim and the words "we Austrians will elect whom we want." The general secretary of the ÖVP, Michael Graff, proclaimed that "Waldheim's election on May 4 will...become a patriotic act." This deliberate stoking of Austrian nationalism often drew applause from neo-Nazi and extreme-right individuals. At an election rally in the province of Carinthia, for example, Waldheim's speech was greeted with neo-Nazi and anti-Semitic comments from some members of the audience. Asked by a reporter if he was not seeking applause from the wrong crowd, Waldheim replied that "these are very proud people" and that their applause was "a healthy, natural reaction to the many acts of meanness, to the clumsy attempt to influence elections in Austria."[96]

Since the Waldheim affair, the ÖVP as a party has not altered fundamentally its views about the Nazi past. In the summer of 1988, for example, conservative opposition nearly blocked the construction of the Monument against War and Fascism (Mahnmal gegen Krieg und Fascismus) in Vienna. As its name suggests, the monument does not draw any distinctions between the victims of racial persecution, fallen Austrian soldiers, or the victims of Allied bombings. In fact, the monument was to be built on the Albertinaplatz, a square in central Vienna and the final resting place of several hundred civilian victims of an Allied bombing campaign. It is thus a very different type of monument than the Holocaust Monument in Berlin, since its primary focus is Austrian suffering rather than Austrian complicity.

The plans for the monument were first presented to the Viennese city council in 1983, and the ÖVP members voted for it. But in the wake of the Waldheim affair, the ÖVP changed its position. The party now made the curious argument that the final resting place of the bombing victims should not be disturbed by a monument to them.[97] It argued that the Morzinplatz in Vienna, the site of the former Gestapo headquarters,

[96] *Kurier*, 22 April 1986.
[97] Matti Bunzl, "On the Politics and Semantics of Austrian Memory: Vienna's Memorial against War and Fascism," *History and Memory* 7 (1995): 7–40.

was a more appropriate location for the monument. Yet, as one ÖVP city councillor frankly noted, the root of their objections was that the Albertinaplatz was "too prominent" a spot for the monument. Indeed, the Morzinplatz is located far from the city center and is surrounded by a gas station and a freeway. In the end, the Social Democratic mayor of Vienna made an executive decision and the monument was built in central Vienna. But the ÖVP's objection to a monument that recognized Jewish as well as Austrian suffering revealed its resistance to any sustained examination of Austria's Nazi past.

In the fall of 1988, Christian Democrats again opposed a work of art that raised questions about the Nazi period. The theater director Claus Peyman had commissioned Thomas Bernhard, Austria's best-known contemporary author, to write a play to commemorate the 100th anniversary of Vienna's famous Burgtheater. Both author and director had already drawn the ire of the Austrian right – Bernhard for his relentless criticism of Austria's political culture in his novels and Peyman for insulting Waldheim in an interview with the German weekly *Die Zeit*. On October 7, the *Krone* ran a story quoting several lines out of context from the secret script of the play, titled *Heldenplatz*, which it assumed to be a critique of Austria's relationship to the Nazi past.

Before *Heldenplatz* opened, leading Christian Democrats condemned what they assumed to be a state-subsidized insult to the Austrian nation. The cultural spokesman of the ÖVP, Erhard Busek, called for a boycott.[98] Vice-Chancellor Alois Mock (ÖVP) argued that "we won't allow ourselves to be insulted by someone who makes a profit from taxpayer's money," noting that "Austrians know that they have made mistakes...such as others have as well."[99] The conservative daily *Die Presse* also considered *Heldenplatz* an insult to national pride and warned that it would provide a "party for Austro-masochists."[100] When the play finally opened, however, it became clear that such claims were exaggerated and that the *Krone* had instigated the entire debate.

The opening of the Wehrmacht exhibit in Austrian cities between 1995 and 1997 provided for further rounds of conflict over the Nazi past. As I noted in Chapter 3, many German Christian Democrats initially opposed the exhibit. Yet as the debate in Germany evolved, many conservatives

---

[98] Ruth Wodak et al., *Die Sprachen der Vergangenheit* (Frankfurt am Main: Suhrkamp, 1994), 117.
[99] *Krone Zeitung*, 9 October 1988.
[100] *Die Presse*, 13 October 1988.

came to view the discussion about the crimes of the Wehrmacht as beneficial for reestablishing Germany's relationship to the military. During its
stops in Germany, some Christian Democrats even supported it. When the
exhibit reopened in 2000, there was no Christian Democratic opposition
at all. In Austria, however, Christian Democrats universally opposed the
first exhibit as well as the second, and the case of Salzburg shows the
extreme measures members of the ÖVP used in protest.

Several months before the exhibit was scheduled to open, the veterans' organization (the Salzburg chapter of the Kamaradschaftbund) distributed a flier to every household in Salzburg (82,000 copies in total)
warning parents to protect their children from the leftist propaganda
against the war generation. Leading ÖVP politicians quickly announced
their opposition to the exhibit. Helmut Scheibner (ÖVP), president of
the Salzburg state parliament, promised that he would do everything
he could to prevent the exhibit from opening.[101] He argued that the
exhibit "injected society with poison" and that teachers were presenting
a "manipulated view of history."[102] Scheibner quipped that "during fascism the schools were more objective than today."[103] Franz Schausberger
(ÖVP), the governor of Salzburg, pledged that the "honor of the veterans must remain intact and that no tax money will be used to fund this
shame of an exhibit."[104] He praised the Salzburg Kamaradschaftsbund
as a "model interest group" and an "ideal forum for discussion."

Veterans' groups like the one Schausberger lauded are important fix-
tures in most Austrian villages and towns.[105] In the province of Salzburg,
the Kamaradschaftsbund numbers over 36,000 – nearly a tenth of the
total population.[106] Members include veterans of the Second World War,
reserves of the Austrian Bundeswehr (Austria's national army), and other
individuals who identify with the military. The official organ of the
Salzburg Kamaradschaftsbund, *Kamaradschaftsaktiv*, lauds the heroism
and sacrifice of Wehrmacht soldiers who "defended the homeland" from
the Soviets. The idea that the German army launched a preventive war

[101] *Der Standard*, 10 December 1997.
[102] Helga Embacher, "Mein Vater war kein Mörder," in *Eiszeit der Erinnerung*, ed. Ulf
Brunnbauer, ed. (Vienna: Promedia, 1999), 32.
[103] *Der Standard*, 1 March 1999.
[104] Quoted in Embacher, "Mein Vater," 33.
[105] The German equivalent lacks the membership and political power of the Austrian *Kamaradschaftsbund*.
[106] Helga Embacher, "...dass die Ehre der Kameraden unangetastet bleiben müsse...," in
Helga Embacher, Albert Lichtblau, and Günther Sandner eds., *Umkämpfte Errinerung*
(Vienna: Residenz Verlag, 1999), 97.

against Stalin – a staple of right-wing political ideology – is a mainstream position among members of the veterans' organization, as is the idea that Stalinism was a greater evil than Nazism. While the Kamaradschaftsbund provides a much-needed venue for former soldiers to discuss their traumatic wartime experiences, it cannot be said that the organization facilitates critical reflection. Many veterans view themselves as either heroes or victims and fail to see the Wehrmachts' complicity in any wartime atrocities.[107]

The local political constellation in Salzburg prevented the *Wehrmachtsausstellungs'* opponents from banning the exhibit. The Salzburg city council was controlled by the SPÖ and the Greens. In contrast to many other local SPÖ groups, the Salzburg SPÖ supported the *Wehrmachtsausstellung* (the Greens universally supported it) and the ÖVP could not muster the votes to block it. But Christian Democratic politicians and members of Kamaradschaft IV took alternative measures. Scheibner became the head of the hastily formed "Working Group for Objective History" that organized a counterexhibit to the *Wehrmachtsausstellung*. The Salzburg mayor's office of Josef Dechant (ÖVP) refused to spend any public funds on the *Wehrmachtsausstellung* and forced the organizers to pay rent for the use of the city-owned cinema where it was held. Yet Dechant gave the Working Group for Objective History free use of the old town hall to present its own exhibit. Dechant also took the *Ehrenschutz* (the title of honorary sponsor) for this counterexhibit that opened one week before the *Wehrmachtsausstellung*.

The primary sources for the Working Group's exhibition were the paintings of Walter Gross, a former member of the Waffen-SS, who spent several years in a Soviet prisoner-of-war (POW) camp. Gross described these paintings as efforts to work through his traumatic wartime experience. How the paintings of one individual were more objective than the photographs and documents in the *Wehrmachtsausstellung* was never made clear. The exhibit also dealt solely with the suffering of Austrian soldiers and the brutality of their Russian captors. When Gross was invited to deliver the exhibit's opening address, he described himself as a "friend of the Russians." Several minutes into his speech, however, Gross explained that "you can't speak with the Russians as you would with a small girl; you must speak with them like you would with a dog."[108]

---

[107] Ibid., 103–124.
[108] Embacher, "Mein Vater," 35.

The victim narrative is not confined to local and state-level Christian Democrats. In 2000, Chancellor Wolfgang Schüssel (ÖVP) embraced the victim narrative in a controversial interview with the *Jerusalem Post* on November 9, the anniversary of *Pogromnacht*. Schüssel stated that "the sovereign state of Austria was literally the first victim of the Nazi regime.... They took Austria by force. They [the Austrians] were the very first victims."[109] While the chancellor added that Austrians also had a "moral responsibility" for their past, Schüssel emphasized the formal dissolution of the Austrian state through German annexation and ignored the fact that Austrian Nazis had laid the groundwork for an *Anschluss* from within.[110] By identifying Austrians as the victims of Nazism first, and recognizing their moral responsibility only second, the chancellor clearly sided with those who emphasized Austrian victimization rather than Austrian culpability. Schüssel authorized the interview before its publication.[111] The chancellor's decision to choose the anniversary of *Pogromnacht* to restate the old victim narrative in an Israeli newspaper was viewed as insensitive even by some of his supporters. The historian Erika Weinzierl, who has close ties with the ÖVP, objected that Schüssel made his statements at the "wrong time," in the "wrong place [the *Jerusalem Post*]," and "with the wrong emphasis."[112]

However, interviews conducted after the publication of the *Jerusalem Post* article suggest that most Christian Democrats agreed with the chancellor. Many politicians stressed the dire economic conditions that forced Austrians to look toward union with Germany.[113] Echoing another common theme, one ÖVP politician argued that while Austrians wanted the *Anschluss* with Germany, they did not want it with Hitler.[114] Several Christian Democrats also noted that "if the majority of Austrians were for the *Anschluss*, then Hitler would not have needed to march in."[115] The argument that Austria was left alone by the international community in 1938 also appears to be deeply embedded in the ÖVP's historical view.

[109] *Jerusalem Post*, 10 November 2000.
[110] Hans Rauscher, "Lernen wir Geschichte," *Der Standard*, 21 November 2000; Eva Weissenberger, "Wir, die Opfer," *Die Presse*, 18 November 2000; Günther Traxler, "Aufreger Schüssel," *Der Standard*, 22 November 2000.
[111] Weissenberger, "Wir, die Opfer."
[112] Interview in *Der Standard*, 23 November 2000.
[113] Interview with member of parliament (ÖVP), Vienna, 12 June 2002; interview with member of parliament (ÖVP), Vienna, 13 June 2002.
[114] Interview with member of parliament (ÖVP), Vienna, 13 June 2002.
[115] Interview with member of parliament (ÖVP), Vienna, 14 June 2002.

As one Christian Democrat who does not share such an interpretation laments, "positions within the ÖVP have not changed fundamentally since the Waldheim affair."[116]

Indeed, many Christian Democrats remain fundamentally suspicious of the process of coming to terms with the past. One charged that "some people are interested in showing that Austrians were only perpetrators."[117] Another complained that contemporary Austrians living in economic prosperity have no right to judge the actions of those living in misery in the 1930s, arguing that "those who present Austrians as perpetrators are judging the people."[118] Perhaps the most common position toward coming to terms with the past is the outright rejection of responsibility for the crimes of previous generations. Many Christian Democrats argued that "they will not apologize for things they didn't do" and want to see "the chapter [on the Nazi past] closed."[119] As one Christian Democrat sympathetic to critical examination lamented, "it is not easy for the ÖVP to be honest" about Austria's Nazi past.[120] If over the course of the 1980s and 1990s German Christian Democrats adopted the key tenets of the contrition narrative, Austrian Christian Democrats continued to downplay Austria's responsibility for Nazism's crimes.

The Contrition Frame and the Other Austria

The primary opposition to Waldheim emerged outside of established political parties and newspapers. Such opposition began on a very small scale. Journalists, intellectuals, artists, political activists, and concerned citizens on the left of the political spectrum began meeting in living rooms to discuss the Waldheim affair and its implications for Austria. The consensus was that they "needed to show that there was another Austria," an Austria that was willing and able to critically examine the Nazi past.[121] From the very beginning, the issue was more than getting the history right. One of the founders of this movement, Silvio Lehmann, described Austria as a "sick patient" whose "view of the past was hindering it from developing further."[122] These individuals saw in Waldheim, and in the chauvinistic

[116] Interview with member of the Styrian state parliament (ÖVP), Graz, 11 January 2001.
[117] Interview with member of the Graz city council (ÖVP), Graz, 15 January 2001.
[118] Interview with member of parliament (ÖVP), Vienna, 12 June 2002.
[119] Interview with member of the Graz city council (ÖVP), Graz, 11 January 2001.
[120] Interview with member of the Styrian state parliament (ÖVP), Graz, 5 January 2001.
[121] Interview with Hans Rauscher, Vienna, 5 February 2001.
[122] Interview with Silvio Lehmann, Vienna, 19 December 2001.

reaction of the Austrian right, a "moral crisis of state."[123] The erosion of the victim discourse, a pillar of Austrian national identity, had permitted a foundational debate about the basic values of their political community. They recognized that the SPÖ's failure to mount any opposition to Waldheim presented them with an enormous window of opportunity for political mobilization.[124]

Members of the other Austria began by holding press conferences to make public statements against Waldheim and participating in actions designed to remind Austrians of the crimes of Nazism. Many devoted themselves full-time to political activism, such as the *Mahnwache* (vigil) organized by Friedrunn Huemer.[125] Twenty-four hours a day during June 1987, people stood silently and held signs in front of St. Stephen's Cathedral in the heart of downtown Vienna to remember the victims of the Second World War. Their presence drew crowds of onlookers and provoked heated debates among them.[126]

The anti-Waldheim movement founded an organization to coordinate its meetings and protest activities: the Republican Club. Like the German '68ers, they attacked entrenched ideas about the Nazi past as part of a broader critique of the political and social establishment. Like the '68ers, members of the other Austria argued that there had been no clear break with the political culture that had both paved the way for fascism and incorporated many of its elements. In particular, left-liberals saw in the Christian Democratic reaction against the WJC the resurgence of the Austrian-fascism of the 1930s. In addition, they argued that Austria's ambiguous relationship to the Nazi past placed it outside of the Western European community of values.

The formation of this small civic movement was a novel development in Austria. Before the Waldheim affair, political activism was almost completely monopolized by political parties. Most secondary organizations were linked with one of the three political camps, which constituted distinct subsocieties well into the 1970s and still persist in attenuated forms today.[127] The coalescence of a left-liberal social movement organized around the theme of confronting the Nazi past was thus an important

---

[123] Interview with Lehmann.

[124] Interview with Walter Manoscheck, Vienna, 17 June 2002.

[125] Interview with Marie Steinhauser, Vienna, 19 December 2001.

[126] For an analysis of the discussions surrounding the *Mahnwache*, see Wodak et al., *"Unschuldige Täter,"* 254–281.

[127] For a study of Austrian subsocieties, see G. Bingham Powell, *Social Fragmentation and Political Hostility: An Austrian Case Study* (Palo Alto: Stanford University Press, 1970).

step in the development of an Austrian public sphere. The movement for the other Austria emerged as a new political actor that increased its political profile by organizing the two largest demonstrations against postwar Austria. In 1992, left-liberal activists organized a national candlelight march to protest Jörg Haider's petition to deport foreigners living in Austria and impose de facto segregation in elementary schools. Over 300,000 Austrians participated in this "sea of light" (*Lichtermeer*) for tolerance. In 2000, the same individuals who came together during the Waldheim affair organized the protests against the formation of the ÖVP-FPÖ government that drew several hundred thousand people in Vienna alone.

Changing Ideas in the SPÖ

During the Waldheim affair, the SPÖ failed to criticize Waldheim's relationship to the Nazi past. This silence was surprising, since the party had at first hoped to profit from Waldheim's biography. In the fall of 1985, Chancellor Fred Sinowatz supposedly intimated that Waldheim's "brown past" could be used against him in the upcoming election.[128] But as we have seen, this was a dramatic misreading of public sentiment, and the SPÖ's alleged instrumental use of history proved counterproductive. The party was caught completely off guard by the Waldheim debate and spent the rest of the affair trying to limit the damage. Within the first week after the publication of the *Profil* article (March 3, 1986), the SPÖ distanced itself fifty-three times from revelations about Waldheim's past.[129] None of the SPÖ's leading politicians took a critical stand against Waldheim or showed any interest in Austria's Nazi past. Jolanda Offenbach summed up the mood of the party: "After forty years, there must finally be an end!"[130] The SPÖ's candidate, Kurt Steyrer, also refused to criticize Waldheim's past, arguing instead that "we need to come to the vital questions of the future and finally leave the fruitless discussion about the past behind us."[131] In an interview with Austrian state television (ORF), Steyrer stated, "Kurt Waldheim's past is not an issue for me. The discussion about it is extremely regrettable. It damages Austria's international reputation when 'mastering the past' is attempted during an election campaign."[132]

---

[128] Interview with SPÖ politician, Vienna, 26 November 2000.
[129] Heindl, "*Wir Österreicher,*" 150.
[130] *Arbeiter Zeitung*, 13 June 1986.
[131] *Wiener Zeitung*, 5 June 1986.
[132] Quoted in Heindl, "*Wir Österreicher,*" 147.

The SPÖ was indeed concerned about Austria's declining international reputation. Not only were journalists covering the Waldheim affair and Austria's Nazi past for the major international newspapers, but international historians were also writing longer articles on the same issues for leading weekly magazines. Robert Knight, the British historian who had discovered and published the unflattering records of cabinet meetings on reparations, wrote an article for the *Times Literary Supplement* arguing that Austria had ignored the Nazi past.[133] In response to Knight's article, Austrian Foreign Minister Peter Jankowitsch (SPÖ) wrote a letter to Austrian academics asking them to "rebut the dangerous theses put forward by Professor Knight" and "to prevent gross distortions of history."[134] Jankowitsch wanted Austrian historians to write articles for foreign journals, give lectures abroad, and organize symposiums attacking Knight. But Jankowitsch's plan to restore Austria's international reputation failed, for many Austrian academics agreed with Knight's thesis. Dr. Karl Stuhlpfarrer, for example, wrote the following to Jankowitsch:

I share the view that after the liberation from fascism – by allied forces and not by our own people – enormous effort was applied to ignore Nazi crimes and Austria's share of responsibility.... If Austria's image has deteriorated, we ourselves are to blame ... there is no need to panic over commentaries that remind us of facts that we have collectively sought to push into the subconscious.[135]

One of the ramifications of the Waldheim debate, and an unwelcome one for Jankowitsch and other politicians, was the growth of academic scholarship about Austria's Nazi past. The years 1938–1945 had been a blind spot in historical scholarship, and most of those works that covered the period at all were devoted to the tiny Austrian resistance movement. As the victim narrative became discredited within academic circles, historians, political scientists, and sociologists began to concentrate on popular support for Nazism in Austria, as well as on the level of Austrian complicity in Nazism's crimes. In addition, academics also analyzed postwar efforts to conceal the Nazi past and to deny restitution to Jewish groups.

It was not until 1991 that a Social Democratic politician, Chancellor Franz Vranitzky, recognized Austrian complicity in the Holocaust during a parliamentary speech. Although Vranitzky's statements marked a radical departure from Kreisky's legacy and an important step in the Social Democrats' examination of the Nazi past, they did not lead the party to

[133] Robert Knight, *Times Literary Supplement*, 3 October 1986.
[134] Quoted in Pick, *Guilty Victim*, 166.
[135] Quoted in ibid., 166.

adopt the contrition discourse of their German counterparts. Vranitzky's admission of responsibility in 1991 was in fact buried in a speech about the Yugoslav crisis. Although foreign correspondents were alerted in advance that the chancellor would make a statement about Austria's complicity, domestic journalists were notably not informed, and the story did not make the headlines in the Austrian dailies.[136]

Vranitzky probably knew that his views did not command wide support in his party, especially at the state and local levels. In Graz, for example, Social Democratic opposition to the Wehrmacht exhibit nearly prevented it from opening. The exhibit's Austrian coordinators found that all conceivable venues in Graz, many of which were controlled by Social Democrats, were closed to them.[137] The Austrian coordinators announced that they would have to cancel the opening in Graz, which would have made it the only city in Germany or Austria to have rejected the Wehrmacht exhibit. In the end, several academics at the Karl-Franzens University in Graz found space in lecture halls. The Social Democratic mayor of Graz, Alfred Stingl, at first protested but then later decided to appear at the exhibit. His decision was certainly not supported by the majority of the party, many of whom believed that supporting the exhibit would cost it votes in the upcoming communal elections.[138]

Only after the formation of the ÖVP-FPÖ coalition did the SPÖ commit to a more critical examination of the Nazi period. On April 7, 2000, the new leader of the SPÖ, Alfred Gusenbauer, issued a document detailing the party's postwar "brown spots." Gusenbauer's "declaration" acknowledged that Karl Renner, the party's leader and first president of the Second Republic, had supported the *Anschluss*. It admitted that the SPÖ had played a central role in creating the VdU, the forerunner of the FPÖ, for tactical reasons. And it condemned Bruno Kreisky's policy of integrating former Nazis and his scathing attacks on Simon Wiesenthal.[139]

Such an admission of culpability after years of silence appears to have been driven by two factors. First, the SPÖ wanted to differentiate itself from both the ÖVP and the FPÖ on the issue of the Nazi past. By examining its own internal party history, the SPÖ could then call on the other parties to release theirs. Since this was unlikely to happen, the SPÖ could then claim the moral high ground. Second, the trial of Herman Gross

---

[136] Interview with Therizija Stoisits (Greens), Vienna, 4 July 2002.
[137] Interview with Walter Manoscheck, Austrian coordinator of the Wehrmacht Exhibit, Vienna, 15 June 2001.
[138] Interview with city councilor (SPÖ), Graz, 24 January 2001.
[139] Markovits and Rabinbach, "The Dark Side of Austrian Social Democracy," 15.

for the murder of children, which began in the winter of 2000, publicly exposed the SPÖ's connections with Nazi criminals. Gross had joined the Nazi Party in 1932 and conducted euthanasia programs on children in Vienna during the Nazi rule. After the war, however, Gross became a member of the SPÖ and was "accorded every accolade, honor, and privilege that the Austrian Republic could bestow."[140] Gusenbauer's declaration was thus also a form of damage limitation. Whatever the precise reason for his declaration, it was widely backed by the party's rank-and-file. Having admitted their sins, Social Democrats then began to criticize the ÖVP and FPÖ for their ambiguous relationship to the Nazi past.[141]

Step Two: Elite Polarization

Historical debates became increasingly frequent in Austrian politics after the so-called *Wende* (turn) that occurred with the formation of the first ever ÖVP-FPÖ national government in February 2000. After the publication of Schüssel's statements in the *Jerusalem Post*, Alexander Van der Bellen, the leader of the Greens, criticized the chancellor's remarks as "an unbelievable step backward in Austria's process of confronting history."[142] This sparked a month-long public debate between politicians, historians, and intellectuals in the pages of *Die Presse* and *Der Standard* about the veracity of the victim narrative. The results of in-depth interviews conducted in 2001 and 2002, and presented in Figure 4.1, show that political elites differ on whether Austrians were victims or perpetrators.

Many Austrians argue that there can be no clear answer to the victim–perpetrator question. If many Austrians welcomed the *Anschluss* and participated actively in the crimes of Nazism, there were Austrian victims as well. Although the Austrian resistance movement was tiny in comparison to that in other occupied states, there were Austrians who opposed the Nazis and suffered for their beliefs. Given these historical facts, how can one say anything other than that Austrians were both victims and perpetrators?

The issue, however, is which aspects of complex historical events one emphasizes. Consider the changing interpretations of May 8th among German political elites. Before the mid-1980s, most Germans viewed

---

[140] Ibid., 18.
[141] One of my general findings from interviews with members of all political parties is that conflicts over history have become more frequent and salient since the *Wende*.
[142] *Der Standard*, 18–19 November 2000.

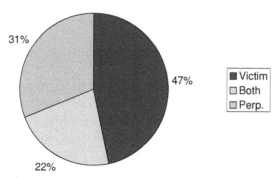

FIGURE 4.1. Victim or perpetrator?

this date as the anniversary of Germany's defeat. When President Von Weizsäcker recast May 8th as the day of liberation, he was criticized by conservatives who argued that East Germans, who then suffered under occupation, and German expellees from the eastern territories certainly did not experience May 8th as such. These were valid historical objections. Nevertheless, German politicians after Weizsäcker increasingly chose not to emphasize the victimization that the term defeat implied, but rather to commemorate the liberation from National Socialism and the chance for the rebirth of German democracy. Politicians across the political spectrum now describe May 8th as a day of liberation, a consensus on terminology that underscores the broader consensus on the meaning of the Nazi past.

By contrast, the ongoing debate about the meaning of the *Anschluss* demonstrates the enduring polarization of Austria's historical consciousness.

This polarization can be represented graphically. As in Germany, I conducted semistructured interviews with politicians from each of the four political parties represented in parliament. From left to right on the graph in Figure 4.2, these included the Greens, the SPÖ, the ÖVP, and the FPÖ. During these interviews, I asked a series of questions about the Nazi past and then scored each interview on a contrition index using a coding procedure outlined in the appendixes. Four out of five questions used to gather answers for the contrition composite were identical in Germany and Austria, allowing me to compare contrition scores across the two cases. Figure 4.2 represents the strong correlation between party ideology and contrition scores. Also, notice that over half of the politicians interviewed (twenty-five out of forty-nine) scored less than 0 on the contrition index, indicating hostility to coming to terms with the Nazi past. The

TABLE 4.1. *Average Party Contrition Scores in Austria and Germany*

Party	Austria	Germany
Christian Democrats	−2.6	+1.3
Socialists	+2.2	+3.7
Greens	+4.1	+5.0

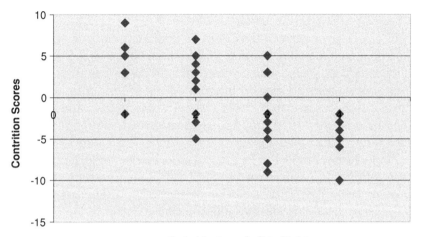

FIGURE 4.2. Contrition and party: Austria.

average contrition scores are lower for every Austrian political party than for its German equivalent, as Table 4.1 makes clear.

Austrians are just beginning to debate aspects of the Nazi past that have long been settled in Germany. For decades, elites from all parties (except the Greens) viewed May 8th as a day of mourning and participated in wreath-laying ceremonies at the graves of former Wehrmacht soldiers, including members of the Waffen-SS. In 2002, however, Austrian Greens declared that May 8th was the day of liberation and condemned wreath-laying as a right-wing practice. The SPÖ held a "festival for democracy" and urged Austrians to see May 8th as a positive day in Austrian history. The ÖVP was silent, while politicians from the FPÖ held speeches in which they referred to May 8th as a day of defeat. Interviews conducted in June 2002 reflect this left–right division over the meaning of May 8th: eight politicians (all but one from the left) referred to May 8th as a day of liberation, while twelve (all but two from the right) refused to use this term.

Interviews also suggest that many of the ideas about the Nazi past that have become common sense in Germany are disputed in Austria. For example, while over 80 percent of German politicians interviewed consider the Holocaust to be singular, less than one-half of Austrian politicians interviewed do. While the term *Vergangenheitsbewältigung* (mastering the past) is controversial in Germany because it implies an end to discussion about the Nazi past, few Austrian politicians interviewed objected to the term (seven out of forty-nine, or 14 percent, compared with nearly 50 percent in Germany). In addition, nearly 25 percent of Austrians, as opposed to less than 10 percent of Germans, expressed hostility toward the idea of coming to terms with the past at all. And while a mere 4 percent of Germans interviewed claimed that that they were "proud to be a German," nearly every Austrian politician interviewed found the phrase "I am proud to be an Austrian" unproblematic and used the phrase themselves.

Why did public debates in Austria produce elite polarization rather than convergence, as in Germany? The result of the Waldheim affair conceivably could have been a newfound sensitivity to the Nazi past and a convergence of elite ideas around something similar to the contrition frame. To put the question another way, why did the Austrian right and many newspapers continue to offer apologetic views of the Nazi past even as Austria's role in the Holocaust was confirmed by historical research?

As in the German case, agency played an important role in the outcome of public debates. Kurt Waldheim could have admitted that he did not fully reveal his wartime past and explained his reasons for doing so. Rather than presenting himself as a victim, he might have found some words for the victims of the Holocaust. He might have condemned the anti-Semitic discourse that surrounded the debate rather than contributing to it. He might have, in other words, used the opportunity to recognize Austrian complicity in Nazism's crimes and called for a critical examination of the past. But such actions would have been completely out of character. Even after his term as president, Waldheim continued to view himself as a victim and has never admitted any form of wrongdoing.

The events that triggered the debate also shaped its outcome. The fact that the allegations against Waldheim were raised by external actors, and particularly by the WJC, permitted the Waldheim camp to frame the debate as one pitting Austrians against foreigners. This stood in marked contrast to debates in Germany, which were internally generated.

The position of Austria's most powerful paper was also critical. While the German *Bild* called for an honest confrontation with the Nazi past and for German–Jewish reconciliation, the *Krone* disseminated the new victim frame and anti-Semitic stereotypes. As the facts of Austria's complicity in the Holocaust became known, the *Krone* stepped up its attacks on coming to terms with the past rather than toning them down. The *Krone*, in short, ensured that Austrians were repeatedly presented with apologetic interpretations of the Nazi past.

The specter of Jörg Haider's FPÖ was a final factor that pushed conservatives, as well as many Social Democrats, toward apologia. As will become clear in Chapter 6, the defense of Austria's history was a potent weapon in Haider's political arsenal, and Austrian politicians were afraid of giving him opportunities to use it. In explaining his opposition to the *Wehrmachtsausstellung*, for example, the head of the Styrian SPÖ said that he "could already hear Jörg Haider's speeches [condemning the exhibit] in the town square."[143] As Haider's power grew, politicians increasingly feared taking contrite positions on the Nazi past and thus opening themselves to Haider's attacks.

Step Three: Changes in Political Discourse

Although the ÖVP had a history of anti-Semitism and many postwar politicians were unabashed anti-Semites, they did not normally make anti-Semitic statements in public.[144] The Waldheim affair marked an abrupt departure from this practice. As I argued previously, ÖVP politicians and journalists employed by bourgeois papers (such as *Die Presse* and *Die Kleine Zeitung*), as well as those from the *Kronen Zeitung*, drew on anti-Semitic arguments in defense of Waldheim.[145] While many readers might not have recognized these articles as such, some leading ÖVP politicians made their points even more clearly. In an interview with a journalist, the general secretary of the ÖVP, Michael Graff, said that "so long that it isn't

[143] Interview with SPÖ politician in Graz, 22 January 2001.
[144] Leopold Kunschack, the founder of the ÖVP and a concentration camp survivor, was an unabashed anti-Semite. In a speech before thousands of people protesting the presence of Jewish-Polish displaced persons, Kunschack said that "he had always been an anti-Semite and continued to be one. No Jews, domestic nor foreign, had any business in Austria." Quoted in Oliver Rathkolb, "Zur Kontinuität antisemitischen und rassistischer Vorurteile in Österreich 1945–50," *Zeitgeschichte* 16 (May 1989), 168.
[145] Anti-Semitism in Austria is largely one without Jews. Only 7,000 Austrians (0.1 percent of the population) are registered with the official Jewish organization (Kultusgemeinde).

proven that he [Waldheim] strangled six Jews with his bare hands, there is no problem."[146] Carl Hödl (ÖVP), the deputy mayor of Linz, wrote a public letter to Edgar Bronfmann, president of the WJC, warning him that "you Jews got Christ; but you will not get Waldheim in the same manner."[147] Hödl added:

Your co-religionists two thousand years ago had Jesus Christ condemned to death in a show trial because he did not fit in with the ideas of the rulers of Jerusalem.... An eye for an eye, a tooth for a tooth is not our European way. The promulgation of this fundamental talmudic tenet throughout the world was left to you and your kind.[148]

Both Hödl and Graf had gone too far even in the environment of the Waldheim affair. The opposition called for their heads, and members of the ÖVP convinced them to resign. Graf, however, was quickly rehabilitated and became the ÖVP's official spokesman for judicial affairs.[149] Graf and Hödl also represent rare cases of Austrian politicians suffering negative political fallout for anti-Semitic remarks. One of the hallmarks of post-Waldheim politics has been the use of code words, such as "east coast" (*Ostküste*) or "certain circles" (*gewisse Kreise*), to invoke the specter of an international Jewish lobby. While it was Christian Democrats who initiated this practice in the course of the Waldheim affair, it was Jörg Haider and other FPÖ politicians who would make frequent use of it thereafter. And by purveying anti-Semitic discourses themselves, Christian Democrats extended the bounds of the discursive space to include positions that had hitherto been confined to extreme-right circles.

While historical apologia ends political careers in Germany, Austrian politicians are sanctioned only when they deny the Holocaust or highlight the positive aspects of National Socialism, since such statements are punishable offenses under Austrian (as well as under German) law. In 1995, the FPÖ Viennese City Council member John Gudenus referred to the existence of the gas chambers as "dogmatic history." Gudenus was forced to give up his seat, but returned to politics a year later and is currently a member of the Bundesrat.[150] In 1991, Jörg Haider praised the employment policies of the Third Reich and was removed as the governor of Carinthia.

---

[146] Quoted in Heindl, "*Wir Österreicher,*" 160.
[147] *New York Times,* 10 November 1987.
[148] Quoted in Pelinka, *Austria,* 193.
[149] Mitten, *Anti-Semitic Prejudice,* 237 (fn.)
[150] *Profil,* 19 August 2002, 36.

But as I argue in Chapter 6, Haider's career was in fact strengthened by this episode, and he continued to make apologist statements about the Nazi past throughout his career.

After the Waldheim affair, historical revisionism began to appear in Austria's popular press as well as in political discourse. The *Krone* in particular published editorials and readers' letters that contained revisionist elements. In the spring of 1992, for example, the columnist Richard Nimmerichter (Staberl) wrote a string of editorials disputing the "conventional wisdom" about the Holocaust. On April 11, Staberl questioned whether 6 million Jews had really been killed. In a column titled "Methods of Mass Murder" that appeared on May 11, 1992, he claimed that "relatively few Jews were gassed."[151] He accused third-generation Jews of using the "Saga of Martrydom" of those Jews who were gassed in the same way that Christians use the death of Jesus on the cross. Alluding to a pseudoscientific study that Holocaust denialists cite as evidence against the existence of gas chambers, Staberl wrote that "specialists have been able to prove that it would have been technically impossible to kill so many people with gas." Most Jews, according to Staberl, were beaten, frozen, or starved to death. He claimed that "according to reports from survivors" of both Nazi concentration camps and Russian POW camps, both groups were killed in a similar fashion. By denying the central role of the gas chambers in the extermination of European Jews, Staberl equated their fate with those of German and Austrian POWs, and by extension with those of other groups who died from hunger or disease during war and its aftermath. This revisionist editorial that appeared in Austria's largest daily drew little response from the Austrian government or other political parties. Although the Austrian Jewish community charged that Staberl had violated Austrian law, its protest was not followed by action from public prosecutors or the courts.[152]

It is unthinkable that such editorials would appear in the *Bild* or in any German paper that does not explicitly address a right-wing extremist audience. Edmund Stoiber (CSU) once remarked that any politician who made apologist statements about the Nazi past would be required to resign within fifteen minutes. In Austria, as one Green politician lamented in an interview, "nearly everything goes" and the boundaries between right-wing extremist conceptions of history and mainstream interpretations are fluid.

---

[151] "Methoden eines Massenmordes," *Neue Kronen Zeitung*, 11 May 1992.
[152] Reinhold Gärtner, "Right-Wing Press in Austria," in *Austro-Corporatism*, 306.

To what extent do attitudes among the Austrian population reflect those of political elites? As in the German case, answers to this question are constrained by the lack of time-series public opinion data about the Nazi past. The existing evidence, however, is consistent with the hypothesis that mass attitudes follow the patterns of elite discourse.

Polls conducted by the research institute IMAS before and after the Waldheim affair demonstrate that elements of the new victim frame were absorbed by the Austrian populace. In 1985, 57 percent of Austrians said that it would be better not to discuss the Nazi past anymore. After the high point of the Waldheim debate in 1987, 75 percent of Austrians agreed with this statement.[153] This was exactly the message the ÖVP and the *Kronen Zeitung* disseminated during the Waldheim debate. The 18 percentage point jump in rejecting the most basic element of coming to terms with the past occurred within less than two years, indicating just how sensitive mass attitudes are to elite-led public debates.

Mass attitudes toward the Nazi past also appeared to have shifted between the early and mid-1990s in response to elite cues. Recall that in 1991 Chancellor Vranitzky (SPÖ) made the first official apology for Austria's complicity in Nazi crimes. As I demonstrated earlier, the Austrian left increasingly picked up elements of the contrition discourse during this period. Public opinion surveys conducted by Gallup for the American Jewish Committee (AJC) in 1991 and 1995 support the hypothesis that as elites called for a more open confrontation with Nazism, ordinary Austrians saw coming to terms with the past as increasingly necessary. In 1991, 53 percent of respondents agreed with the statement that "it is time to put the memory of the Holocaust behind us." By 1995, that number had dropped 20 percentage points to 33 percent.[154]

Polls conducted since the mid-1990s support the hypothesis that the polarization of elite discourse produces a polarization of mass attitudes. As I argued earlier, Austrian elites have frequently debated whether Austria was primarily a victim or a perpetrator during the Second World War. In 1995, a Gallup poll conducted for the AJC found that only 29 percent of Austrians are prepared to acknowledge that Austria shares some complicity in Nazi crimes. By 2001, that number had risen to 45 percent. At the same time, the percentage of Austrians who believed

[153] IMAS Public Opinion Institute.

[154] Quoted in Richard Mitten, "Austria All Black and Blue: Jörg Haider, the European Sanctions, and the Political Crisis in Austria," in *The Haider Phenomenon in Austria* (New Brunswick: Transaction Books, 2002), 191.

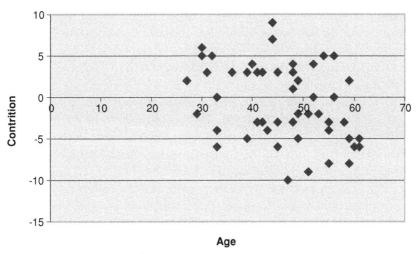

FIGURE 4.3. Contrition and age: Austria.

that Austria was Hitler's first victim rose from 28 percent in 1995 to 34 percent in 2001. These figures strongly suggest that ordinary Austrians have become increasingly divided on whether Austria was a victim or perpetrator, reflecting a similar split among elite opinion makers.[155]

Conclusion

This chapter has argued that domestic politics, and more specifically an elite-led public debate, is responsible for the current polarization of Austria's historical consciousness. In contrast to the German case, generational change played little role in this outcome. Recall that the generation of '68 in Austria did not challenge the victim narrative. Moreover, change came quickly and suddenly in the mid-1980s, not gradually, as a generational explanation would predict. Finally, as Figure 4.3 demonstrates, the correlation between age and attitudes about the Nazi past is weak.

International factors also did not matter in the way one might have expected. One might have predicted that a small state heavily reliant on international trade would have cared deeply about its international reputation and done everything to demonstrate that it was taking responsibility for its painful history. Yet exactly the opposite occurred during the

---

[155] "Large Plurality of Austrians Oppose Holocaust Compensation Accord" (http://www. charitywire.com/charity11/00701.html).

Waldheim affair as Austrian elites thumbed their noses at international censure. As we will see in Chapter 6, there was a similar "rally round the flag" effect after the ÖVP formed a government with the FPÖ and the fourteen member states of the European Union (EU) placed symbolic sanctions on Austria.

It is often claimed that Austria, unlike Germany, has done next to nothing to confront its Nazi past. This claim needs to be qualified. The movement for the other Austria has kept the Nazi past in the political spotlight and, along with the Green Party, has pushed for material and symbolic restitution for Holocaust victims. The SPÖ has recently become more willing to examine its internal party history and to take a more contrite position on the Nazi past. Moreover, there are some individuals within the ÖVP, and even within the FPÖ, who embrace a critical confrontation with the Nazi past and argue that Austria should do more for the victims of the Holocaust. In 2000, the ÖVP–FPÖ government signed a law providing restitution for slave laborers and is currently coping with the issue of stolen and art aryanized property.[156]

The Waldheim debate thus pushed some Austrian political actors toward contrition. But the fact remains, as I have argued, that a significant section of the Austrian political and media establishments remains hostile to efforts to come to terms with the Nazi past. The Waldheim debate not only produced the movement for the other Austria, but also created a golden opportunity for a right-wing populist party to enter the political spectrum. Although it was the ÖVP that used history, or more precisely the defense of history, as a political weapon, it was Jörg Haider who ultimately capitalized on this issue. As some members of the other Austria predicted during the Waldheim debate, "those who sow Waldheim will reap Haider." As I argue in Chapter 6, this was a prophetic warning.

---

[156] It must be noted that the government was under extreme international pressure to demonstrate its seriousness in confronting the Nazi past.

5

Combating the Far Right in Germany

Over the past two decades, the rise of the far right has dramatically altered party landscapes across Western Europe. Right-wing populist parties have captured double-digit vote shares in national parliamentary elections in eight different Western European states.[1] In Italy, Austria, the Netherlands, and Sweden, far-right parties have entered national coalition governments. In both Norway and Denmark, the national government currently depends upon the toleration of the right-wing populist parties. On the subnational level, far-right parties have become the largest parties in many regions and cities in Western Europe.

For all the attention lavished upon them, it is often overlooked that the electoral success of right-wing parties in Western Europe has not been uniform. In some states, no right-wing populist party has emerged.[2] In both Sweden and the Netherlands, such parties imploded after brief successes. In Germany, the subject of this chapter, the REP failed to consolidate itself in the party system despite persistently high unemployment, a large foreign-born population, and a host of shocks associated with absorbing

---

[1] These include Austria, Belgium, Denmark, France, Italy, the Netherlands, Norway, and Switzerland; I use the terms "right-wing populist" and "far right" interchangeably in this study. Other scholars have described these parties as right-wing extremist or part of the extreme-right party family. I avoid the term "extreme" because I draw a conceptual distinction between parties that seek to overturn the existing political order (right-wing extremists) and those that accept parliamentary democracy (right-wing populist and far-right parties).

[2] These include Finland, Greece, Iceland, Ireland, Malta, and Spain. In the United Kingdom, there are two neofascist parties (the National Front and the British National Party) but no right-wing populist party.

a former Communist state. Other right-wing political and intellectual movements in Germany have fared little better.

Why has the far right succeeded in some states and failed in others? Existing explanations focus on immigration, unemployment, electoral institutions, and the political program of right-wing populist parties. Using Germany as a case to evaluate these arguments, this chapter shows that none of them provide a compelling account for the failure of the REPs. I then use the German case to develop a new theory about the divergent success of right-wing populist parties.[3] Rather than looking at the ecological correlates, electoral institutions, or political coalitions that influence electoral support, I focus on the response to the far right from established political parties, the national media, and civil society. These political and social actors have adopted different strategies to deal with the rise of right-wing populist parties. In some countries, established political parties have sought to tame the far right by giving it governmental responsibility. In others, some parties have attempted to stimulate right-wing populist parties to damage their political rivals.[4] In Germany, however, political parties sought to coopt, discredit, and marginalize the far right as soon as it emerged. The national media denounced the REPs after their initial electoral breakthrough in the 1989 West Berlin state elections and warned the German public of the dangers of right-wing populism. German civil society protested against the REP wherever the party appeared and stigmatized its members. The combined reactions of political parties, the media, and civil society produced a host of organizational and recruitment problems for the REPs. Germany's culture of contrition proved too powerful for a small party trying to gain a permanent foothold in German politics.

The Rise and Demise of the REP

In 1983, Franz Handlos, Ekkehard Voigt, and Franz Schönhuber founded the REP in the state of Bavaria.[5] Handlos and Voigt were prominent

---

[3] On using case studies to create theories, see Stephen Van Evera, *Guide to Methods for Students of Political Science* (Ithaca: Cornell University Press, 1997), 67–73.
[4] In France, for example, François Mitterrand changed the electoral system in 1986 from majoritarianism to PR to help the National Front and divide the French right. I explore the French case in more detail in Chapter 7.
[5] For more on the REPs, see Hans-Gerd Jaschke, *Die Republikaner* (Bonn: Verlag J. H. Dietz Nachf., 1993); Richard Stöss, *Die Extreme Rechte in der Bundesrepublik* (Opladen: Westdeutscher Verlag, 1989); Hans-Georg Betz, "The Politics of Resentment: Right-Wing

CSU politicians who left the party after Franz Josef Strauss agreed to a major bank loan for the German Democratic Republic (GDR), which they denounced as a stabilization of the Communist regime. Schönhuber had been a CSU member, journalist, and popular host of the radio program *"Jetzt red I"* ("Now I Talk"), in which he traveled around Bavaria and encouraged people to air their political grievances. Schönhuber lost his job, however, after he published an autobiography titled *Ich War Dabei* (*I Was There*) that glorified his wartime service in the Waffen-SS. After internal power struggles, Schönhuber emerged as leader of the REPs in 1985.

Unlike other right-wing parties in Germany, the REPs were not founded by right-wing extremists with ties to neo-Nazi groups, and the party consistently distanced itself from such elements. The REPs initially sought to attract German conservatives who were disappointed by Helmut Kohl's promise of a political-moral turnaround. As the liberal faction of the CDU/CSU gained power in the mid-1980s, many voters looked for an alternative to the right of the Union. The REPs developed a more populist, xenophobic program in the middle to late 1980 when they began calling for an end to political asylum and immigration. Blaming immigrants for unemployment, the housing crunch, and rising crime, they decried Germany's "ethnic overalienation" (*Überfremdung*). In addition, the REPs charged that foreigners were straining the welfare state and demanded that benefits be reserved for native Germans.

The party's core ideology is German nationalism, and the defense of German history has always been an important theme. During speeches at the REP's first party congress, the party founders called for an end to mastering the past and for Germans to develop a healthy national identity.[6] This was an especially important issue for Schönhuber, who repeatedly raised the issue of German masochism in election rallies and public statements. It struck a chord with many other Germans, who joined the party specifically because of the REPs' defense of German history. The former head of the REPs in Berlin, for example, joined the party to "defend the reputation of the German Wehrmacht."[7] The leader of the REPs in Baden-Württemberg, who had previously been a swing voter,

Radicalism in West Germany," *Comparative Politics* 23, no. 1 (October 1990): 45–60; Jürgen R. Winkler and Siegfried Schumann, "Radical Right-Wing Parties in Contemporary Germany," in Hans-Georg Betz and Stefan Immerfall, eds., *The New Politics of the Right* (New York: St. Martin's, 1998), 96–110.
[6] Katharina Behrends, *NPD–REP* (Regensburg, Germany: Roderer Verlag, 1996), 117–118.
[7] Interview with Dr. Konrad Voigt, Berlin, 24 January 2002.

heard Schönhuber denounce coming to terms with the past at a rally in Bavaria and joined the party soon after.[8]

Revisionist ideas occupied a prominent place in the party's official documents. The very first page of the REP's 1987 party program laments that "the war propaganda of the victorious powers has entered our history books, and our youth must believe their exaggerations and falsifications to a large degree because an objective history is still not possible."[9] The REP's 1990 program repeats these basic points, adding that German political parties have exaggerated the importance of the twelve years of Nazi rule.[10] An "objective history," according to the REPs, would "decriminalize" the Nazi past by showing that the Allies committed atrocities as well, that German soldiers behaved honorably in combat, and that Germans suffered enormously as a result of both Allied occupation and retribution in Europe.

The REPs were unsuccesful outside the state of Bavaria, where they captured only 3 percent of the vote in the 1986 state elections, until their dramatic breakthrough in West Berlin in 1989. The REPs had captured the public's attention during the election campaign by airing a television ad that linked German immigrants with the death of German culture. They shocked the political establishment by scoring 7.5 percent in the Berlin election and entering a state parliament for the first time. The party gained momentum in the summer of 1989 in the elections for the European Parliament, winning 7.1 percent of the vote nationwide and 14.6 percent in Bavaria. After a brief hiatus following unification, the REPs won 10.9 percent in the 1992 state elections in Baden-Württemberg. Many commentators predicted that the REPs would clear the 5 percent hurdle in the 1994 national elections and thereby transform Germany into a five-party political system.[11]

Yet 1992 marked the REPs' high point. Although the party won 9.1 percent of the vote in the 1996 Baden-Württemberg election, it never again came close to winning 5 percent in other state elections and won a mere 2.6 percent in the 1994 national elections. The party is now politically irrelevant. As one politician lamented in 2001, "our significance

---

[8] Interview with head of REPs in Baden-Württemberg, Stuttgart, 16 April 2002.
[9] Die Republikaner, *Parteiprogram* (1987).
[10] Die Republikaner, *Parteiprogram* (1990).
[11] See, for example, Dieter Roth, "Sind die Republikaner die fünfte Partei?" *Aus Politik und Zeitgeschichte*, B41–42/89 (October 1989): 10–20; F. U. Pappi, "Die Republikaner im Parteisystem der Bundesrepublik," *Aus Politik und Zeitgeschichte*, B21/90 (May 1989): 37–44.

is now so minimal that we ask ourselves if we should even continue at all." [12]

As the REPs collapsed during the 1990s, right-wing populist parties across Western Europe made extraordinary gains. Only in Germany, Sweden, and the Netherlands did existing right-wing parties fail to tally a double-digit electoral return in a national parliamentary election between 1986 and 2001. On the local and regional levels, the differences are even more pronounced. In Austria, the FPÖ captured 42 percent in the 1999 state elections in the state of Carinthia. In Belgium, the Vlaams Blok won nearly 30 percent in municipal elections in the city of Antwerp. The National Front won enough votes in municipal elections to win the major's office in four major French cities. The Northern League became the largest political party in several northern Italian cities and even entered the government in Milan. The REPs never approached these results.

Explaining the Success and Failure of the Far Right

How can we account for the divergent success of right-wing populist parties across Western Europe? Given the xenophobic rhetoric of most far-right parties, immigration is an obvious factor to consider. Many scholars have hypothesized that rising immigration is positively correlated with the electoral success of the far right. Using vote intention as her dependent variable, Pia Knigge finds that rising immigration increases latent electoral support for right-wing populist parties. [13] But as Matt Golder notes, this result is open to question since only six countries, all of which possessed right-wing populist parties, were included in the sample. [14] The problem of selection bias undermines the validity of this and other studies in which countries without a right-wing populist party are either not included or coded as 0. [15] Using a new data set including all nineteen Western European

---

[12] Interview with Günther Reich, Berlin, 8 April 2002.

[13] Pia Knigge, "The Ecological Correlates of Right-Wing Extremism in Western Europe," *European Journal of Political Research* 34, no. 2 (October 1998): 249–279.

[14] Matt Golder, "Explaining Variation in the Success of Extreme Right Parties in Western Europe," *Comparative Political Studies* 36, no. 4 (May 2003): 432–466.

[15] As Golder argues, studies that include countries without right-wing parties but code electoral support for these parties as zero assume that unemployment and immigration have no effect on extreme right support in these countries. To solve this problem, Golder uses a Tobit model with a maximum likelihood estimator to avoid this form of selection bias. For more on Tobit models, see Gary King, *Unifying Political Methodology: The Likelihood Theory of Statistical Inference* (New York: Cambridge University Press, 1994), 210.

countries and a Tobit model, Golder finds that immigration does in fact increase support for right-wing populist parties. However, since Golder only uses the percentage of foreign-born population for his immigration variable, his study does not address the question of whether an increase in immigration is correlated with the electoral success of right-wing populist parties.[16] Moreover, in a larger cross-national study, Pippa Norris finds no significant relationship between the proportion of nonnationals living in a country and the national vote share of the far right, a finding that dovetails with Herbert Kitschelt's earlier assessment.[17]

There is thus a scholarly debate about whether immigration matters for the success of right-wing populist parties, and whether the relevant independent variable should be static (the percentage of foreign-born) or dynamic (the increase in the percentage of foreign-born). Neither of these independent variables, however, helps make sense of the German case. The proportion of foreigners in the total population in Germany averaged around 9 percent throughout the 1990s; Luxembourg and Switzerland were the only European countries that posted significantly higher numbers. During the late 1980s and 1990s, Germany also experienced the largest absolute increase in its foreign-born population in Europe.[18] Between 1987 and 1997, the percentage of the foreign-born population jumped from 6.9 percent to 9 percent, an increase of 30 percent.

Perhaps more important than the number and flow of immigrants was the prevalence of xenophobic attitudes among the German population. In 1992, 55 percent of Germans believed there were too many non EU nationals living in Germany (the EU average was 50 percent).[19] In 1997, this figure was still at 52 percent, while the EU average had fallen to 45 percent.[20] In another *Eurobarometer* poll conducted in 1997, 79 percent of Germans agreed with the statement "Our country has reached

[16] Christopher Wendt argues that sharp rises in immigration increase electoral support for right-wing populist parties. Wendt, "Toward a Majoritarian Mobilization Model for Western Europe: Explaining Changes in Far Right Vote Support," paper presented at the annual meeting of the American Political Science Association, August 28–31, 2003.

[17] Pippa Norris, *Radical Right: Parties and Electoral Competition* (New York: Cambridge University Press, forthcoming); Herbert Kitschelt, in collaboration with Andrew J. McGann, *The Radical Right in Western Europe: A Comparative Analysis* (Ann Arbor: University of Michigan Press, 1995), 610.

[18] John Salt, "Current Trends in International Migration in Europe," Council of Europe, November 2001.

[19] *Eurobarometer*, No. 37 (June 1992).

[20] *Eurobarometer*, No. 48 (Autumn, 1997).

its limits; if there were to be more people belonging to these minority groups we would have problems." The EU average for this response was 65 percent and only Greece (85 percent) and Belgium (82 percent) ranked higher than Germany.[21] Despite a large foreign-born population, a significant increase in immigration, and an anti-immigration public opinion environment, Germany failed to develop a successful right-wing populist party. Moreover, in a cross-national study, Terri Givens found that in Germany, the far right does not do better in areas with more foreigners.[22]

Is Germany an outlier? If one takes the average electoral performance of right-wing populist parties between 1986 and 2002 (see Table 1.1), rather than individual national elections, as the dependent variable, several other countries do not fit the immigration explanation. For example, in Italy the extreme right has gained 12.4 percent of the vote over this time, while the percentage of the foreign-born population has risen from only 0.8 percent to 2.2 percent. Although this represents nearly a threefold increase, the absolute numbers are still extremely low. In Norway, the far right's vote share averaged 12.3 percent between 1986 and 2002, while the percentage of foreign born increased from 2 percent to 4 percent – again, a sharp increase in percentage terms but a small increase in absolute terms. In Belgium and France, the only two Western European countries where the percentage of foreign born declined between 1981 and 1999, the far right averaged 7.5 percent and 11.8 percent, respectively, between 1986 and 2003. When one looks at the long-term success of the far right in different countries, the hypothesis that immigration alone (measured either in static or dynamic terms) translates into far-right success appears dubious.

A second variable that scholars have linked with the electoral success of right-wing populist parties is unemployment. The hypothesis is that unemployment increases the political appeal of parties that find easy scapegoats, that is, foreigners, for economic problems. In a cross-national statistical analysis, Jackman and Volpert find that unemployment is positively correlated with the vote share of right-wing populist parties.[23] Knigge, however,

---

[21] *Eurobarometer*, No. 47 (Spring 1997).

[22] Terri Givens, "The Role of Socioeconomic Variables in the Success of Radical Right Parties," unpublished paper, Department of Political Science, University of California, Los Angeles.

[23] Robert Jackman and Karin Volpert, "Conditions Favouring Parties of the Extreme Right in Western Europe," *British Journal of Political Science* 26, no. 4 (October 1996): 501–520.

finds that unemployment actually reduces the vote share of these parties and hypothesizes that voters prefer left-wing parties when the national economy sours.[24]

Unemployment, whether measured in static or dynamic terms, has clearly not helped right-wing populist parties in Germany. The unemployment rate doubled between 1991 and 1999 (from 4.2 percent to 8.4 percent) and was one of the most politically salient issues throughout the 1990s. But rather than increasing their support, the REPs collapsed over this period. Moreover, the REPs achieved their best state election results in Baden-Württemberg, the state with the lowest unemployment rate in Germany over the past two decades. The REPs also originated in Bavaria, the state with the second lowest annual unemployment rate since 1984.[25]

A brief glance at other European countries calls into question the causal effect of unemployment. The two states with the most electorally successful right-wing populist parties since 1986, Austria and Switzerland, possessed the lowest average unemployment rates over the past two decades in Western Europe (not counting Luxembourg). Despite an unemployment rate of 3.2 percent in 1999, Norway's Progress Party hovered near 30 percent in public opinion polls. Moreover, in states plagued by double-digit unemployment during the 1990s, such as Ireland, Spain, and Finland, right-wing populist parties failed to emerge.

What about the combination of immigration and unemployment? Golder finds that only when foreigners comprise more than 6.3 percent of the population does unemployment affect the vote share of right-wing populist parties. Of the nineteen Western European countries, only six have ever reached this high a percentage of foreign born. Germany is one country that fits this profile, but the combination of rising unemployment, a large foreign-born population, and an increase in immigration has clearly not produced a successful right-wing party there. If one excludes Luxembourg from the sample, then only Austria, Switzerland, France, and Belgium remain.[26] As noted earlier, unemployment rates in Austria and Switzerland have been extremely low over the past two decades, so the argument that unemployment coupled with immigration is not a persuasive explanation for the rise of the Austrian FPÖ or the Swiss People's Party. Thus, in only two cases, France and Belgium, might the

---

[24] Knigge, "Ecological Correlates," 1998.
[25] *Bundesanstalt für Arbeit*, 1999.
[26] Since most foreigners in Luxembourg are citizens of other EU countries, there is good reason to exclude it from the universe of cases.

immigration plus unemployment hypothesis explain part of the electoral success of right-wing populist parties.

The preceding discussion is not to deny that immigration, and possibly unemployment, do matter. There can be little doubt that the wave of immigration that hit Western Europe beginning in the mid-1980s produced new political issues that right-wing populist parties could exploit. The point is that we still know little about how these variables, either separately or in combination, influence electoral support for right-wing populist parties. The German case also suggests that unemployment and immigration alone cannot produce a successful right-wing populist party and that we should study how they interact with other variables, such as electoral rules.

There is a large literature on how electoral rules influence both the size of political parties' representation in parliament and their vote share.[27] When electoral laws favor large parties over smaller ones, voters perceive votes for small parties as wasted and instead choose parties that have a better chance of being represented. Proportional representation (PR) is thus more favorable to small parties than majoritarianism. "District magnitude," defined as the number of representatives elected in a district, also influence disproportionality among PR systems.[28] In many PR systems, legal thresholds rather than district magnitude determine the vote share a party needs for representation. To compare different types of electoral systems, Lijphart developed the "effective threshold," which estimates the percentage of the vote a party must receive to gain parliamentary representation.[29]

Since all right-wing populist parties were originally small, it is reasonable to expect that they have done better in states with lower effective thresholds than in those with higher ones. Jackman and Volpert's cross-national analysis tests this hypothesis and finds strong support

---

[27] The conventional starting point for this literature is Maurice Duverger, *Political Parties: Their Organization and Their Activity in the Modern State* (London: Methuen, 1954). Other studies include Rein Taagepera and Matthew Soberg Shugart, *Seats and Votes: The Effects and Determinants of Electoral Systems* (New Haven: Yale University Press, 1989); Arend Lijphart, *Electoral Systems and Party Systems: A Study of Twenty Seven Democracies 1945–1990* (New York: Oxford University Press, 1994); Gary W. Cox, *Making Votes Count: Strategic Coordination in the World's Electoral System* (Cambridge: Cambridge University Press, 1997); Richard S. Katz, *Democracy and Elections* (New York: Oxford University Press, 1997).

[28] Douglas W. Rae, *The Political Consequences of Electoral Laws* (New Haven: Yale University Press, 1967).

[29] Lijphart, *Electoral Systems*, 25–30.

for it.[30] But when Golder replicates and interprets their results, he finds that their claim is not supported by their own data.[31] In another cross-national statistical analysis, Elisabeth Carter finds that the correlation between effective thresholds and vote share of the extreme right is not statistically significant.[32] Moreover, she finds that right-wing populist parties do not perform less well under majoritarian formulas than under PR formulas.[33] Golder, however, does find that electoral rules, captured by district magnitude and upper-tier seats rather than by effective thresholds, have a strong impact on support for right-wing populist parties.[34]

While this scholarly debate is sure to continue, it is clear that electoral rules have not worked against the German REPs. Germany has a PR system with a 5 percent effective threshold, which is only slightly higher than the European average. More importantly, Germany uses the Hare formula – considered the most proportional of all PR formulas – to distribute seats.[35] The German Green Party is one example of a small party that was able to establish itself in the German party system. Small parties that develop a regional base can also enter parliament if they win three districts outright. The former Communist Party (the PDS) maintained its representation in the Bundestag between 1990 and 2002 by winning three districts in East Berlin during parliamentary elections. In sum, the German electoral system is not, in comparative terms, hostile to small parties like the REPs.

Two comparative studies that have sought to explain the electoral success of the extreme right, written by Hans-Georg Betz and Herbert Kitschelt, have not placed primary emphasis on either ecological correlates or electoral rules.[36] Rather, Betz and Kitschelt view the transition to postindustrial society as the driving force behind the appearance of right-wing populist parties. According to Betz, these parties are "the reflection and expression of profound and widespread anxieties in the face of a

[30] Jackman and Volpert, "Conditions Favouring Parties of the Extreme Right in Western Europe."

[31] Matt Golder, "Electoral Institutions, Unemployment and Extreme Right Parties: A Correction," *British Journal of Political Science* 33, no. 3 (July 2003): 525–531.

[32] Elisabeth Carter, "Proportional Representation and the Fortunes of Right-Wing Extremist Parties," *West European Politics* 25, no. 3 (July 2002): 125–146.

[33] Ibid., 133–134.

[34] Golder, "Explaining Variation."

[35] Lijphart, *Electoral Systems*, 24.

[36] Hans-Georg Betz, *Radical Right-Wing Populism in Western Europe* (New York: St. Martin's Press, 1994); Kitschelt, *Radical Right*.

radically changing world."[37] The shift from industrial to postindustrial capitalism has dissolved established subcultures and produced a new division among winners, who have the "cultural capital" to prosper, and losers who are "confronted with deteriorating prospects with regards to their life chances."[38] In Betz's account, right-wing populist parties represent the anxieties of the losers of postindustrialization. Although Kitschelt also begins with postindustrial change, he highlights a shift in citizens' preferences, rather than in their psychological state, as the central factor favoring right-wing populist parties.

Kitschelt tries to account for the variation in the far right's success and offers testable hypotheses. He begins with postindustrialization, his "master variable," and adds a theory of political institutions and strategic choices to explain the variation among different states. He argues that postindustrialization has created a new political cleavage dividing left-libertarians from right-authoritarians in European welfare states, and that catalysts such as economic crisis and immigration have further shifted preferences towards neoliberalism and xenophobia.[39] One key shift is that blue-collar workers are, as a result of postindustrial transformation, becoming less economically leftist while still retaining xenophobic political attitudes. Another is that the growth of white-collar employees in the private sector is decreasing support for the welfare state and increasing support for market-oriented policies.[40] In order for right-wing populist parties to prosper in this new environment, they must create a "cross-class" coalition by expressing both neoliberalism and xenophobia. Parties that fail to develop this "winning formula" will not succeed. Another necessary condition for success is a favorable "political opportunity structure," which Kitschelt conceives of as an ideological convergence between the other major political parties. The only two cases in which all of these conditions have been met are France and Denmark. In Italy and Austria, the radical right has not developed this winning formula (Kitschelt claims that they have not adopted xenophobia) but has been enormously

---

[37] Betz, *Radical Right-Wing Populism*, 170.

[38] Ibid., 33.

[39] Kitschelt argues in *Radical Right* that the existence of a mature welfare state is a necessary condition for a successful right-wing populist party. This is why, in his view, there are no right-wing populist parties in Greece, Ireland, Spain, and Portugal.

[40] Kitschelt, *Radical Right*, 9–10; For more on this transformation, see Kitschelt, *The Transformation of European Social Democracy* (New York: Cambridge University Press, 1994).

successful because it has created antistatist parties attracting a cross-class coalition rebelling against a patronage-based system.

Before assessing Kitschelt's argument in general, let us consider his explanation for the failure of the German far right. His central claim is that the cognitive framework of National Socialism was transmitted to postwar German right-wing activists and that this legacy prevented right-wing populist parties from developing the winning formula of neoliberalism and xenophobia. Since the German far right inherited the Nazis' anticapitalism, parties like the REPs were unable to develop market-liberal appeals and instead focused on welfare chauvinism, a program for saving the embattled welfare state by denying benefits to non-Germans. The REPs were thus unable to build the cross-class coalition necessary for enduring electoral success. In sum, "the German extreme Right has not been electorally 'rational' and has not brought together an electoral coalition under the winning formula of market-liberal and authoritarian appeals because its activists, as well as its leaders, have inherited nationalist and socialist patterns of thought that limit the parties' strategic flexibility."[41]

The predictions that follow from Kitschelt's view of the German far right are that blue-collar voters supportive of welfare chauvinist and xenophobic appeals will be overrepresented in the REPs' voter base and that small-business and other groups favoring liberal market policies will be underrepresented. Drawing on limited evidence from a 1990 World Values survey and secondary studies of elections until 1993, Kitschelt concludes that the REPs are a "distinctly working-class and lower social status party."[42] In another study, Jürgen Falter finds that individuals with less education and lower incomes than average are overrepresented in the REP electorate.[43] Yet Falter also discovers that the REPs' electoral coalition possessed a disproportionate share of both working-class and old middle-class voters, a fact that is difficult to square with Kitschelt's prediction.

Another fact that belies Kitschelt's account is that the REPs did adopt elements of neoliberalism beginning in the early 1990s.[44] As the party tried to extend its voter base beyond the so-called losers of modernization, the REPs demanded lower taxes, an end to government subsidies for large

---

[41] Kitschelt, *Radical Right*, 239.

[42] Ibid., 232.

[43] Jürgen Falter, in collaboration with Marcus Klein, *Wer Wählt Rechts?* (Munich: Verlag C. H. Beck, 1994), 154.

[44] Thomas Saalfeld, "The Politics of National-Populism: Ideology and Policies of the German Republikaner Party," *German Politics* 2, no. 2 (August 1993): 177–199.

businesses, and changes in a welfare state that was discouraging individual initiative and encouraging private abuse.[45] This neoliberal trend increased when Rolf Schlierer, a young attorney from Baden-Württemberg, took control of the party in 1994. The strategic flexibility of the REPs was thus not as constrained by the National Socialist legacy as Kitschelt suggests.

It is also far from clear that the winning formula in Germany would have indeed been a coalition of blue-collar workers, small businessmen, and farmers. In the two Baden-Württemberg state elections (1992 and 1996) in which the REPs posted their best scores ever (10.9 percent and 9.1 percent, respectively), blue-collar workers were the only socio-economic group that was overrepresented.[46] Cross-national comparisons also suggest that strong blue-collar support, rather than a cross-class coalition, can also be a winning formula for right-wing populist parties. In French national elections since 1988, only workers were consistently overrepresented among National Front voters. Nonna Mayer and Pascal Perrineau found that Le Pen's voters in the 1988 presidential elections were less pro-market than those for other parties on the right.[47] As Betz pointed out in 1994, right-wing populist parties across Europe began in the early 1990s to place far more emphasis on their xenophobic appeals and downplay, or even jettison, their neoliberal elements.[48] A final development in the 1990s that is hard to square with Kitschelt's prediction is the electoral success of the Nationalist Alliance (AN), formerly the Italian Social Movement (Movimento Sociale Italiano, MSI). This neofascist party captured 16 percent in the 1996 Italian elections and became the first party of the extreme right to enter a national coalition government in 1994. The AN is also currently a member of Silvio Berlusconi's ruling coalition. Since the strategic flexibility of this party, like that of far-right parties in Germany, is, according to Kitschelt, limited by its fascist heritage, the MSI should not have been able to succeed.

Although some of its predictions proved wrong, Kitschelt's analysis usefully focuses our attention on the partisan political context in which right-wing populist parties emerge and attempt to grow. While immigration, unemployment, and electoral rules have received much attention,

[45] Die Republikaner, *Parteiprogram* (1990), 9–12.
[46] Dieter Roth, "*Volksparteien* in Crisis?: The Electoral Success of the Extreme Right in Context – the Case of Baden Württemberg," *German Politics* 2, no. 1 (April 1993): 1–20.
[47] Nonna Mayer and Peter Perrineau., eds. *Le front national à découvert* (Paris: Press de la Fondation nationale des sciences politiques, 1989).
[48] Betz, *Radical Right-Wing Populism*, 1994.

the interaction between right-wing populist parties and existing political parties has rarely been systematically explored.[49] The strategy that established political parties adopt to deal with the far right, I will argue, is a critical variable in the success and failure of right-wing populist parties.

Several scholars have noted that established political parties attempt to coopt right-wing populist parties by adopting their central messages and implementing elements of their program. Students of German politics have employed this argument to explain the failure of the REPs. Brigitte Young, for example, argues that the challenge of the REPs pushed German politics rightward and cites the tightening of Germany's asylum law in 1993 as the primary evidence for this shift. As the CDU and SPD adopted elements of the REPs' program and discourse, they left the party without an original message and a pressing problem to address.

There is little doubt that the CDU/CSU did attempt to coopt the REPs; Christian Democratic politicians openly admitted this during interviews with the author. In 1991, Volker Rühe circulated an election strategy paper within the CDU/CSU that called on the party to keep the asylum issue at the center of political debate.[50] Many Social Democrats, not wanting to leave "the entire topic [of asylum] to the right," also called for constitutional changes to stem the flow of asylum seekers.[51] In 1993, both the SPD and the CDU/CSU voted in favor of modifying Article 16 of the Basic Law that guaranteed asylum to "every politically persecuted individual."[52] As a result, the number of asylum seekers dropped dramatically, from 438,200 in 1992 to 127,200 in 1994.[53]

---

[49] There are some important exceptions: William M. Downs, "Pariahs in Their Midst: Belgian and Norwegian Parties React to Extremist Threats," *West European Politics* 24, no. 3 (2001): 23–42; Michael Minkenberg, "The Radical Right in Public Office: Agenda-Setting and Policy Effects," *West European Politics* 24, no. 4 (2001): 1–21; Bonnie Meguid, "Competition Between Unequals: The Role of Mainstream Party Strategy in Rising Party Success in Western Europe" (Ph.D. diss. Harvard University, 2002); Tim Bale, "Cinderalla and Her Ugly Sisters: The Mainstream and Extreme Right in Europe, Bipolarising Party Systems," *West European Politics* 26, no. 3 (2003): 67–90.
[50] Quoted in Brigitte Young, "The German Party System and the Contagion from the Right," *German Politics and Society* 13 (Spring 1995), 68.
[51] The quote is from Rudolf Schärping, former secretary of defense and chancellor candidate for the SPD. Quoted in Young, "Contagion," 68.
[52] The German parliament added two restrictions to Article 16. First, persons seeking asylum from countries listed as "secure" will be immediately returned. Second, persons entering Germany through a secure third nation (such as Poland or Austria) will be returned to that third nation.
[53] Young, "Contagion," 69.

But did this strategy of cooptation weaken the REPs? The evidence suggests otherwise. The REPs did well in the 1996 Baden-Württemberg state election, which was dominated by immigration themes. The 1993 changes in the asylum law did not produce a shift in public opinion that weakened support for xenophobic appeals. As noted earlier, between 1992 and 1997 the percentage of Germans who "believed that there were too many foreigners living in their country" dropped from only 55 percent to 52 percent. Moreover, when the two major parties voted to change the German citizenship laws in 1999 and admitted that Germany needed more immigrants to remain economically competitive and to finance its pension system in 2000, the German public reacted with skepticism. In sum, immigration remained a salient political issue long after the 1993 changes to Article 16 and one that the REPs should have been able to exploit.

This cooptation hypothesis is also not supported by evidence from other European states. In Austria, Belgium, Denmark, France, the Netherlands, Norway, and Sweden, the vote share of right-wing populist parties increased after governments passed tougher immigration laws.[54] As some scholars have suggested, cooptation might boost electoral support for right-wing populist parties by endowing them with legitimacy and keeping immigration a salient item on the political agenda.[55] When tough immigration laws are passed, right-wing populist parties can not only claim victory but may also be emboldened to press for even tougher measures.

Political Choices and Strategies: Combating the Far Right

The German case suggests an alternative explanation for the success and failure of right-wing populist parties. Although postindustrialization, immigration, and unemployment have created pressures that augur well for right-wing parties, these pressures themselves do not translate into success. Like the cooptation hypothesis, I consider the dynamic interaction between established political parties and their right-wing populist challengers. But cooptation is only one possible pattern of interaction. Existing political parties can choose to cooperate with the far right and integrate it into the party system. This process often begins at the municipal and state levels, and can result in the formation of coalition governments including

---

[54] Wendt, "Toward a Majoritarian Mobilization Model."
[55] Virginie Guiraudon and Martin A. Schain, "The French Political 'Earthquake' and Extreme Right in Europe," *European Studies Newsletter* 32, no. 1/2 (September 2002).

right-wing populist parties at the national level. Although participation in government weakens right-wing populist parties in the short run by eliminating their protest votes, I suggest that cooperation and integration strategies contribute to the consolidation of right-wing populist parties.

The most effective strategy for neutralizing right-wing populist parties, I hypothesize, is a combination of cooptation, confrontation, and marginalization – what I term the combat strategy. Why does this response weaken right-wing populist parties? First, the possibility of eventual cooperation with other parties is essential for small parties to survive in PR systems. If small parties are to become anything more than protest parties, they must convince their voters that they might have some tangible effect on the political process. Small parties also need to claim some sort of achievement while in parliament, whether on the communal, regional, or national level. If all of their proposals are rejected in principle, an essential component of the combat strategy, small parties cannot claim any achievements and gain a reputation for ineffectiveness and incompetence. A vote for them comes to be perceived as wasted by the electorate.

The reaction of the national media is another variable that influences the success of right-wing populist parties. In some national contexts, major newspapers have given right-wing populist parties either tacit or direct support, and I explore this effect in Chapter 6. In other cases, the national media have universally condemned right-wing populist parties and waged campaigns against them. Given their mass circulation and their blue-collar readership, the role of national tabloid papers is especially important. Since one of the most consistent empirical findings about right-wing populist parties is that their voters are less educated than those from other parties, there is a large overlap between the readership of tabloid papers and the potential clientele of the far right. Thus, if a national tabloid newspaper wages a campaign against the far right, it will decrease support for right-wing populist parties.

The reaction of civil society to the appearance of right-wing populism also influences the development of the far right. Large, frequent protests against right-wing populist parties not only demonstrate that a significant portion of the population considers them politically illegitimate, but sustained protest can also create organizational and recruitment problems. The mundane tasks of political organization, such as finding places to meet, running information stands, and disseminating election materials, become infinitely more difficult when protestors disrupt these activities. Individuals are also less willing to work publicly for a party that is socially stigmatized.

In sum, my explanation for right-wing success or failure focuses less on the far-right parties themselves than on the reactions to them by the other political parties, the media, and civil society. These political actors have choices, and the choices they make help determine the success or failure of right-wing populist parties. Although these choices are sometimes guided by strategic calculation (interests), generally they are more influenced by ideas about the legitimacy of right-wing populist ideas. Elite norms against right-wing populism, I hypothesize, are more developed and entrenched in some countries than in others.

Combating the REPs

The notion that elite norms against right-wing populism, a legacy of German debates about the Nazi past, contributed to the REPs' demise has received only a passing nod from a few scholars.[56] In fact, several students of right-wing movements deny that elite norms exist or that they make any difference. The political scientist Richard Stöss, for example, explains the REPs' success in part as a product of German elites' inability to "come to terms with the past."[57] During interviews with the author, German politicians often denied that the REPs' failure had anything to do with Germany's intense confrontation with the Nazi past. They claimed that more work needed to be done in this regard; that although the far right was currently weak, it could rise again; and that Germans must remain vigilant.

Such warnings, however, speak volumes about the prevalence of elite norms. In interviews, many German politicians stated that they felt compelled to react to the slightest sign of right-wing resurgence. Given that the REPs and the New Right received far more attention than their success or influence merited, German academics might have felt a similar duty.[58] This also might explain in part why the majority of German studies account for the REPs' success and offer solutions for containing them rather than analyzing their failure. This culture of vigilance and, one might argue, overreaction to the far right is part of political correctness, German style. When the REPs broke through in West Berlin, German elites reacted as if

[56] One example is Roth, "*Volksparteien* in Crisis?" 19.
[57] Stöss, *Extreme Rechte*, 239.
[58] It is telling that the REPs, despite their limited electoral success, received far more scholarly attention than similar right-wing parties in Western Europe. Cas Mudde, "The War of Words: Defining the Extreme Right Party Family," *West European Politics* 19, no. 2 (April 1996), 234.

German democracy itself was under threat. While scholars have ignored or downplayed this reaction, I will argue that the measures that German political parties, the media, and civil society took against the REPs played the central role in the party's failure to gain a foothold in German politics.

On the eve of the Berlin elections, politicians from the SPD and the Greens gathered in spontaneous demonstrations against the REPs' entry into the state parliament. They announced that members of their party would actively fight the REPs at every opportunity. When the REP politician Andres made his first speech in the Berlin state parliament, every Green politician rose and held a single letter that together spelled "Wehret den Anfangen ("beware of the beginnings" – an illusion to Hitler's rise to power)." During a parliamentary session in Berlin on April 20th, the anniversary of Hitler's birth, members of the Green Party presented REP politicians with a brown birthday cake and mockingly congratulated them on their leader's birthday. For the rest of the 1990s, the SPD and the Greens helped organize protests whenever the REPs held meetings or election rallies. The DBG, the German confederation of trade unions closely aligned with the SPD, also played a major role in organizing demonstrations.

As Greens, SPD politicians, and trade unionists explained in interviews with the author, they believed that demonstrating against the far right was their political duty.[59] The question of cooperating with or secretly encouraging the REPs was never raised. Yet there certainly existed a strategic reason for doing just that. By strengthening the REPs, or at least not committing scarce resources to combat them, the SPD could have damaged the CDU/CSU. Even if the REPs captured only 5 percent of the vote in Bavaria, they would eliminate the CSU's absolute majority that had allowed the regional party to play at the national level for decades. Since the REPs drew more voters from the CDU/CSU than the SPD, a strong showing in national elections would redound to the SPD's advantage.[60]

The West Berlin elections produced a dilemma for the Union. Some Christian Democrats saw a tactical interest in cooperating with the far

---

[59] One trade unionist stated that organizing and participating in demonstrations, although they are costly in terms of both time and money, is a "matter of course" (*Selbstverständlichkeit*) for the DGB and that they could not allow any right-wing demonstration to proceed without a counterdemonstration. Interview with Dieter Pougin, DBG, Berlin, 14 November 2001. Many other politicians repeated this general argument about the moral necessity of demonstrating against the far right during interviews with the author.

[60] Winkler and Schuman, "Radical Right-Wing Parties in Contemporary Germany," 106–107.

right. Heinrich Lummer, for example, believed that the REPs were a suitable coalition partner for the CDU in the Berlin state parliament. This option, however, was quickly ruled out in Berlin, and the CDU/CSU's national leadership prohibited any form of cooperation with the REPs several months later. In several cases, this policy forced the CDU either to give up political power or enter into unwelcome coalitions. For example, in both 1992 and 1996, the CDU in Baden-Württemberg chose to enter into a highly unpopular Grand Coalition with the SPD rather than form a minority government reliant on the toleration of the REPs.

What explains the Union's refusal to consider cooperating with the far right? The longtime leader of the CSU, Franz Josef Straus, once stated that "there must never be a democratic party to our [the Union's] right." This statement has become party doctrine, and is underpinned by both strategic and normative considerations. If a party were to emerge to its right, the CDU/CSU would be unable to integrate right-wing extremist voters into the political mainstream. This would not only cost the Union votes, but would also potentially undermine the quality of German democracy. German politicians from all political parties recognize the Union's historic achievement in helping turn nationalist and conservative Germans into democrats, and they view the Union's integrating role as proper and legitimate.[61]

Having decided to isolate and combat the REPs, the Union needed to justify this policy. The REPs and the CDU/CSU did not differ dramatically on immigration issues. Both parties also stressed law-and-order themes and the preservation of traditional family values. One issue over which the REPs and the CDU did differ, however, was the Nazi past. As mentioned earlier, the REPs offered apologetic narratives of the period and decried the self-masochism associated with coming to terms with the past. By the end of the 1980s, the CDU had abandoned efforts to normalize the Nazi past and had adopted the key tenets of the contrition frame. Now standing on the politically correct side of the debate, the Union was free to use the Nazi past as a weapon against the REPs.

Immediately after the Berlin election, the idea that the REPs' views on the Nazi past rendered them an unacceptable coalition partner won strong backing inside the Berlin state CDU.[62] This became national policy

---

[61] Interview with Green member of the Bundestag, Berlin, 15 July 2001; interview with SPD member of the Bundestag, Berlin, 20 June 2001. This point was confirmed in many other interviews with politicians from parties besides the CDU/CSU.

[62] Interview with Monica Gruetters (CDU), member of the Berlin State Parliament, Berlin, 21 February 2002.

when the head of the CDU/CSU, Heiner Geissler, justified *Ausgrenzung* (marginalization) in an internal party report that argued that the REPs were not a possible coalition partner because they sought to trivialize the Nazi past.[63] Edmund Stoiber (CSU) also justified *Ausgrenzung* in part based on the REPs' "irresponsible dealing" with the past and their similarities to Nazi demagoguery.[64]

The CDU's position was critical in the erection of a *cordon sanitaire* against the far right. All parties followed a policy of marginalization that ruled out any form of cooperation with the REPs. *Ausgrenzung* prohibited personal contact with REP politicians, reliance on REP votes to pass legislation, and support for any REP candidate or proposal. This occurred at every political level. Party members in communal parliaments were instructed to vote against even the most mundane proposals of the REPs, such as the installation of a traffic light, on principle.[65] Members of the CDU and FDP who violated the policy of *Ausgrenzung* were immediately kicked out of their parties.[66]

Ausgrenzung made life exceedingly difficult for the REPs. The party stood no chance of passing legislation and benefited from none of the informal cooperation that eases committee work in communal and state parliaments. REP politicians appeared ineffective and harassed, and inflated the party's reputation for incompetence. Strict *Ausgrenzung* also sent a strong message that the REPs were an illegitimate political actor. In other national contexts, collaboration with the far right at local levels has marked the first step in their political integration. German politicians were determined not to let this happen.

While the CDU and other parties ignored the REPs, they also took other measures to combat them. Several states placed the REPs under the observation of the *Verfassungschutz* (Office for the Protection of the Constitution) after the party's electoral breakthrough. This institution is charged with monitoring groups that potentially threaten Germany's Basic Law and is empowered to ban parties that violate it.[67] For the

---

[63] Stöss, *Extreme Rechte*, 215.

[64] Jaschke, *Die Republikaner*, 59.

[65] Interview with a member of the Berlin state parliament (SPD), Berlin, 7 February 2002.

[66] Politicians from the CDU, CSU, and FDP, who preferred to remain anonymous, stated that there were several cases of party banishment. Most party members, however, followed the policy of *Ausgrenzung*.

[67] This has occurred twice in postwar Germany. In 1953, the *Verfassungschutz* banned the Socialist Reich Party (SRP), the successor of the Nazi Party. The German Communist Party (KPD) was banned in 1956.

REPs, observation means that government officials monitor all of their gatherings. Although the REPs have tried for years to escape this stigma, although they consistently proclaim their allegiance to the Basic Law, and although no incriminating evidence has ever been found against them, the CDU in particular has succeeded in keeping the party under observation. During public statements and election rallies, CDU and CSU politicians constantly remind potential voters that the REPs are being monitored by the Office for the Protection of the Constitution and refer to the party as an enemy of democracy.

In sum, German political parties adopted a mix of strategies to combat the REPs. If they did to a certain extent seize on their issues, they also battled them with all the political-cultural and institutional resources at their disposal.

The German media reacted quickly and decisively to the appearance of the REPs. Many newspapers, particularly *Bild*, tried to discredit the party by invoking the Nazi past. Following the REP breakthrough in West Berlin, *Bild* began a relentless campaign against the party, drawing comparisons between it and the Nazis and constantly reminding its readers of Schönhuber's glorification of the Waffen-SS. The paper regularly referred to Schönhuber as the *Führer* (an allusion to *The Führer*, Adolf Hitler) of the REPs instead of using the more neutral term *Chef*, or "chief". It also placed the name of the party in quotation marks (*"Republikaner"*) to indicate that it did not agree that the REPs were devoted to the Federal Republic. The editorial that appeared the day after the Berlin election is typical:

Franz-Schönhuber – The *Führer* of the "Republikaner"

...He considers himself the avenger ...

...volunteered for the Waffen-SS. He was a corporal in the SS-*Leibstandarte Adolf Hitler* [Hitler's elite bodyguard division]...in October 1981 he published a book: "I Was There," a personal avowal of his time with the Waffen-SS. The right-wing extremist "Deutsche National-Zeitung" voted it book of the year.

Then something happened to the "Nazi of the Bavarian Radio" something that he had never imagined: The CSU, the Munich community, the Bavarian Radio, they all dropped him. Therein lies the motive for his revenge.[68]

Bild explained the Berlin election as a protest vote and a horrible mistake. The paper published interviews with well-meaning citizens who had

---

[68] *Bild*, 31 January 1989 (boldface in the original).

voted for the REPs. As one taxi driver explained, "we really wanted to send those in charge a message . . . but we never thought it would come to this. We didn't want this at all."[69] Several days later, *Bild* placed a story about the reaction in Turkey, where Schönhuber owned a vacation house, in the middle of its politics section:

"He was always so nice," said the newspaper seller Mehmet Akine (24): "But he never showed his true face in Turkey." But now many residents of the Turkish vacation resort Bodrum believe they have seen the true face of the foreigner from Germany – the face of Franz Schönhuber (66), the Führer of the xenophobic "Republikaner."

In the past week the citizens of Bodrum (20,000) marched to Schönhuber's villa and draped his nameplate with a black towel. . . . "We symbolically gave him a black face. We took him without knowing who he is. We took him in our arms like a friend. It was a shock as we realized that we had a poisonous snake among us.[70]

Articles like this appeared throughout 1989 and in the early 1990s. Schönhuber once complained that the paper had turned him into the "national bogey-man," and other REP politicians claimed that *Bild*'s hostility was an important factor in the party's demise. The leader of the REPs in Bavaria, for example, called the media campaign against the party "our chief problem."[71] Although the exact effects of *Bild*'s coverage have not been measured, it is difficult to imagine that the open hostility of Germany's largest paper did not adversely affect the REPs' political fortunes

The German print media as a whole were also openly hostile to the REPs. There exist a "journalistic ethos" and an "unwritten law" in Germany that writers and editors have a duty to warn the population of the danger of right-wing populism. Like *Bild,* most newspapers placed the name of the party in quotation marks and drew connections between it and the Nazis. The specter of the Nazi past provided "the easiest method of transport" for sensitizing the population. The journalist feels a compulsion to react in this manner and "would also face the allegation that he is covering up the dangers of right-wing extremism" from other journalists if he failed to. The fact that German journalists in Weimar did not combat the Nazis early enough serves as a constant reminder against complacency. The journalistic norms that are part of political correctness, German style often cause journalists to overreact to small surges of

---

[69] *Bild*, 2 February 1989.
[70] *Bild*, 7 February 1989 (boldface in the original).
[71] Interview with Johann Gärtner, head of the REPs in Bavaria, Kissing, 22 April 2002.

right-wing radicalism. As one admits, "we sometimes turn ants into right-wing elephants," but one must always "beware of the beginnings."[72]

Elements of German civil society responded quickly and decisively to the rise of the REPs. Only hours after the results of the 1989 Berlin election were announced, over 10,000 Berliners joined in spontaneous protests holding signs that read "We don't need any Nazis" and yelling "Nazis out!" When REP politicians entered the Berlin parliament for the first time in March 1989, they were forced to use a back door under police protection to avoid the hundreds of protestors blocking the front entrance. Similar protests occurred whenever the REPs held party meetings or election events, forcing the party to meet in remote locations with police protection. A typical REP party caucus, for example, took place in a tent surrounded by police in the middle of an open field.

The constant protests created a host of everyday organizational problems for the REPs. The party was unable to rent public rooms for meetings since other political parties controlled access to them. The REPs also had trouble finding private venues, either because restaurant and hotel owners were hostile to the REPs or because they feared the reputational, and often material, damage from the protests that inevitably accompanied REP meetings. During election campaigns, the REPs had to hang their signs from high trees, or else they were immediately torn down. They had problems finding members who were willing to run information booths during election campaign, for the booths were quickly surrounded by protestors.[73]

In the fall of 2001, I witnessed a REP rally before the Berlin state elections. Several local REP politicians appeared with the party's national leader, Rolf Schlierer. Thirty policemen separated the REPs from a crowd of about a hundred protestors. There was an information booth behind the police lines, and one could gain access only by convincing the police that one was genuinely interested in collecting REP party literature. Several protestors persuaded the police that they wanted to collect the REPs' campaign flier, but then proceeded to hold signs in front of the REP speakers and chant "Nazis Raus [Nazis Out], Nazis Raus!" The crowd roared in approval as the protestors were led away and chanted so loudly that Schlierer was forced to interrupt his speech every minute or so. It was not that anyone was actually listening to him; the REPs' election rally

---

[72] The quotes in this paragraph are from an interview with Wolfgang Molitor, journalist for the *Stuttgarter Nachtichten*, Stuttgart, 16 April 2002.

[73] Many REP politicians I interviewed stressed these points.

only attracted protestors and the police required to monitor them. Similar scenes have been replayed hundreds of times across Germany.[74]

During interviews, REP politicians claimed that they faced a host of social pressures in their daily lives. The leader of the REPs in one German state claimed that he lost at least a third of his friends after he joined the party. Three of his cars were set aflame in front of his house. When he went to a political function at the town hall in one town, he claimed that there were over a hundred police on hand to protect him. Given these pressures, it is perhaps not surprising that he questioned "whether he did the right thing by putting all his efforts into politics."[75]

Members also faced pressure at work to quit the party. After the REPs were put under the observation of the *Verfassungschutz*, employers were legally allowed to ask if potential employees belonged to the party. Many of those who sympathized with the REPs did not join the party for fear that they would doom their chances for promotion. The leader of the REPs in one state actually claimed that he advised professional people to leave the REPs for the sake of their careers. REPs who were "out," meaning that their party affiliation was public knowledge, also stood little chance of holding leadership positions in the voluntary associations and clubs (*Vereinen*) that play an especially important role in German society.

REP politicians repeatedly claimed in interviews that they had lost many of their best people because of the occupational and social pressures they faced. Several claimed that they had found highly educated and upstanding members of the community to head the party list in elections, only to lose them after they became aware of the consequences for their reputation. After their initial success in 1989, the REPs lost 40 percent of their membership within a single year (25,000 to 15,000). Most REP politicians attributed this drop in part to the myriad social pressures that REP members faced. By the end of the 1990s, the party consisted mainly of unskilled workers, pensioners, and others who, as one leading REP politician put it, "had nothing else to lose"[76]

The Failure of Other Right-Wing Movements

Elite norms against right-wing populism caused German political parties, the media, and civil society to combat the REPs. The combined

---

[74] Participant observation, Berlin, October 2001.
[75] Interview with leader of the REPs in a German state.
[76] Interview with Gärtner.

reactions of these actors fatally weakened the right-wing populist party. To strengthen this argument, this following section examines the fate of the other important right-wing movements and individuals who sought to establish themselves in German politics in the 1990s. As I will argue, the same general dynamics explain the failure of the so-called New Right, the "Haiderization" of the FDP, and the presidential candidacy of Steffen Heitmann. In each case, conservative actors sought to carve out space for nationalist ideas by challenging the culture of contrition and offering apologetic narratives of the Nazi past. Such historical revisionism produced immediate reactions from political, media, and social actors that viewed such attempts as illegitimate and dangerous.

The New Right was a movement of young intellectuals who sought to renew, and relegitimate, the core ideas of German conservative political thought. These included the defense of the nation as a political organizing principle, the creation of a strong state, and the promotion of national interests in foreign policy. They drew on the thoughts of German intellectuals like Carl Schmitt and Armin Mohler, and modeled their strategy of winning "cultural hegemony" on that of the French *Nouvelle Droit*. Several of its leaders had studied under the conservative historians, such as Ernst Nolte, who had battled Habermas and others during the Historians' Debate. Thus, it was hardly surprising that the New Right sought to overturn the contrite narratives of the Nazi past to clear space for their conservative ideas. As one scholar notes, "from the start, the New Right sought political legitimacy through the struggle over 'culture', which primarily came to mean 'history', rather than staking out present constitutional positions or policy prescriptions."[77] None of their strategies to normalize the Nazi past were strikingly new. Like Hillgruber and others, they published histories that extracted some usable history from the Nazi past.[78] They wrote polemical essays attacking the political correctness that prevented Germans from departing from the contrition narrative. And returning to a familiar theme among the German right, New Right intellectuals stressed German victimization both during and after the war.

Many New Right intellectuals initially found support for their ideas in the years following German unification, during which some conservatives perceived a window of opportunity for the revival of nationalist thought.

[77] Jan Müller, "From National Identity to National Interest: The Rise (and Fall) of Germany's New Right," *German Politics* 8 (December 1999): 1–20.
[78] Many of these studies focused on the modernizing aspects of the Third Reich.

Rainer Zitelman, the most prominent member of the New Right, became
editor of the weekend culture section of the conservative daily *Die Welt*.
Zitelman then used his position to disseminate right-wing interpretations
of the Nazi past and spirited essays against political correctness. The New
Right won influence within the Ullstein publishing house, which began
to print revisionist histories of the Second World War. In 1994, the New
Right published a collection of polemical essays, titled *Die Selbsbewusste
Nation* (*The Self-Confident Nation*), which laid out its vision of domestic politics and strategy for gaining cultural hegemony.[79] The next year,
they released a similar collection called *Westbindung* that outlined their
conception of German foreign policy.

The New Right received enormous attention from German intellectuals and the media. Within several years, over a dozen book-length studies
of the New Right appeared in Germany, most of which carried dire warnings about the New Right's growing power. From the titles, it seemed that
German democracy itself was in imminent danger; *Is the Republic Tip-
ping?* and *Brown Danger* were two of the most alarmist. Some American
observers viewed the New Right in similar terms. In an article in *Foreign
Affairs*, Jacob Heilbrunn warned that the New Right was leading a "deep
change" in Germany "at the intellectual level."[80]

This was certainly an exaggeration of the New Right's power. At its
height, the movement could only claim several positions in the mainstream
press. Its success, moreover, was short-lived.[81] By the mid-1990s, New
Right intellectuals had been chased from their perches in the media and
publishing houses. After printing a particularly apologist article about the
Nazi past, the editors of *Die Welt* signed a petition protesting the paper's
"slide to the right." Zitelman was dismissed from his position and soon
left the paper.[82] As I will note, Zitelman's attempt to continue his political
activism within the FDP also failed. By the end of the 1990s, the former
cover boy of the New Right had left politics and was selling real estate in
the suburbs of Berlin. The New Right also lost its position in the Ullstein
publishing house as public criticism of its revisionist histories mounted.[83]
As Josef Joffe noted in a reply to Heilbrunn's *Foreign Affairs* article, if

[79] *Die Selbsbewusste Nation* (Berlin: Ullstein, 1997).
[80] Jacob Heilbrunn, "Germany's New Right," *Foreign Affairs* 75, no. 6 (November–
December 1996): 80–98.
[81] Josef Joffe, "Mr. Heilbrunn's Planet; On Which the Germans Are Back," *Foreign Affairs*
76, no. 2 (March–April 1997): 152–157.
[82] *Süddeutsche Zeitung*, 12 March 1994.
[83] Joffe, "Heilbrunn's Planet," 155.

the New Right "was a cancer, the German body politic soon released powerful antibodies."[84]

Another significant right-wing movement appeared within the small German liberal party (FDP) in the early 1990s. After unification, the FDP failed to cross the electoral hurdle in many state elections and was running well under 5 percent in national public opinion polls. The party was fighting for its political life, and many within it offered new solutions. Eying Jörg Haider's transformation of the FPÖ from a small liberal party to a growing nationalist one, some politicians argued that the FDP should seize upon nationalist themes and seek votes to the right of the CDU. Many new party members from eastern Germany found this strategy appealing. Such a move would not be entirely alien to the FDP, for the party was founded as a coalition between liberals and nationalists after the Second World War. Although the nationalist element had become smaller over the years, it was still significant in some states, such as Hessen and Berlin.

New Right intellectuals and politicians flocked to the FDP. As a small party undergoing an identity crisis, the New Right saw the FDP as an institution ripe for capture. Rainer Zitelman and other castoffs from the Ullstein publishing house focused on locations where the nationalist wing of the FDP had achieved some success and tried to win control of party organizations in Berlin and Hessen. The history and theology teacher Heiner Kappel led the nationalist wing in Hessen and was soon dubbed "Hessen's Haider."[85] Berlin was the most promising target, given the influx of "new Berliners" from the former capital Bonn and the presence of eastern Germans. Nationalist members of the FDP feverishly recruited new party members in several Berlin districts and were able to "tip" several of them. FDP politicians asked Jörg Haider to speak to their organizations, and the Austrian accepted several of these invitations. Alexander von Stahl, Rainer Zitelman, and Wolfgang Mleczkowski emerged as the leaders of the nationalist wing of the Berlin FDP.

Partly out of conviction and partly to position itself to the right of the CDU, the nationalist movement within the FDP pushed for the normalization of German history. As part of this endeavor, Zitelman, Von Stahl, Mleczkowski, and others collected signatures for a full-page paid advertisement titled "Against Forgetting" that appeared in the *Frankfurter Allgemeine Zeitung* on May 8th, 1995, the fiftieth anniversary of the end

---

[84] Ibid.
[85] *Der Spiegel*, 9 January 1995.

of the Second World War. The advertisement called for memory of the German victims of the war, such as the East Germans and the expellees, whose suffering began, rather than ended, in 1945. The advertisement failed to mention those victim groups who had suffered from 1933 to 1945 and described May 8th as a defeat rather than as a liberation. It marked the only elite protest against the culture of contrition that was, as I demonstrated in Chapter 3, on full display in May 1995.

The publication of the *Aufruf* (appeal) "Against Forgetting" marked the first time that the nationalist wing of the FDP had won national attention. It brought the struggle between liberals and nationalists in Berlin and Hessen to the attention of the FDP's national leadership. Leading members of the FDP were furious with the advertisement and demanded the resignation of those responsible for it, calling their "understanding of history an unbearable burden for any party."[86] The national FDP signed a resolution prohibiting Haider's appearance at FDP functions. The Junge Liberalen (Young Liberals – the FDP's youth party) decried that nationalist push as "anachronistic" and initiated inner-party trials against members of the nationalist wing, several of which ended in party banishment.[87] While politicians recognized that cultivating a nationalist profile might bring electoral gains, they were, in the words of one party member, "not willing to pay any price for power." Winning votes from the right wing was not "consistent with the character of the party." As another politician in Berlin put it, she could live with a small liberal party but not with a larger nationalist one. Like other political parties in Germany, the FDP as a whole placed its party identity and ideology above its strategic interests. "Even if we would get more votes," one politician explained, "the danger of turning nationalist was too strong."

If the *Aufruf* marked the high point of the nationalist wing in the FDP, the reactions it provoked contributed to its decline. There were intense debates with the Berlin FDP about historical consciousness. In a battle for the final place on the party list, one that pitted the liberal Erwin Lossmann against Mleczkowski, Lossman used the *Aufruf* as a weapon against Mleczkowski and easily won the vote.[88] By signing the *Aufruf*, nationalists within the FDP opened themselves up to charges of historical revisionism and pandering to right-wing extremists, and liberals within the Berlin FDP

---

[86] Quoted in Alice Brauner, *Die Neue Rechte in Deutschland* (Opladen: Leske and Budrich, 2001), 164.

[87] Interview with Birgit Homburger (FDP–MdB), former leader of the *Junge Liberalen*, Berlin, 15 February 2002.

[88] Interview with Erwin Lossman, Berlin, 8 April 2002.

seized upon this line of argument.[89] By the mid-1990s, it was clear that the nationalist wing of the FDP was on the wane. In the election for the party leadership, the liberal Wolfgang Gerhardt captured 86 percent of the vote, while the nationalist Heiner Kappel won less than 10 percent. The national FDP also took action against Kappel, who was thrown out of the FDP parliamentary fraction in Hessen in 1997 and soon left the party entirely. Von Stahl, Zitelman, and many other national liberals followed soon after. By the end of the 1990s, the attempted Haiderization of the FDP had clearly failed.

The nationalist wing of the FDP made another brief and disastrous appearance during the national parliamentary election campaign of 2002. Jürgen Molleman, the maverick vice-president of the FPD known for his support of the Palestinians, spent much of the election criticizing Israel and several German Jews. Mölleman's chief political advisor, Fritz Georgen, was an Austrian who believed that the FDP needed the votes of far-right voters to break the 10 percent barrier. The liberal leadership tried, without success, to stop what were widely interpreted as Mölleman's overtures to the far right. In early June, polls in *Die Zeit* showed that Mölleman's behavior was costing the party electoral support.[90] Mölleman dropped the Israel issue for several months but returned to it in the final phases of the campaign. Predicted to win over 10 percent of the vote and hoping for much more, the FDP captured less than 8 percent. Leading FDP politicians viewed Mölleman's behavior as the primary reason for the party's humiliating defeat, and he was forced out of the party's leadership. In March, Mölleman quit the FDP entirely and on June 5 apparently committed suicide during a parachute jump.[91]

Steffen Heitmann was a theologian, lawyer, and minister of justice in the state of Saxony (part of the former GDR) before Chancellor Kohl hand-picked him to succeed President Richard von Weizsäcker, whose term ended in 1994. Kohl wanted an eastern German to become president of the newly reunified Germany, and Heitmann's deeply conservative worldview – strong state, strong family, strong laws against criminals and asylum seekers – appealed to the right wing of the CDU and the Bavarian CSU. But Heitmann, perhaps because he was an easterner and unfamiliar with the culture of contrition of the Federal Republic, made apologetic statements about the Nazi past that immediately sparked controversy.

[89] Interview with Christian Meyer, FDP-Berlin, Berlin, 11 February 2002.
[90] *Die Zeit*, 29 May 2002.
[91] *International Herald Tribune*, 6 June 2003.

Heitmann spoke of the normalization of Germany history and called for a "de-tabooization" (*Enttabuisierung*) of the Nazi past.[92] Departing from discursive norms, Heitmann described both the Holocaust and the crimes of other nations as singular events.[93]

The CDU leadership initially tried to limit the damage by keeping Heitmann's public appearances and statements to a minimum. But the FDP, the CDU's coalition partner, indicated that they would not support Heitmann's candidacy. Prominent CDU politicians also turned against Kohl's candidate. President von Weizsäcker, Bundestag President Rita Süssmuth, former CDU chairman Heiner Geissler, Minister of Defense Völker Ruhe, and other Christian Democrats publicly voiced their objections to Heitmann. Süssmuth accused Heitmann of "trivializing the Nazi past" and making "statements about the overcoming of German history" that resembled those of the REP leader Franz Schönhuber.[94] With only the right wing of the CDU standing behind Heitmann, Kohl was forced to drop his preferred candidate in favor of Roman Herzog (CDU).

Although Herzog created unease early in his presidency by asserting that Germans should be less "uptight" (*unverkrampft*) about their history, he developed into one of the best practitioners of the contrition discourse. On an official trip to Poland in 1996, Herzog delivered a speech at the site of the Warsaw ghetto uprising in which he "asked for forgiveness for what the Germans did to you."[95] Recall from Chapter 3 that Herzog championed the idea of turning January 27 (the anniversary of the liberation of Auschwitz) into a national holiday dedicated to the victims of National Socialism. During a speech to the Bundestag marking the first occasion of the holiday in 1996, Herzog noted that the plight of the Jews "was reported on the radio and in the newspapers. It was something anyone could have known about who had eyes to see with and ears to hear with." Emphasizing that anti-Semitism "gradually became a part of public opinion," Herzog made the most critical statement to date about the complicity of ordinary Germans in the Holocaust. While Weizsäcker introduced this topic and Jenninger fumbled it, Herzog – an arch-conservative in other matters – got it as close to right as a German politician can.

[92] *Der Spiegel*, 41, 1993; *Der Spiegel*, 11 October 1993.
[93] *Der Spiegel*, 15 November 1993.
[94] *Der Spiegel*, 25 October 1993.
[95] *Die Zeit*, 5 August, 1994.

Conclusion

As one German commentator wrote in 1992, "the conditions for the far right's success were never so favorable as they are today."[96] However, elite norms against historical revisionism and right-wing populism led German political parties, the media, and civic activists to combat right-wing movements as soon as they appeared. The combined reaction of German political and social actors created insurmountable problems for the REPs and was the primary reason for their collapse. In the Conclusions and Extensions, I note that this combat strategy has been pursued in other countries. Yet I also suggest that an alternative strategy, one that relies on cooperating with and attempting to tame extremist parties, has been far more common, both in contemporary confrontations with the far right in Western Europe and with other forms of extremist parties in other times and places.

---

[96] Richard Stöss, "Rechtsextremismus in einer geteilten politischen Kultur," in *Politische Kultur in Ost- und Westdeutschland*, eds. Oskar Niedermayer and Klaus von Beyme (Opladen: Leske und Budrich, 1996), 136.

6

Taming the Far Right in Austria?

In October 1999, the Austrian Freedom Party (FPÖ) captured nearly 27 percent of the popular vote in national parliamentary elections. Several months later, after negotiations between the Social Democrats (SPÖ) and the People's Party (ÖVP) collapsed, the FPÖ formed a coalition government with the ÖVP. The domestic and international reactions to the formation of the Black-Blue coalition (the colors of the FPÖ and ÖVP, respectively) were dramatic. Members of the new government were forced to enter parliament through tunnels to avoid the largest political demonstration in postwar Austrian history. The fourteen other states of the European Union (EU) downgraded diplomatic relations with Austria to a technical level, an unprecedented action against another member state.[1]

As international attention focused on Austria for the second time since the Waldheim affair, many observers asked the following question: how was it that a right-wing populist party could become so strong in a state with solid economic growth, low unemployment, and a generous welfare state? Scholars have offered three main explanations for the "Haider phenomenon." First, the FPÖ fostered, and benefited from, popular

---

[1] Many observers noted that EU states had not taken similar measures when the postfascist National Alliance in Italy joined a coalition government in 1994. If rejection of the far right alone drove the sanctions against Austria, then the response of the EU fourteen was surely inconsistent. But as Walter Manoscheck argues, "Austria's political isolation at the hands of the rest of the EU partners has two causes: the participation of the FPÖ in the government and the inadequate review and reappraisal of National Socialism in Austria. Only the combination of the two makes the categorical reaction of the EU partners understandable." Manoscheck, "FPÖ, ÖVP, and Austria's Nazi Past," in *The Haider Phenomenon in Austria*, Ruth Wodak and Anton Pelinka, eds. (New Brunswick; Transaction Books, 2002), 4.

discontent with Austria's sclerotic system of consociational democracy.[2] Thirteen straight years of the SPÖ-ÖVP coalition had left many Austrians with the impression that their country lacked any political opposition, and the FPÖ's promises to shake up the system resonated with them. Second, the FPÖ played on xenophobic fears following a massive wave of immigration in the late 1980s and early 1990. As the ÖVP and the SPÖ bickered over immigration policy, the FPÖ offered clear solutions. Third, Jörg Haider was simply a brilliant politician. His charisma, as well as his vast personal fortune, helped him win over voters and recruit party members in droves.[3]

All of these arguments shed light on the success of the FPÖ. Yet, there is still a puzzle that needs explaining. Simply put, how could nearly one-third of Austrian voters cast their votes for a party whose members disseminate revisionist accounts of the Nazi past and regularly make explicitly racist statements? The Austrian press and Austrian specialists often assert that only a small percentage of FPÖ voters are from the extreme-right circles, and survey evidence supports this claim.[4] It is thus probably true that many FPÖ voters support the party *in spite* of its Nazi apologia and overt racism. But why are so many Austrians willing to overlook these positions? Why have Haider's statements, and those of other FPÖ politicians, not been a handicap, but arguably a boon, in the party's steady rise?

This chapter argues that the success of the FPÖ must be understood in the broader context of Austria's confrontation with the Nazi past. In Chapter 4, I noted that the VdU, the forerunner of the FPÖ, was the party of former Nazis. During the 1960s and 1970s, however, the party's leadership tried to turn the FPÖ into an Austrian version of the German FDP. This liberalization, in addition to Bruno Kreisky's apologetic interpretations of the Nazi past, made the FPÖ an acceptable ally and coalition partner. Yet there was always tension between the liberal leadership and

---

[2] See, for example, Herbert Kitschelt, in collaboration with Andrew J. McGann, *The Radical Right in Western Europe: A Comparative Analysis* (Ann Arbor: University of Michigun Press, 1995), 159–201.

[3] Exit poll interviews from parliamentary elections between 1989 and 1999 corroborate these arguments. In 1994, for example, 44 percent voted for the FPÖ because it fought against the abuses of consociationalism, 32 percent because of its tough stand on immigration, and 31 percent because Haider and the FPÖ would bring "fresh air into Austrian politics." Fritz Plasser and Peter Ulram, *Radikaler Rechtspopulismus in Österreich. Die FPÖ unter Jörg Haider* (Vienna: Fesell +GFK, 1994).

[4] See, for example, Richard Mitten, "Austria All Black and Blue: Jörg Haider, the European Sanctions, and the Political Crisis in Austria," in *The Haider Phenomenon in Austria*, eds. Ruth Wodak and Anton Pelinka (New Brunswick: Transaction Books, 2002), 179–212.

an essentially nationalist base. When the so-called Reder–Frischenschlager affair exposed this rift in 1985, a young politician named Jörg Haider used the Nazi past to rally the nationalists against the liberals. The Waldheim debate that broke out a year later brought anti-Semitic, nationalist, and apologist discourse into the political mainstream, and it was the FPÖ that was ideally positioned to benefit from this shift in discursive space. It was no coincidence that Haider's electoral breakthrough occurred in November 1986, during the midst of the Waldheim debate.

But if the Waldheim debate provided the immediate opportunity for the FPÖ's electoral breakthrough, it was the reactions to it by other political parties, the media, and civil society that were critical for its consolidation. Recall that when the German REPs polled 7.5 percent in the Berlin state election, politicians and the media behaved as if German democracy was at risk. Yet, when the FPÖ captured nearly 10 percent in *national* elections, Austrian political and social actors did not behave as if the far right was an illegitimate political actor. The ÖVP never ruled out a national coalition with the FPÖ, and both it and the SPÖ cooperated with the FPÖ on the local and state levels. Austria's largest newspaper, the *Kronen Zeitung*, supported Haider's policies on immigration and positions on the Nazi past, and defended him from his domestic and international critics. Although Austrian civil society would mobilize against the FPÖ in the late 1990s, there were no significant protests until the FPÖ was polling nearly 20 percent nationally. Whereas Germany's confrontation with the Nazi past rendered politicians, journalists, and ordinary citizens enormously sensitive to right-wing political movements and historical revisionism, public debates over that past in Austria not only failed to discredit movements like Haider's but legitimated them.

The Reder Affair and the Rise of Jörg Haider

When Bruno Kreisky failed to secure an absolute majority for the SPÖ in the 1983 elections, he turned to the FPÖ as a coalition partner. This so-called small coalition (*die kleine Koalition*) was made possible by a liberal turn within the FPÖ over the course of the 1970s. Under Friedrich Peter, Norbert Steger, and Friedhelm Frischenschlager, the FPÖ tried to shed its image as the party of former Nazis and model itself on the German liberal party (FDP), which made the party palatable to many Social Democrats. Yet, it was unclear to what extent the liberalization of the FPÖ's elite had changed the nationalist orientation of the party's base. In 1985, the Reder–Frischenschlager affair exposed the yawning gap between the FPÖ's national leadership and party rank-and-file, weakened the small coalition beyond repair, and marked the beginning of the rise of Jörg Haider.

The Reder–Frischenschlager affair began with a handshake between Walter Reder and Friedhelm Frischenschlager (FPÖ), the minister of defense in the small coalition. Reder had joined the SS in 1932 at the age of seventeen and left for Germany in 1934 to join the Austrian legion, a group devoted to the *Anschluss* cause. He attended the school for SS leaders in Braunschweig and served in the SS's Totenkopf-Standorte, from which death camp guards were recruited, before becoming the commander of an SS tank division in northern Italy. In September 1944, Reder led reprisals for partisan attacks on the civilian population of Marzabotto. According to eyewitness accounts, German soldiers threw grenades into churches where civilians were seeking protection, raped and tortured women and children, and killed over 1,800 civilians in two days of attacks.[5] Following the war, Reder was sentenced to lifelong imprisonment by an Italian military tribunal. In 1985, the Italian government announced that it would release Reder to the Austrians on the condition that the handover be conducted discretely.

In keeping with Italy's wishes, Minister of Defense Frischenschlager arranged to have Reder flown to an airport in Graz and met him personally when he landed. The two men shook hands as Frishenschlager told Reder, "Welcome home, I am very happy for you."[6] The day after this handshake, several leading members of the SPÖ denounced Frischenschlager's behavior and demanded his resignation. They did not criticize Reder's release – indeed, Kreisky and other SPÖ politicians had pleaded with the Italian government for it – but rather Frischenschlager's official state reception of a convicted war criminal. The ÖVP, seeing a chance to break apart the small coalition, also demanded Frischenschlager's resignation and forced an emergency parliamentary session to seek a vote of no confidence in the government. All this took place while the executive committee of the WJC was meeting in Vienna. Its members were stunned and demanded Frischenschlager's resignation.

Although members of the FPÖ unanimously defended Frischenschlager's conduct, the liberal leadership of the party reacted very differently to the affair than the nationalist base. Liberals like Vice-Chancellor Norbert Steger cautiously defended Frischenschlager while trying to

[5] *Profil*, 28 January 1985.
[6] Ibid.

appear sensitize to the domestic, and the growing international, criticisms. The nationalist wing positively cheered Frischenschlager, and the loudest applause came from a young politician in Carinthia, Jörg Haider, who praised Frischenschlager's action as "exemplary."[7]

Jörg Haider, born in 1950 in the province of Upper Austria, was the son of a shoemaker who joined the Hitler Youth in 1932 and the Nazi Party in 1937. Nostalgia for the Nazi period, sadness for the lost war, and opposition to the Allied "reeducation" campaigns were pervasive in Haider's childhood and adolescence. As a student, Haider joined the right-wing Österreichischen Turnerbund (ostensibly a sports club) and later the pan-Germanist fraternities Albia and Sylvania.[8] A gifted speaker, Haider won several competitions in rhetoric before becoming the head of the RFS (the FPÖ's student organization) and completing a degree in law. Haider also inherited a massive estate in Carinthia, which originally belonged to Jews and was sold far below its market value to Haider's uncle in 1938. Haider's revenues from this property, known as the Bärental, have allowed him to maintain a lavish lifestyle and devote himself full-time to politics. He rose quickly within the ranks of the Carinthian FPO and was trying to enter the national stage when the Reder–Frischenschlager debate provided him with an ideal opportunity.

Haider positioned himself during the crisis as the most vibrant spokesman for the "war generation," meaning all those Austrians who had experienced the Second World War as youths or young adults. He argued that Walter Reder's "fate is the tragic life story of a soldier, whose acts cannot be compared to the horrible acts of the Nazi regime. Our fathers could have shared Walter Reder's fate." Defending the war generation from criticism, Haider also noted that "he who is ashamed of Walter Reder shoots the generation of our fathers, who fulfilled their duty as soldiers, in the head."[9] When asked if he considered Reder a war criminal, Haider answered that "if Reder is, then the English are as well. They bombarded Dresden. Atrocities are indivisible."[10]

When the liberal leadership appeared to cave in to international pressure, Haider saw his opportunity. Several weeks after the handshake, the Israeli daily *Yediot Achronot* published an article quoting Frishcenschlager as apologizing to the entire Israeli population for

[7] *Die Presse*, 31 January 1985.
[8] Fraternities in Austria (*Burschenschaften*) have traditionally had a romantic nationalist, right-wing political orientation.
[9] Jörg Haider, "Die Wahrheit, eine Gasse," *Kärtner Nachrichten*, 14 February 1985.
[10] Ibid.

receiving Reder.[11] The next day, Haider called for a special meeting of the FPÖ party leadership to discuss the situation. He repeated that Frischenschlager had behaved correctly in the first place, and there was no need for him to apologize at every opportunity. Within the FPÖ, Haider presented Frischenschlager, and indeed the entire liberal leadership, as spineless and cowering to international, and especially Israeli, pressure.[12]

This move proved highly successful, as Haider was able to rally the FPÖ's nationalist base around him and against the liberal leadership. Apologetic interpretations of the Nazi past proved to be an effective means of mobilizing the rank-and-file, and Haider used this tactic throughout his career. In addition, Haider's strong statements about the Nazi past won him the attention of the Austrian media and turned him nearly overnight into a national figure. In short, Haider used the Reder–Frischenschlager affair to rise within his own party and to gain national attention for the first time.[13]

The Haiderization of the FPÖ

In September 1986, Haider completed his purge of the liberals and was elected leader of the FPÖ at the party convention in Innsbruck. Haider received 59.5 percent of the votes, while Steger mustered only 40.5 percent. The newly elected head of the FPÖ played to the euphoria of the party's nationalist base. In his acceptance speech, Haider promised to defend the war generation and Austrian history from its international critics. He attacked artists like Thomas Bernhard, Austria's most famous contemporary writer, for criticizing their homeland during the Waldheim affair. During the convention, several FPÖ delegates wore Nazi regalia and shouted that Steger deserved to be "gassed." The normally FPÖ-friendly *Krone* columnist Viktor Reimann wrote of "a drunken atmosphere" marked by "heckling and verbal attacks that reminded one of the Nazi period."[14] The Liberal International (an umbrella group of liberal parties, of which the FPÖ was then a member) was concerned about the

---

[11] Frischenschlager denies that he ever offered such an apology. Once the article appeared, however, he felt that he had no way of backing out without "receiving applause from the wrong crowd" (Haider and the nationalist wing of the party). Interview with Friedhelm Frischenschlager, Vienna, 29 November 2000.

[12] Interview with Heide Schmidt, Vienna, 29 November, 2000.

[13] Interview with Frischenschlager. See also Anton Pelinka, *Die Kleine Koalition* (Vienna: Böhlau, 1993), 46–50.

[14] *Kurier*, 15 September 1986.

conduct of the Innsbruck convention. The vice-president of the Liberal International, Urs Schöttli, stated that "the tones that appeared at Innsbruck were shocking" and decided to send observers to monitor the FPÖ during the upcoming national parliamentary elections.[15] The group stated that the atmosphere at Innsbruck was grounds for ejecting the FPÖ from the Liberal International.[16]

The Austrian press and political parties, however, took little notice of Innsbruck. Although *Die Presse* covered the party convention, it did not mention the Nazi slogans and regalia that accompanied it. Nor did the *Kronen Zeitung*. The *Salzburger Nachrichten* caught this story, but only mentioned it nearly a week after the convention.[17] Within Austria's mainstream press, only the left-liberal weekly *Profil* covered the Innsbruck party convention in any depth and argued that it represented the nationalist takeover of the FPÖ. An editorial in *Die Presse* captured the consensus position: "a turn rightward? Certainly, that cannot be denied. But was it not in reality a return to where this party always stood in the political landscape?"[18]

Yet Haider's victory in Innsbruck marked a dramatic reorientation of the FPÖ. Friedrich Peter, the former chairman and architect of the liberalization of the FPÖ, left the party less than a week after Haider's victory, beginning what would become a veritable exodus of liberals. Norbert Steger announced a week after Innsbruck that "if Haider does not distance himself from the Nazis, then I will leave the party."[19] Although Steger officially left the party several years later, he was no longer active in it after Haider's purge. Some liberals, such as Heide Schmidt and Friedhelm Frischenschlager, remained in the party for several years but, with the party lurching toward right-wing extremism, left the FPÖ in January 1993 and founded their own political party, the Liberal Forum (LiF). The creation of the LiF marked the final collapse of liberalism within the FPÖ.

As liberals left the party in droves, right-wing extremists and members of the neo-Nazi scene flocked to it.[20] Haider played a central role in this transformation, personally anointing the right-wing extremist

---

[15] *Profil*, 22 September 1986; *Profil*, 6 October 1986.
[16] *Salzburger Nachrichten*, 22 September 1986. The FPÖ was ejected from the Liberal International in 1993.
[17] *Salzburger Nachrichten*, 20 September 1986.
[18] *Presse*, 15 September 1986.
[19] *Profil*, 22 September 1986.
[20] Brigitte Bailer-Galanda and Wolfgang Neugebauer, *Haider und die Freiheitlichen in Österreich* (Berlin: Elefanten Press, 1997), 39.

Andreas Mölzer, the editor-in-chief of the *Kärtner Nachrichten*, the FPÖ's official newspaper. Mölzer had previously edited right-wing extremist journals that printed articles questioning the existence of gas chambers at Auschwitz.[21] On the local and state levels, the FPÖ allowed individuals with links to right-wing extremist organizations, such as the German National Democratic Party (Nationaldemokratische Partei Deutschland, NPD), to appear on party lists and hold political office.[22]

Many foreign scholars have argued that the FPÖ is less xenophobic than other right-wing populist parties, such as the German REPs, the French National Front, or the Belgian Vlamms Blok.[23] This might have described the situation in the late 1980s, when immigration had yet to become a salient issue. Indeed, immigration was not even on the list in a survey of Austria's political problems in 1989 and ranked only tenth in 1990. By 1992, however, it had jumped to second after the influx of immigrants and asylum seekers following the end of the Cold War.[24] Beginning in the early 1990s, the FPÖ made halting immigration a centerpiece of its political program. In the 1991 Vienna city elections, in which the FPÖ won 22.5 percent of the vote, the party ran on an anti-immigrant platform.

When one looks at the discourse of leading FPÖ politicians, it becomes even more difficult to deny that xenophobia is a central element of the party. Haider has referred to black Africans as "bush negroes" and "drug dealers." After a visit to Namibia, he noted that "it is such a problem with blacks. Even when they are in the majority, they can't achieve anything."[25] During a parliamentary speech, the longtime FPÖ politician Helen

[21] Brigitte Bailer-Galanda and Wolfgang Neugebauer, "Vom Liberalismus zum Rechtsextremismus," in Stiftung Dokumentation des österreichischen Widersandes ed., *Handbuch des Österreichischen Rechtsextremismus* (Vienna: Wiener Verlag, 1993), 384.

[22] Ibid., 385.

[23] Making this argument is Kitschelt, who writes in *Radical Right* that "it is misleading to equate the FPÖ with the National Front or other pure New Rightist parties." He supports this argument by drawing on a survey, conducted in 1990, of FPÖ voters' motivations. Sixty-two percent cited disaffection with the two big parties, 44 percent wanted to teach the big parties a lesson, 42 percent liked Haider's personality, and only 39 percent mentioned immigration as a reason for voting for the FPÖ. Data from Fritz Plasser and Peter A. Ulram, "Überdehnung, Erosion und rechtspopulistische Reaktion-Wandlungsfaktoren des österreichischen Parteinsystems in Vergleich," *Österreichische Zeitschrift für Politikwissenschaft* 21, no. 2 (1992): 147–164.

[24] Peter A. Ulram and Wolfgang C. Mueller, "Die Ausgangslage fuer die Nationalratswahl 1994: Indikatoren und Trends," in *Wählerverhalten und Parteienwettbewerb. Analysen zur Nationalsratswahl 1994*, Wolfgang C. Mueller, Fritz Plasser, and Peter A. Ulram eds. (Vienna: Signum, 1995).

[25] Quoted in Hubertus Czernin, ed., *Wofür Ich Mich Meinetwegen Entschuldige: Haider, beim Wort genommen* (Vienna: Czernin Verlag, 2000), 86.

Patrik-Pable reached the following conclusion about black Africans: "they don't only look different... they are different, and indeed they are particularly aggressive. That is apparently in their nature. The majority of them are here illegally, the majority of them are drug-dealers, and they are tremendously aggressive."[26] Patrik-Pable was chosen to head the FPÖ's party list in the 2001 Vienna state elections. Thomas Prinzhorn, the head of the FPÖ's national party list in 1999, once stated that foreigners were receiving free hormones from the Austrian social services to increase their fertility and thereby posed an even greater threat to Austrians.[27]

As the FPÖ lurched rightward in the 1990s, the traditional social basis of the party shifted as well. Rather than attracting the winning coalition of blue-collar chauvinists and white-collar neoliberals that Kitschelt considered necessary for right-wing populist parties to thrive, the FPÖ became predominantly a party of the working class. By 1999, the FPÖ captured 47 percent of the working-class vote, far outpacing the Social Democrats, which claimed only 35 percent.[28] As one scholar concluded: "the FPÖ has become the party of choice for the least educated segments of Austrian society, while it has virtually disappeared among the country's intelligentsia and attained a minoritarian position among its professional sectors. Sociologically speaking, the party under Haider has assumed the profile of a traditional party of the Old Left."[29]

Although immigration later became an important issue, the FPÖ's central strategy in the mid-1980s was to attack Austria's consociational democracy, meaning the political domination of the two major parties. During the 1986 election campaign, Haider stressed this theme in his stump speeches. But he also defended the war generation at every opportunity, and this message apparently resonated with many Austrians in the wake of the Waldheim affair. The 1986 election, the first election after the Waldheim debate, was imbued with nationalist discourse and symbolism. Former Chancellor Kreisky critized politicians for using "too much red and white" (the colors of the Austrian flag) in the campaign. This was ideal terrain for a right-wing populist party with openly apologist views on the Nazi past. When the votes were counted on November 23, 1986,

[26] *Tiroler Tageszeitung*, 20 May 1999.

[27] Hans-Henning Scharsach and Kurt Kuch, *Haider: Schatten über Europa* (Cologne: Kiepenheuer and Witsch, 2000), 211.

[28] Fritz Plasser, Peter A. Ulram, and Gilg Seeber, "(Dis)Kontinuitäten und Spannungslinien im Wählerverhalten," in *Wählverhalten und Parteienwettbewerb*.

[29] Andrei Markovits, "Austrian Exceptionalism: Haider, the European Union, the Austrian Past and Present," in *Haider Phenomenon*, 116.

the FPÖ had captured nearly 10 percent of the vote, doubling its vote total from 1983 and establishing Haider as the election's real winner.

Reacting to the FPÖ

After Haider had renationalized the FPÖ and engineered its electoral coup of 1986, Austrian political parties, the media, and civil society were confronted with how to react to the reemergence of the far right. In Chapter 5, I laid out the combat hypothesis and illustrated it with evidence from Germany. In this section, I outline the logic of the "taming hypothesis," which states: *when established political parties, the media, and civil society cooperate with right-wing populist parties, offer them tacit or overt support, or otherwise fail to combat them, the far right will be able to establish itself as a permanent actor in the political landscape.* It was this strategy that political and social actors largely pursued in Austria.

The reaction of other political parties is important because it affects the ability of right-wing populist ones to garner votes, recruit party members, and gain the multiple advantages that political incumbency provides. When political parties do not rule out cooperation with the far right, voters do not consider a vote for the far right as wasted or merely a protest vote.[30] Moreover, when established political parties publicly consider electoral coalitions with the right-wing populist challengers, they signal to voters that such parties are indeed legitimate political actors and do not represent a threat to democracy. In terms of party recruitment, the possibility of effecting legislation and winning powerful positions in government increases the ability of right-wing populist parties to attract qualified and ambitious individuals from society. Finally, when far-right parties actually hold power, which normally occurs with the consent of established political parties, they become political incumbents and can consolidate their power by delivering resources to local constituencies and improving their name recognition.

The media's role in aiding right-wing populist parties is straightforward. Ceteris paribus, positive coverage and endorsements in the form of editorials will increase support for right-wing populist challengers. The magnitude of this effect depends on the circulation rate of the newspaper and the degree to which it endorses the far right. Tabloid papers are likely to have a greater effect than quality papers, both because they have a

---

[30] On wasted votes and strategic voting, see Gary Cox, *Making Votes Count* (New York: Cambridge University Press, 1997).

186 The Politics of the Nazi Past in Germany and Austria

higher circulation rate and because their readership corresponds with the potential constituency of the far right.

The reaction of civil society to right-wing populist challengers is also consequential for the latter's development. When ordinary individuals do not protest far-right rallies, when employers do not dissuade employees from engaging in far-right political activity, and when the daily lives of right-wing populist party members are not adversely affected by their political involvement, right-wing populist parties face few hurdles in recruiting new members. Having outlined the logic of the taming hypothesis, let me illustrate it with evidence from Austria.

When Haider took control of the FPÖ from Norbert Steger on September 16 at the Innsbruck party convention, Chancellor Franz Vranitzky (SPÖ) declared the end of the small coalition. New elections were scheduled for November 23, and Vranitzky made it clear that his party would not enter a national alliance with a renationalized FPÖ. On the one hand, then, the SPÖ decided on a strategy of marginalization (*Ausgrenzung*) from the moment Haider took control of the FPÖ. The national party held to this strategy throughout the late 1980s and 1990s and continues to practice it today.

Yet, the SPÖ's *Ausgrenzung* of a right-wing populist party was never as complete and active as that of its German counterpart. Recall that the SPD protested against the REPs, refused to participate with them at any political level, and justified their opposition with reference to German history. Although Vranitzky was undoubtedly an antifascist, he hardly made this the basis of his rejection of Haider's FPÖ. In fact, neither Vranitzky nor other SPÖ politicians ever explained their opposition to Haider in much depth to the Austrian public.[31] The SPÖ could not draw on norms versus right-wing populism and Nazi apologia, since the Waldheim affair had largely legitimated nationalist appeals and revisionist interpretations of the Nazi past.

Moreover, and in marked contrast to Germany, *Ausgrenzung* did not occur at all political levels. Social Democrats in communal and state parliaments continued to cooperate with their FPÖ counterparts to pass legislation. Kreisky had made the FPÖ a party of government, and local and communal politicians did not change their views about their FPÖ counterparts, even though the Haiderization of the party had changed it fundamentally. They also never received orders to do so from the SPÖ's national leadership.

[31] Interview with Armin Thurnher, editor-in-chief of *Falter*, Vienna, 5 February 2001.

The combination of *Ausgrenzung* at the national level but cooperation at the local and state levels contributed directly to the FPÖ's success. As Haider railed against a political system that was excluding him from office, angry voters cast their ballots for the FPÖ's communal and state parliamentary lists. A vote for the FPÖ was hardly a wasted one, as a vote for the REPs was in Germany, since FPÖ politicians played an active role in devising and passing legislation. After its breakthrough in 1986, the FPÖ gained ground in one state election after another. In 1987, it topped 7 percent in Burgenland and Vienna. In 1989, it won 15.4 percent in Salzburg, 15.6 percent in Tirol, 16.1 percent in Vorarlberg, and 35 percent in Haider's stronghold in Carinthia.

As the FPÖ did well in state elections and crossed the 20 percent mark in national ones, leading politicians within the SPÖ publicly questioned the *Ausgrenzung* strategy. In 1996, the head of the Styrian SPÖ, Peter Schachner, called for a "radical change of course" in SPÖ–FPÖ relations. Similarly, the governor of the Burgenland, Karl Stix (SPÖ), argued that his party should include the FPÖ in political dialogue. After a strong showing by the FPÖ cost the SPÖ their long-held absolute majority in the Viennese state assembly, the mayor of Vienna, Michael Häupl, invited the FPÖ to official discussions about Vienna's future.[32] Such open rejections of the *Ausgrenzung* policy further signaled to voters that the SPÖ was willing to work with the FPÖ, and that it was only a matter of time before the marginalization strategy was abandoned entirely. Although the SPÖ renewed its *Ausgrenzung* strategy after the 1999 elections, leading SPÖ politicians, such as Kurt Schlöggl, have continued to recommend cooperation with the FPÖ.

If the SPÖ's *Ausgrenzung* was far from complete, the ÖVP did not pursue such a strategy at all. From the 1986 elections to the formation of the ÖVP–FPÖ government in February 2000, the ÖVP never ruled out a national coalition with the FPÖ. Indeed, ÖVP leaders often played the "Haider card," the threat to leave the Grand Coalition and side with the FPÖ, to extract concessions from the SPÖ. It was also ÖVP politicians who helped Haider become the governor of the state of Carinthia in 1989, after the FPÖ gained 35 percent to the ÖVP's 21 percent (the SPÖ led with 46 percent). By handing Haider governmental responsibility and endowing him with the substantial media attention that provincial governors receive, the ÖVP both legitimated the FPÖ and helped Haider consolidate his power in Carinthia. In the state elections of 1999, the FPÖ

---

[32] Bailer-Galanda and Neugebauer, *Haider*, 136–137.

captured over 42 percent of the vote, making it the largest party in the state and giving Haider a strong popular mandate.

Although there were isolated politicians within the ÖVP who objected to cooperation with the FPÖ, the majority never saw any reason for refusing. While Christian Democrats in Germany labeled the far right a threat to German democracy and attacked its apologist reading of German history, the ÖVP never made similar claims about the FPÖ. Indeed, as many Austrian journalists have noted, many politicians from the ÖVP agree in principle with Haider's reading of the Nazi past.[33] Semistructured interviews with Christian Democratic politicians, presented in Chapter 4, largely support this claim.

In sum, the flawed marginalization of the SPÖ and the perpetual openness of the ÖVP to a coalition with Haider created an ideal climate for the FPÖ to consolidate and expand. But it was the Austrian media that gave Haider the explicit support, endorsements, and protective cover that helped turn the FPÖ into a mass political party. After the 1986 national elections, there were few persons in Austria who saw Haider's victory as problematic for Austrian democracy. In fact, even liberal columnists argued that his victory was beneficial, since it would provide a check on the two larger parties.[34] When the first scholarly work on Haider appeared, the author was criticized for labeling him a politician of the far right.[35] While nearly a dozen monographs on the REPs appeared within a year of the 1989 West Berlin election, it was not until the FPÖ was garnering 20 percent nationally that studies about Haider and the FPÖ began to appear in Austria.

Most importantly, the FPÖ was supported by the *Krone*. Recall that it is read daily by over 2.4 million of Austria's 8.2 million people, making it proportionally the most widely read national paper in the world.[36] During the Waldheim affair, the *Krone* had acted as "a sort of self-appointed pro-Waldheim journalistic hit squad" and disseminated the new victim discourse.[37] After Haider took control of the FPÖ at Innsbruck, the *Krone*

---

[33] Interview with Hans Rauscher, Vienna, 5 February 2001. See also Hans Rauscher, "Eine geschlossene Verdrängungskette," in *Haider: Österreich und die rechte Versuchung*, Hans Scharsach ed. (Hamburg: Rowohlt, 2000), 24.

[34] *Profil*, 24 November 1986.

[35] Interview with Brigitte Bailer-Galanda, Vienna, 30 November 2000.

[36] The circulation figure is from 1996. Reinhold Gartner, "Right-Wing Press in Austria," in *Austro-Corporatism*, ed. Günter Bischof and Anton Pelinka (New Brunswick: Transaction Books, 1996), 305.

[37] Richard Mitten, *The Politics of Antisemitic Prejudice: The Waldheim Phenomenon in Austria* (Boulder: Westview Press, 1992), 199.

turned its attention to him. During the national parliamentary election campaigns in the fall of 1986, the *Krone* gave Haider, the head of a party that had polled less than 3 percent in public opinion polls that summer, twice the coverage of any other Austrian paper.[38] From 1986 to February 2000, the *Krone* stuck to a pro-Haider line. The tabloid's most widely read columnist, Richard Nimmerichter, whose column appeared an amazing six days a week for over two decades, once referred to Haider as "an unfaltering representative of the truth and indispensable ally of the average man."[39]

Apart from giving Haider favorable coverage and lauding him in editorials, the *Krone* proved to be a critical ally when the FPÖ suffered political setbacks. For instance, in 1991 Haider appeared to have cast himself in the political wilderness after defending the positive achievements of Nazism. During a debate in the Carinthian parliament on June 13, 1991, Haider castigated the national government's employment policies and lauded those of the Third Reich. This statement provoked an outcry from the SPÖ's parliamentary fraction, which convinced an ÖVP that was already looking to get rid of Haider to vote for a motion of no confidence in the governor. Haider was dismissed several weeks later, and many considered his political career over.

But the *Krone* came to Haider's defense. Its editorial staff defended Haider's statement, argued that the Nazis had indeed created jobs, and printed a barrage of editorial and readers' letters portraying Haider as the victim of the machinations of the two major parties.[40] Star columnist Richard Nimmerichter wrote five columns in succession about the Haider affair, which he described as a "man hunt." Reminding Austrians of the Waldheim affair, Nimmerichter wrote:

> It is completely unclear...why Jörg Haider is being demonized as a Nazi in a smear-campaign (*Sudelkampagne*), of the sort that only the democratically elected Austrian president Waldheim has ever had to withstand, merely because he stated in an unimportant interjection that there was an orderly employment policy in the Third Reich.[41]

In a previous editorial, Nimmerichter had noted that Haider's statement had a "certain justification in the facts," since Hitler had virtually

[38] Fritz Plasser, "Die populistische Arena: Massenmedien als Verstärker," in *Populismus in Österreich*, Anton Pelinka ed. (Vienna: Junius, 1987), 100.
[39] *Kronen Zeitung*, 9 February 1992.
[40] *Kronen Zeitung*, 22 June 1991.
[41] *Kronen Zeitung*, 23 June 1991.

eliminated unemployment in Austria within six months after the *Anschluss*. While Haider would have been wise to qualify his statement, Nimmerichter continued that Haider's interjection became "a state affair" when the SPÖ, the ÖVP, and the Greens "saw their chance to finally get rid of their annoying competitor Haider."[42]

During the summer of 1991, the *Krone* published no fewer than fifty readers' letters about the "Haider affair," as the paper termed it, forty-four of which either lauded Nimmerichter's commentary about Haider or defended the FPÖ politician. Nimmerichter himself wrote that "in 27 years, I have never received so many supportive letters as in the 'Haider' case. Only during the Waldheim affair . . . did I receive so much incoming mail."[43] Some representative selections of these letters are as follows:

The hypocrisy of the campaign by the two big parties against Jörg Haider cannot be topped. Anyone who studies history knows that Haider's statements about the Third Reich's employment policies are accurate for the period from January 1933 to August 1939.   – Franz Wiedl[44]

Behind the campaign against Haider are the same powers that invented the "brown past" of presidential candidate Waldheim.   – Karl Schmölzer[45]

"Staberl" is a Nazi because he writes the truth! Haider is a Nazi because he speaks the truth! I am a Nazi because I read "Staberl" and vote for Haider!
                                                             – Dr. Karl Schnell[46]

What is our democracy really worth, when an indiscrete interjection by a Haider leads to a political hanging-machine?   – Hans Pfeiffenberger[47]

Deeply disgusted by the rest of the media hunt against Haider, I would like to take my hat off to you for your fair and objective news coverage in this "matter." Nearly all of my friends feel this way as well. Many of them will discontinue their other newspaper subscriptions and order the *Krone* because of its reputable stance.   – Dr. Edward Huemer[48]

Let me sign up with the FPÖ! Dr. Haider is the up-and-comer.
                                                       – Professor Josef Griessler[49]

In addition to publishing these readers' letters, the *Krone* covered pro-Haider rallies in Carinthia and included a special report on Haider's

[42] *Kronen Zeitung*, 20 June 1991.
[43] *Kronen Zeitung*, 23 July 1991.
[44] *Kronen Zeitung*, 25 June 1991.
[45] *Kronen Zeitung*, 25 June 1991
[46] *Kronen Zeitung*, 2 July 1991.
[47] *Kronen Zeitung*, 9 July 1991.
[48] *Kronen Zeitung*, 9 July 1991.
[49] *Kronen Zeitung*, 2 July 1991.

politics, printed FPÖ advertisements supporting the former governor, and featured several combative photos of Haider on the paper's all-important front cover. At a time when Haider was considered politically dead by many observers, the *Krone* did all it could to resuscitate him. Although it is difficult to measure the precise effect of the *Krone's* campaign, the results of the September 1991 state elections in Vienna suggests that it succeeded. The FPÖ won 22.5 percent of the vote, more than doubling its total from 1987 and robbing the SPÖ of the absolute majority it had enjoyed since 1954. Throughout the rest of the decade, the *Krone* would continue to support Haider and passionately defend him against charges of right-wing extremism and Nazi apologism.

During February 2000, the largest political demonstrations in postwar Austria took place in Vienna in protest against the new ÖVP–FPÖ government. Judging from these events, one might have imagined that the FPÖ had had to overcome such protest in its rise to power. Yet this was decidedly not the case. Austrian civil society did not react to the FPÖ with the same vigor as German civil society did to the German REPs. Recall that when the REPs gained 7.5 percent in the Berlin state elections, tens of thousands of protestors took to the streets in spontaneous anti-REP demonstrations after the results were announced. When the FPÖ captured nearly 10 percent in national elections, there were no protests in Austria. As members of the other Austria admit, their failure to organize against Haider at an early stage was a critical mistake.[50] Haider faced little protest from Austrian civil society until he won over 20 percent of the vote in national elections, and even then, the protests were sporadic and largely confined to Vienna. Trade unions and church groups also did little to protest the FPÖ.

My participant observations of FPÖ rallies confirm this pattern of nonprotest. During the fall of 2000, I attended nearly a dozen FPÖ rallies leading up to the Styrian state elections. On October 11, for example, Haider came to Graz, the capital of the state of Carinthia and Austria's second largest city, to speak in the old town square. An hour before his scheduled appearance, a crowd of local politicians and several hundred supporters had gathered under a tent. There were several policemen at the event, but not significantly more than would be patrolling the town hall on any Saturday morning. When Haider finally arrived – he normally makes it a point to be at least a half an hour late – he was mobbed by men

[50] Interview with Marie Steinhauser, co-founder of the Republican Club, Vienna, 20 December 2001.

and women of all ages who wanted his autograph. After nearly twenty minutes of autograph signing and handshaking, Haider took the podium and proceeded to lash out against the SPÖ for approximately thirty minutes.

Since this scene took place only several months after the Viennese demonstrations of 2000, I was surprised by the lack of protest in Austria's second largest city. The anti-Haider protestors in Graz numbered fewer than twenty. When they tried to mount anti-Haider chants (such as *"Haider ist ein Rassist!"*), they were drowned out by screams from Haider's supporters. Indeed, Haider appeared to enjoy having a small gang of straggly-looking protestors at his rally, as he made fun of their ragged appearance throughout his speech. During other appearances in smaller towns in Styria, Haider found no protestors to entertain himself with during his rallies. Such scenes, of course, contrast with those that occurred at REP rallies in Germany (see Chapter 5). They also demonstrate the extent to which the FPÖ has become an accepted political actor by ordinary Austrians.

The FPÖ in Government: The Party Self-Destructs

Between 1986 and 1999, Haider turned a liberal party garnering around 5 percent of the vote into a right-wing populist party capturing over five times that number. But the international uproar over the formation of the ÖVP–FPÖ government, coupled with domestic protests, led Haider to resign as head of the FPÖ. Although still governor of Carinthia, Haider claimed that he would become a "simple party member" and allow his appointed team of politicians to work without his interference. No one expected his retreat from national politics to be permanent, and the simple party member continued to determine the FPÖ's policies behind the scenes.

Since entering government, there have been dramatic changes within the FPÖ in terms of both party ideology and leadership structure. In response to intense international pressure, the FPÖ in 2000 backed legislation providing restitution for slave laborers under the Nazis. The FPÖ politicians who held cabinet positions in the first ÖVP–FPÖ government largely avoided making xenophobic statements or apologist references to the Nazi past. When Ewald Stadler (FPÖ), a politician in Lower Austria with close connections to right-wing fringe groups, argued in June 2002 that the Allied occupation of Austria from 1945 to 1955 was as brutal as that of the years 1938 to 1945, several prominent FPÖ politicians distanced themselves from him.[51]

In 2002, the FPÖ had its worst electoral performance since 1986, capturing only 10 percent of the vote.[52] Many observers concluded that the FPÖ's participation in the national government had weakened it and that the ÖVP's taming strategy had been a success. Yet, while it is no doubt true that the FPÖ lost some of its support as a governing party, public opinion polls several months before the election showed the party winning about 20 percent. Finance Minister Karl-Heinz Grasser (FPÖ) was widely considered to be Austria's most popular politician, and Vice-Chancellor Susanne Riess-Passer (FPÖ) was also running high in the numerous "likability" polls published by Austrian weeklies. Thus, while the FPÖ would certainly have suffered some losses in a national parliamentary election, it is likely that it would have remained a significant force and probably would have captured at least 15–20 percent of the vote.

It was in fact Jörg Haider's mercurial behavior that, more than any other factor, led to the FPÖ's electoral collapse. Haider had apparently tired of being merely the governor of Carinthia and wanted to reenter national politics. In 2002, he made several surprise trips to Iraq to visit Saddam Hussein, which did not play well with the Austrian electorate. After terrible floods in August 2002, Haider, in an uncharacteristic misreading of public sentiment, urged the government to go through with planned tax cuts rather than delay them for one year and use the money for disaster relief. He then used this issue to bring down the very government that he had created and force new elections.

The fact that FPÖ politicians in the national government enjoyed wider popularity than he did was probably also a factor in Haider's decision to sabotage the governing coalition. In September 2002, with Stadler's help, Haider engineered a revolt from the FPÖ's base against the national leadership, which brought down the government. Riess-Passer, Peter Westenthaler, and Grasser resigned and left the party. The ÖVP quickly scooped up the popular finance minister for the election campaign. Haider, claiming that he feared assassination, refused to lead the FPÖ's party list, and

---

[51] *Der Standard*, 4 July 2002.

[52] For an analysis of the 2002 elections that views the FPÖ's implosion as partly self-inflicted and partly as the result of exogenous factors, see Kurt Richard Luther, "The Self-Destruction of a Right-Wing Populist Party? The Austrian Parliamentary Election of 2002," *West European Politics* 26, no. 2 (April 2003): 136–152.

this task eventually fell to the uncharismatic former veterinarian Herbert Haupt. With the party bitterly divided and the Austrian electorate weary of Haider's ploys, the FPÖ captured only 10 percent of the vote, its worst performance since 1986.

The magnitude of the FPÖ's 2002 electoral defeat only exacerbated interparty infighting. After several years of turmoil, Haider left the FPÖ in April 2005 to found the Alliance for the Future of Austria (BZÖ). The BZÖ remained the junior partner in Schüssel's coalition government, as Haider brought with him several former FPÖ parliamentarians. At the time of this writing, it appears that the BZÖ is positioning itself as a more moderate version of the FPÖ, a feat that might prove difficult given Haider's reputation. It is also unclear whether the BZÖ will be electorally viable or whether it will disappear like the earlier breakaway faction from the FPÖ, the Liberal Forum (LiF).

Did taming work? As scholars have noted, the FPÖ's transition from an opposition party to a party of government was bound to be difficult and result in some loss of electoral strength.[53] But the magnitude of the FPÖ's collapse cannot be explained by this factor alone. It was Haider's exclusion from the government and the FPÖ leadership that ultimately led him to attack a party that was no longer under his sole control.

It was primarily the reaction of the EU fourteen to the formation of the ÖVP–FPÖ coalition that forced Haider into the role of a simple party member, and this was the most profound effect of the international protest against Austria.[54] Through their rhetoric and symbolic sanctions, the EU fourteen resorted to an international version of the combat strategy. The vehemence of the international reaction to the ÖVP–FPÖ coalition prevented Haider from holding a cabinet position, and he formally resigned the chairmanship of the FPÖ in May in favor of Riess-Passer in large part to end the sanctions. Although both domestic and international observers argued at the time that the sanctions were ill-conceived and would produce a nationalist backlash, their longer-term effect was to sever Haider's link with the party he had created. In this sense, the combat strategy employed by the EU fourteen was ultimately effective.

[53] On this point see Kurt Richard Luther, "The FPÖ: From Populist Protest to Incumbency," in *Right-Wing Extremism in the Twenty-first Century*, eds. Peter Merkl and Leonard Weinberg (London: Frank Cass, 2003), 193–218.

[54] For more on the sanctions against Austria, see Marc Howard, "Can Populism Be Suppressed in a Democracy? Austria, Germany, and the European Union," *East European Politics and Society* 14, no. 2 (2000): 18–32.

It remains to be seen whether the FPÖ will recover from its 2002 debacle and whether Haider will continue to play a leading role in the party. Observers of Austrian politics are notably cautious in declaring Haider's demise, for they have been proven wrong several times before. In the Carinthian state elections of 2004, for example, Haider stunned everyone by improving upon his 1999 electoral victory, capturing 43 percent of the vote and remaining governor. Even if Jörg Haider does not mount yet another comeback on the national level, Haiderism survives as a loose political ideology that has permanently changed the face of Austrian politics. The package of fears and resentments that Haider drew on and fostered, and that the *Kronen Zeitung* continues to spread, can potentially be used by politicians from both the FPÖ and other parties.

7

Conclusions and Extensions

The Argument in Brief

A central goal of this book was to explain the divergent strength of the far right over the past two decades in Germany and Austria. My argument largely rejected structural and institutional factors, focusing instead on the political power of historical narratives. Ideas about the legitimacy of the far right shaped the reactions of political parties, the media, and civil society to right-wing populist challengers. These ideas about the lessons of history were forged at critical junctures through elite-led public debates about the Nazi past. These debates, which occurred in the mid-1980s, unfolded very differently in Germany and Austria, and these differences shaped the political culture and partisan politics in their societies.

In Germany, public debates about May 8th, Bitburg, and the singularity of the Holocaust produced the normalization and contrition frames. During the course of these debates, elite opinion converged on the latter. By the early 1990s, even the most conservative political party represented in the Bundestag (the CSU) had made critical examination of the Nazi past and atonement for its crimes a central part of its ideology and identity. The prevailing culture of contrition in Germany was reinforced by a set of discursive norms, a phenomenon I refer to as political correctness, German style. This culture filtered down to the general population. As the Goldhagen debate, the *Wehrmachtsausstellung*, and the development of the November 9th public rituals demonstrated, many ordinary Germans have embraced critical examination of Nazi atrocities.

When right-wing parties and movements appeared in the late 1980s and early 1990s, German political elites actively combated them, both because such movements offered revisionist interpretations of the Nazi past and because their program and discourse bore affinities to National Socialism. German political parties adopted a policy of marginalization, which ruled out any form of cooperation with the REPs and sanctioned politicians who violated it. This denied the REPs any possibility of influencing legislation or holding political office. Voters came to perceive a vote for the REPs as wasted and the party itself as ineffective. The media, particularly the *Bild*, waged a campaign against the far right that further undercut its support. German civil society protested against the REPs and created a host of obstacles for party organization and political recruitment. In the end, social stigma and everyday discrimination associated with being a REP politician or supporter forced all but low-skilled workers and pensioners from the party.

In Austria, the far right found a far more hospitable political environment. The Waldheim debate of 1986 produced a nationalist reaction that brought ideas previously associated with the extreme right into the political mainstream. The defense of Austrian history and apologetic interpretations of the Nazi past became part of the ÖVP's political arsenal, and these views were widely disseminated by the Austrian press. A smaller, and initially less powerful, group of elites offered an alternative frame of the Nazi past during the Waldheim debate – a version of the German contrition frame – and created a new social movement to represent the other Austria. This cleavage over the lessons of the Nazi past became central in Austrian politics, one that divided left and right and became the basis for many future political conflicts. Since elite views polarized rather than converged, no norms on acceptable political discourse developed. The Waldheim debate introduced anti-Semitic code words and revisionist accounts of Nazism into mainstream political discourse. There was no political correctness, Austrian style. As one Green politician laments, politicians can say just about anything about the Nazi past without suffering any adverse consequences.

As Silvio Lehmann predicted during the Waldheim debate, "those who sow Waldheim will harvest Haider." Indeed, the Waldheim debate created an ideal political-cultural terrain for Haider's renationalized FPÖ to engineer an electoral breakthrough and consolidation. The reactions of Austrian political parties, the media, and civil society succeeded in strengthening the far right. The FPÖ's discourse about the Nazi past was not significantly different from that of the ÖVP, which never ruled out a national coalition with Haider. The SPÖ policy of incomplete marginalization proved counterproductive: allowing the FPÖ power at one level of government but not at the other sent a confusing message to voters. The FPÖ became a governing party at the local and state levels, giving it political legitimacy, making it an attractive organization for ambitious new members, and providing the party with the myriad benefits of political incumbency. The unwavering support of Austria's dominant *Kronen Zeitung* from 1986 to February 2000 was akin to free advertising: it legitimated the FPÖ, defended it from critics, and helped it extend its voter base. Austrian civil society did not organize early or actively enough to significantly disrupt the FPÖ's organization. Politicians who openly worked for the FPÖ were not treated as social outcasts, as were REP politicians in Germany. In sum, the FPÖ became such a powerful force in large part because there was no one willing or able to stop it.

What about Eastern Germany?

Austria is not often compared with eastern Germany. Yet there are striking similarities with the ways in which elite actors represented the Nazi past in the postwar era and how those representations created a fertile climate for right-wing political activity. Eastern German politicians, like their counterparts in Austria, largely externalized the Nazi past by placing the blame for Nazism's crimes on the western German capitalists. Eastern German elites congratulated their citizens for their heroic antifascism, which was largely mythical, during the war.

In Chapter 5, I explained how right-wing political and intellectual movements, after a brief moment in the sun, were quickly squashed by German political and social actors. Yet, while the extreme right has failed *politically*, right-wing extremist movements have undoubtedly affected German society, particularly in the east. During the early 1990s and again during the summer of 2000, neo-Nazi gangs burned asylum homes and attacked foreigners. Since 1989, nearly 100 people have been killed by right-wing violence. Despite efforts to ban and infiltrate it, the NPD still has a core following and even dominates some eastern German towns.[1] Neo-Nazis have declared some locales in eastern Germany *national befreite Zonen* (nationally liberated zones), meaning that they control social activities there and have forced youths to conform to their standards. Indeed, in many eastern German towns, neo-Nazism has penetrated the youth culture to such an extent that nonconformists are in the minority.

---

[1] The journalist Toralf Staud has written extensively on this topic in *Die Zeit*. See, for example, "Reise zu den Brandstiftern," *Die Zeit*, 14 September 1998.

Although neo-Nazism is not a new phenomenon in either part of Germany, since the 1990s the problem has been concentrated in eastern Germany. After unification, right-wing extremists from the west rushed to the east and founded local organizations. Although it is beyond the scope of this study to explain why neo-Nazi movements such as the NPD have gained a foothold in some locales in eastern Germany, both political cultural and institutional explanations have some purchase.

The GDR experienced no generation of '68 and no debates about the Nazi past that discredited authoritarian political values and emotional attachment to the nation. When the GDR crumbled, eastern Germans thus had very different ideas about national identity than westerners. Steffen Heitmann's statements, for example, were perfectly acceptable in eastern Germany. Many eastern Germans do not view the NPD and other right-wing extremist groups through the lens of the Nazi past, but consider them orderly and patriotic organizations.

Eastern Germany also lacks the institutions that have combated right-wing extremism in the west. Political parties, unions, church groups, and civic organizations are all relatively weak in the east. Whereas these groups can mobilize thousands of protestors against an NDP rally in the west, counterdemonstrations and protests are smaller and less frequent in the east. Even within the city of Berlin, one can see the differences between west and east. During 1990, there were 132 right-wing extremist events and 81 counteractions in eastern Berlin. In western Berlin, there were only forty-eight right-wing extremist events but sixty-three counteractions. Although it is unclear from the statistics, it is probable that many of the counterdemonstrations in the east were organized by western Berliners.[2] The number of counterdemonstrations in Berlin is also not representative of eastern Germany in general, for antifascist groups are far stronger in Berlin than in any other eastern city.

Although some left-wing youth groups have begun to protest right-wing extremism elsewhere in the east, they have found little sympathy among the general population. Eastern Germans have little, if any, experience with political protest, and many still apparently view it as an illegitimate activity.[3] Local and state politicians in the east have also downplayed the danger of right-wing extremism, and police in many cities and towns

---

[2] Bernd Holthusen and Michael Jänecke, *Rechtsextremismus in Berlin* (Berlin: Schüren Verlag, 1995), 97.

[3] This was the impression I received from numerous interviews with eastern German politicians. I have no public opinion data to confirm this hypothesis.

have not combated neo-Nazi groups as aggressively as the law allows. The local media in eastern German locales also have not made as much of an issue of right-wing violence as their western counterparts for fear of damaging the town's reputation or appearing traitorous.[4]

In this climate, right-wing political movements have been able to thrive. Although the REPs were unable to conquer the east, the right-wing extremist Democratic People's Union (Deutsche Volksunion, DVU) pulled off a coup in the March 1998 Sachsen-Anhalt state elections, winning 12.9 percent of the vote. This result, the best ever for a far-right party in a state election, was surprising since the DVU had no party organization in the state and did not contest the previous elections. Its score was entirely attributable to a mass mailing financed by Gerhard Frey, the millionaire publisher and head of the DVU. Over half of the DVU votes came from former nonvoters who were apparently swayed by the DVU's campaign literature.[5] The fantastic success of this "phantom" party underscored the susceptibility of eastern Germans to right-wing populist and extremist political appeals.

Shocked into action by the Sachsen-Anhalt election, political elites in Mecklenburg-Vorpommen, (Meck-Pomm), an eastern German state with elections scheduled for later in 1998, organized against the DVU. A wide coalition of social actors, including the print media, local politicians, citizens' initiatives, and businesspeople, participated in an "enlightenment" campaign in which they entered into political discussions with potential DVU voters. Rather than appealing to political-moral considerations, these elites argued that Frey's support for social justice was a sham. They exposed DVU candidates as incompetent failures who had no plans for reducing Meck-Pomm's unemployment rate, the highest of any German federal state. Although it is obviously impossible to conclude definitively, this campaign may have had some effect. Despite another mass mailing, the DVU failed to cross the 5 percent hurdle.[6]

It is yet to be seen if the campaign in Meck-Pomm is an isolated event or part of growing sensitivity and activism on the part of elites and the public in the east. The success of both the DVU and the NPD in state elections in Brandenburg and Saxony in 2004 certainly suggests that right-wing

---

[4] Interview with Wolfgang Arnold, head of the Coalition for Democracy and Tolerance, Berlin, 15 July 2001.
[5] Richard Stöss, "Rechtsextremismus und Wahlen 1998," in *Braune Gefahr*, Jens Mecklenburg, ed. (Berlin: Elefanten Press, 1999), 152.
[6] Ibid., 162–163.

extremism is becoming a political force.[7] The transformation of the NPD into a political party capable of winning representation is especially significant since the party is highly organized and has deep roots in eastern society (in constrast to the DVU). The NPD's success had sparked renewed debates about how mainstream parties should combat right-wing extremism. While some argue that the NPD should be banned, others argue that agents and informers working for the *Verfassungshutz* have penetrated the party to such an extent that it can be easily monitored by the state.

Whatever the future of the NPD, it is clear that right-wing extremism has only strengthened the culture of contrition in the west. Millions of Germans have participated in candlelight marches against attacks on foreigners. Politicians from all political parties have marched for tolerance and demanded that Germans show "civil courage" and battle right-wing extremism. The *Bild* has urged its readers to get out and march. German celebrities like former tennis star Boris Becker have demonstrated and produced infomercials on tolerance. Ordinary Germans have formed civic organizations to combat right-wing extremism. In 1992, there were over 200 demonstrations against neo-Nazism in Berlin alone. As of 2001, there were 214 organizations in Berlin dedicated to combating xenophobia and right-wing extremism.[8]

Germany now possesses a quasi-official holiday linking tolerance, vigilance against right-wing extremism, and remembrance of Nazism's crimes. On November 9, 1938, the Nazis incited pogroms throughout the Third Reich in what many scholars consider the first step of the Final Solution. Exactly fifty-one years later, Germans pulled down the Berlin Wall in the first step toward uniting their country. One might have expected that the positive celebration of unification would have eclipsed the commemoration of *Pogromnacht*. Yet, in fact, November 9th has developed into a day of public demonstrations for tolerance and remembrance. In 2000, for example, hundreds of thousands of Germans gathered near the Brandenburg Gate as leading figures from all political parties (except the extreme right) urged civil courage against right-wing extremism and for tolerance. In in-depth interviews, politicians at all levels confirmed that November 9th has become a quasi-official holiday and stated that they are expected to attend demonstrations and commemorations.[9]

---

[7] For more on these state elections, see David Art, "The Wild, Wild East: Why the DVU Does Not Matter and the NPD Does," *German Politics and Society* 22, no. 4 (Winter 2004): 124–133.

[8] Interview with Barbara Simon, civic activist, Berlin, 12 June 2001.

[9] Interview with SPD politician, Berlin, 18 February 2002.

Germans have thus reacted to right-wing extremism by demanding more memory of the Nazi past. In response to a wave of neo-Nazi violence in 1992, the German government founded the organization *Gegen Vergessen für Demokratie* (Against Forgetting, for Democracy). After another wave of right-wing extremism in 2000, the government formed the organization *Bündnis für Demokratie und Toleranz* (Coalition for Democracy and Tolerance). The leader of this organization hopes to change attitudes in eastern Germany by encouraging local reporters to write more about the Nazi past.[10] German judges regularly sentence neo-Nazis to visit former concentration camps, and foreign tourists are often shocked at the sight of groups of skinheads roaming around the memorials at Dachau or Sachsenhausen.[11] As some critics of such practices have noted, invoking the Nazi past to combat right-wing extremism among German youths may not be the most effective method. Many German youths – and right-wing extremism is largely a youth phenomenon – are attracted to Nazi imagery precisely because of its shock value in a society devoted to coming to terms with the past. Some have argued that perhaps the lens of the Nazi past is not the appropriate one for viewing the problem of right-wing extremism.[12] In any event, it remains the central one in Germany, and right-wing violence continues to increase the salience of the Nazi past in German political culture.

The Future of the Past

One central conclusion of this book is that the way in which a society confronts its past, specifically a past marked by massive violations of human rights, affects its long-term political development. Yet, I have also shown that coming to terms with the past is not a one-shot deal: as elites try to mobilize history in political-ideological battles, new interpretations of the past enter the political arena. Since elite ideas about the Nazi past have changed markedly over the course of five decades, one might question the stability of the culture of contrition in Germany and the victim culture in Austria.

Recently, there has been a perceptible shift in German political discourse about the Nazi past. The publication of Günther Grass's novella

---

[10] Interview with Arnold.
[11] Interview with Barbara Distel, director of the Dachau Memorial, Dachau, 26 April 2002.
[12] See Ruud Koopmans, "Rechtsextremismus und Fremdenfeindlichkeit in Deutschland: Probleme von heute – Diagnosen von gestern," *Leviathan* 29 (2001): 469–483.

Im Krebsgang (*Crabwalk*), which centered on the sinking of a ship carrying German refugees, caused the magazine *Der Spiegel* to begin a series about the expulsion from the east (*Die Vertreibung*).[13] In this context, the publication of Jörg Friedrich's study of the fire bombing of German cities elicited further public commentary on the topic of German suffering, both during and after the Second World War.[14] Although some American observers interpreted this as a new development, I have shown that German victimization was the dominant trope in early postwar narratives of the Second World War.[15] Nevertheless, not since the early 1980s had the suffering of Germans been the subject of public debate.

Will Germany's culture of contrition be undermined by narratives of victimization? Will the salience of the Holocaust in German politics and society be eroded by accounts of the fire bombing of Hamburg, the destruction of Dresden, or the suffering of German expellees? Although this is a possibility, there are good reasons to think that historical remembrance is no longer the zero-sum game it appeared to be in the 1980s or that the remembrance of German suffering will be used as a tool for the legitimation of nationalist politics.

For one, the debate about German suffering was sparked by Günther Grass – the same man who called German unification the punishment for Auschwitz and left the SPD in protest after the party voted to restrict the right to political asylum in 1993. Grass, in other words, has been one of the main voices of German contrition, and cannot be accused of introducing German victimization into public discourse to legitimize nationalist political ideas. Following the logic of "Nixon goes to China," it was only an outspoken leftist who could introduce the issue of atrocities against Germans without being accused of trying to downplay the atrocities that Germans committed against others. Grass also appears to have written about German suffering precisely to take control over the theme away

[13] Günther Grass, *Im Krebsgang* (Göttingen: Steidl Verlag, 2002). The Spiegal series began with "Die Flucht der Deutschen: Die Spiegal Serie über die Vertreibung aus dem Osten," Spiegal Special, Nr. 2/2002.

[14] Jörg Friedrich, *Der Brand: Deutschland im Bombenkrieg, 1940–1945* (Munich: Propyläen, 2002). German television stations, such as the ARD, ran special programs on the expulsions and the fire bombing of German cities. The *Bild* printed excerpts from Friedrich's book in November 2002.

[15] Peter Schneider, for instance, writes that "it's almost as if people are discovering that something was very wrong." *New York Times*, 18 January 2003. On early postwar narratives of victimization, see also Eric Langenbacher, "Changing Memory Regimes in Contemporary Germany?" *German Politics and Society*, 21, no. 2 (Summer 2003): 46–68.

from the right, which had repeatedly tried to harness victimization for political ends. As the narrator in *Crabwalk* laments: "Never should we have kept silent about all that suffering simply because our own guilt was overpowering ... for we abandoned the suppressed reality to the right-wingers."[16]

There is also reason to expect that the right will not soon try to exploit the theme of German suffering for political gain. Since their failed attempts in the 1980s and early 1990s, German conservatives have not publicly attacked the contrition narrative. The conservative "Schill Party" that won a stunning 19.4 percent in the Hamburg state elections in September 2001, for example, consciously distanced itself from nationalist discourse.[17] Ronald Schill himself had the proper credentials for a German conservative: membership in the society for Jewish–German cooperation. Although many predicted that Edmund Stoiber would seize on nationalist themes in the 2002 national elections, he unofficially began his campaign by visiting Israel and generally steered clear of far-right discourse. It was the second in command of the FDP, Jürgen Mölleman, who tried to court the far right and dragged his party down as a result.

It was, paradoxically, the German left that mobilized German nationalism to snatch electoral victory from the jaws of defeat. Chancellor Schroeder trailed his rival, Stoiber, by nearly 15 points before seizing upon the "No to Iraq" theme in mid-August 2002. The SPD edged out the CDU by less than 1 percentage point in the September 22 elections. For the first time in postwar German politics, a politician had not only publicly defied the United States but won a campaign by doing so. Schröder invoked what I would term a German "pacifistic nationalism." Germans, Schröder appeared to be saying, knew better than others the perils of war and would take a strong stand for peace. It was a message that resonated with many Germans and even made some proud to be Germans for the first time. In a letter to the *Süddeutsche Zeitung*, one person wrote, "I can say I now feel proud, for the first time in my life, to be German

---

[16] Gräss, *Im Krebsgang*, 90–91.
[17] The Schill party was the creation of Ronald Schill, also known as "judge merciless" for his harsh rulings in the Hamburg court system. He ran on a strictly law-and-order platform, a salient issue given Hamburg's longstanding crime problem and rising crime rate. His tough stand on internal security proved attractive to many voters in the immediate wake of the September 11 attacks. The fact that several of the leading terrorist plotters had lived in Hamburg further discredited the incumbent SPD government. Although some observers predicted that the Schill party would develop into a national party, it has had no success outside of Hamburg. In 2003, Schill was banished from the party and later that year the party failed to cross the 5 percent hurdle in Hamburg.

and privileged to live in a country where the overwhelming majority of the public and its government reject a war in Iraq."

If the culture of contrition survives in Germany, there are signs that apologist narratives about the Nazi past are finding less resonance in Austrian politics. During the course of the 1990s, public opinion surveys suggested that Austrians were becoming more aware of their nation's involvement in Nazi crimes. As noted in Chapter 3, the percentage of Austrians who saw their state as complicit in the crimes of Nazism rose from 29 percent in 1995 to 45 percent in 2001.

It was changes in elite discourse that drove this shift. Whereas Christian Democrats were loath to discuss any form of Austrian complicity in the 1980s, some began in the early 1990s to refer to Austria as both a victim and a perpetrator during the Second World War. Even some FPÖ politicians have recently stressed the complicity of Austrians in Nazi crimes, particularly those from factions of the FPÖ that Haider recently tried to destroy.[18] The persistence of elite debate about the Nazi past after the Waldheim affair also appears to have sensitized the Austrians to the topic. Whereas 53 percent of those surveyed in 1991 believed that "it is time to put the memory of the Holocaust behind us," only 33 percent agreed with that statement in 1995.[19]

Radical Right Parties and Mainstream Politics

Whether or not the FPÖ recovers from its current nadir, its two-decade march to power is important for understanding a general phenomenon: namely, how parties representing the extremes become part of the political mainstream. Conversely, the study of the moribund REP Party helps elucidate the conditions under which such parties, despite auspicious circumstances, fail to establish themselves. In both accounts, the reactions of other political parties, the media, and civil society were central to the story and explain, in large part, the divergent paths of right-wing populism in Austria and Germany.

Although it is a new argument in the literature on the contemporary far right, this type of analysis has been used to explain the rise of Nazism in Weimar Germany. In *Who Voted for Hitler?*, Richard Hamilton makes

---

[18] Susanna Riess-Passer, the former vice-chancellor of the ÖVP-FPÖ coalition, has criticized the victim narrative.
[19] These surveys were conducted by Gallup for the AJC. Österreichisches Gallup-Institute "Antisemitismus in Österreich," June–July–August 1991; American Jewish Committee, "Current Austrian Attitudes Toward Jews and the Holocaust," 1995.

a strong case that the behavior of German political parties across the political spectrum was critical for the success of the Nazi Party.[20] The German Communist Party (KDP) openly welcomed the rise of Nazism, believing that it would hasten the revolution of the proletariat. As one KDP parliamentarian argued, "when the fascists come to power, then the united front of the Proletariat will come into being and sweep everything away.... We are not afraid of the fascists. They will mismanage faster than any government."[21] The SPD, mired in intraparty doctrinal squabbles, also underestimated the Nazi Party and did not muster much opposition to it. Like the KPD, the SPD was rooted in an evolutionary outlook that justified passivity in the face of threats to the democratic order.[22] While the German left was passive, German conservatives saw Hitler as a useful tool for bringing down Weimar democracy. Leaders of the Catholic Center (Zentrum) Party hoped to tame the Nazi Party by governing in a coalition with it. Hamilton concludes that the willingness of the conservative parties of Weimar to collaborate with the Nazis served to legitimize the latter in the eyes of the electorate.

The conservative print media also contributed to Weimar's destruction. The powerful Hugenberg press carried the speeches of Hitler and other prominent Nazis, thus increasing the audience for Nazi propaganda campaigns from thousands to millions. As Hamilton notes, "to millions of Germans who had scarcely ever heard of him before, Hitler now became a familiar figure."[23] Although there was a vibrant left-wing and liberal press in Weimar Germany, Hugenberg controlled over half of Germany's press and dominated the small-town and rural media markets that would become the backbone of the Nazi electorate.[24] In 1931, Hugenburg openly allied himself with Hitler and urged his readers to do the same.

The reaction of German civil society to the Nazi Party was also critical for the latter's growth and success. In his study of a German small town, William Sheridan Allen demonstrates how the Nazis recruited local notables to give the party an aura of respectability in small communities.[25] Contrary to the prediction that associational networks improve the quality and stability of democracy, the Nazis captured the dense organizational

<hr/>

[20] Richard Hamilton, *Who Voted for Hitler?* (Princeton: Princeton University Press, 1982).
[21] Quoted in ibid., 304.
[22] On this point, see Sheri Berman, *The Social Democratic Movement: Ideas and Politics in the Making of Interwar Europe* (Cambridge: Harvard University Press, 1998).
[23] Hamilton, *Who Voted for Hitler?*, 236.
[24] Jack Synder, *From Voting to Violence* (New York: Norton, 2000), 123.
[25] William Sheridan Allen, *The Nazi Seizure of Power* (New York: F. Watts, 1984).

networks that characterized Weimar Germany.[26] As one historian of Nazi Germany notes:

Path-breaking work in recent years on the rise of National Socialism has stressed the importance of local newspapers, municipal notables, and voluntary associations, and points to the buoyancy and vigor of civic traditions. Had bourgeois community life been overly disoriented and fragmented, the body of new evidence indicates, the Nazis would never have been able to marshal the resources or plug into social networks necessary to their political success.[27]

To be sure, the Nazis could not have capitalized on a favorable political-cultural environment had they been incompetent. Hitler's oratorical ability, coupled with the Nazis' organizational skill, was important for the party's success. But it was largely the reactions of German civil society, the media, and, most importantly, other political parties that allowed a party from the fringes to capture political power.

How far does this argument travel beyond Weimar Germany, contemporary Germany, and Austria? Specifically, how might such an analysis help us to understand the variation in the fortunes of right-wing populist parties across Western Europe?

The two other countries in Western Europe in which the far right emerged but failed to gain a political foothold between 1986 and 2002 were the Netherlands and Sweden. Although further research is needed, there is some evidence that political parties, the media, and civil society in these societies reacted to the rise of the far right in a manner similar to that of their contemporary German counterparts.

Beginning in the mid-1980s, the Netherlands possessed all the variables that have been associated with the emergence and success of right-wing populist parties. During the early 1980s, the country suffered from double-digit unemployment and other economic problems that became known as the "Dutch disease." With a foreign-born population of 4 percent in 1992 and 5 percent in 1997, the Netherlands was in a comparable position with Norway and Denmark. The effective electoral threshold in the Dutch PR system is a mere 0.67, the lowest in Western Europe. But despite these favorable background conditions, neither the right-wing populist Center Party (CP), founded in 1980, nor the Center Democrats

[26] See Sheri Berman, "Civil Society and the Collapse of the Weimar Republic," *World Politics* 49, no. 3 (1997): 401–429.

[27] Peter Fritzsche, *Rehearsals for Fascism: Populism and Political Mobilization in Weimar Germany* (New York: Oxford University Press, 1990), 76 (fn. 36).

(CD), founded in 1986, were ever able to gain more than 3 percent in national parliamentary elections between 1986 and 2002.

When these two parties appeared, all other Dutch political parties reacted by boycotting and denouncing them. Members of the CP and CD were prevented by other parties from entering committees with local councils in which they held seats.[28] When the leader of the CP, Hans Janmaat, took his parliamentary seat in 1982 after the CP won 0.8 percent of the vote, antifascist committees were formed all over the Netherlands. These committees disrupted the CP and later the CD whenever these parties held electoral rallies or internal party meetings, even setting fire to a hotel where both parties were meeting in 1986. As a result, members of right-wing parties "tended to keep a very low profile."[29] Although the CP and CD combined polled 3 percent in the 1994 parliamentary election, and although both parties won some seats in major cities, the far right failed to establish itself in Dutch politics between 1986 and 2002.[30]

In 2002, however, the meteoric rise of Pim Fortuyn appeared to change this situation. A former professor of sociology, a political journalist, and a flamboyant homosexual, Fortuyn announced his intention to run for political office in the 2002 national parliamentary elections. After considering other political parties, Fortuyn decided to lead the new party Livable Netherlands (LN) in late 2001. He initially received favorable coverage from the Dutch press. On February 9, 2002, however, Fortuyn was quoted as calling Islam a "backward culture" in an interview in the newspaper *de Volkskrant*. When the LN dismissed him, Fortuyn decided to form his own political party – List Pim Fortuyn (LPF).

Fortuyn dominated and shaped the 2002 election campaign. A different kind of right-wing populist politician, he justified his opposition to immigration with reference to the Dutch value of tolerance. Foreigners, and especially Muslims, were generally less tolerant toward minorities than the Dutch, Fortuyn argued, and thus threatened to undermine the pillar of Dutch political culture. As a homosexual, Fortuyn aired his personal grievances against Islam. But his critique of Islam, and the resonance it found within the Dutch electorate, was also related to

---

[28] Paul Lucardie, "The Netherlands: The Extremist Center Parties," in *The New Politics of the Right*, Hans-Georg Betz and Stefan Immerfall, eds. (New York: St. Martin's Press, 1998), 121.

[29] Ibid., 113.

[30] See Ruud Koopmans, "Die Neue Rechte in den Niederlanden – oder: warum es sie nicht gibt," in *Rechtsextremismus und Neue Rechte in Deutschland*, Wolfgang Gessenharter and Helmut Fröchling, eds. (Opladen: Leske and Budrich, 1998), 241–253.

the aftermath of September 11, 2001, and the fear of further terrorist attacks.

On May 6th, barely one week before the elections, Fortuyn was assassinated in the parking lot of a radio station by an environmental activist. Although Fortuyn had been doing well in public opinion polls, there is little doubt that the LPF benefited from a "sympathy vote" for their murdered leader. On May 15th, the LPF gained 17 percent of the vote and entered into a coalition government with the Christian Democrats (CDA) and the liberals. Yet factional infighting within the LPF began almost immediately, and it ultimately brought down the Dutch government in October 2002. In the 2003 elections, the LPF managed to gain only 5.7 percent of the vote. Lacking elite resources, a strong organization, and an individual who can credibly run an anti-immigrant campaign based on preserving Dutch tolerance, the LFP's future appears bleak. The 2002 election may thus prove to be a momentary aberration in the Netherlands' long rejection of the far right.

Sweden is the third country where the far right achieved brief success but then imploded. The short-lived New Democracy Party won 6.7 percent of the vote in the 1991 elections but disappeared by 1994.[31] Like Germany and the Netherlands, Sweden had both a significant foreign-born population (4.7 percent in 1984 and 6.1 percent in 1994) and periods of high unemployment (8–10 percent from 1993 to 1998). Its effective electoral threshold is rather low at 4 percent. As Jens Rydgren notes, existing explanation for the success and failure of right-wing populist parties cannot account for the Swedish case.[32] There is some evidence that the combat hypothesis obtains in the Swedish case, although further research must be done. As in Germany, Swedish journalists have repeatedly presented right-wing populist parties against the backdrop of the Nazi past. Civic movements in Sweden have organized to fight racism and neo-Nazi violence, as in Germany. Swedish political culture is notably tolerant, and this value might shape elite strategy against the far right. Indeed, there is substantial evidence that Sweden's major political parties agreed not to politicize the immigration issue and attempt to use it for partisan gain.[33]

---

[31] On New Democracy, see Paul Taggart, *The New Populism and the New Politics: New Protest Parties in Sweden in Comparative Perspective* (London: Macmillan, 1996).

[32] Jens Rydgren, "Radical Right Populism in Sweden: Still a Failure, But for How Long?" *Scandinavian Political Studies* 25, no. 1 (2002): 27–56.

[33] In an interview with CNN, Goran Persson, the prime minister of Sweden, noted that "there has traditionally been some type of agreement between all political parties in Sweden, and between media and the political parties, not to give room for the right-wing

Although not unique to contemporary Germany, the combat strategy is far less common than the pattern of reactions I described in Weimar Germany and contemporary Austria. In these two cases, existing political parties cooperated with and tried to tame the far right, important sectors of the media supported it, and civil society did not organize against it. In France as well, political parties share some complicity in the rise of the far right. With the goal of weakening the moderate right, French Socialists sought to ensure the parliamentary representation of the National Front (FN) in the early 1980s. When Jean-Marie Le Pen, the leader of the FN, complained in 1982 that he was not receiving adequate media attention, President François Mitterrand convinced the leaders of France's three public television chains to increase their coverage of the FN.[34] This action obviously helped the far-right party reach a larger audience. In 1986, Mitterrand's government changed the electoral rules for the 1986 presidential and parliamentary elections, replacing the two-ballot majoritarian system with PR. The FN, which had won 9.7 percent of the vote, gained thirty-five seats in the National Assembly. This both gave it a claim to legitimacy and bolstered its national profile. As Kreisky had done in Austria, the French left strengthened the far right in order to weaken the moderate right, their central electoral rival.

The French right, like its Austrian counterpart, cooperated with the far right. During the by-elections in the city of Dreux, in which the FN managed its first electoral coup, the center-right formed a joint list with it in order to defeat the left. As Nonna Mayer notes, "the highly controversial electoral alliance provided the Front National with the political legitimacy and visibility it had craved."[35] Following the 1986 national elections, mainstream rightist parties also struck various tacit and open deals with the FN at the regional level.[36] National-level conservative politicians

extremists to misuse the fact that we in Sweden have at least 10 percent of the population as immigrants. . . . They have contributed to our society, without them we wouldn't have been able to maintain our welfare, we all realise that. Why then create tensions and difficulties letting the right-wing extremists dominate the election campaign? All of the responsible political parties have said no to that, and I think we stick to that policy" (http://edition.cnn.com/2002/WORLD/europe/09/12/oakley.persson.cnna). See also Anders Widfeldt, "Scandinavia: Mixed Success for the Populist Right," *Parliamentary Affairs* 53 (2000): 486–500.

[34] Nonna Mayer, "The French National Front," in *The New Politics of the Right*, Hans-Georg Betz and Stefan Immerfall, eds. (New York: St. Martin's, 1998), 21.

[35] Ibid., 13.

[36] See, for example, Jonathan Marcus, *The National Front and French Politics* (New York: New York University Press, 1995), 133–143.

took different positions on the legitimacy of the FN. While Jacques Chirac, the mayor of Paris, ruled out any deals with Le Pen, other politicians, such as Charles Pasqua and Raymond Barre, were more ambiguous. Pasqua noted in 1988, for example, that the mainstream right shared the same values as the FN, a statement that appeared to legitimate the latter.[37] Conservative voters were also unsure about how best to respond to the FN. Even after Le Pen had referred, in 1988, to the gas chambers as a "minor detail" in the Second World War, nearly one-third of mainstream right sympathizers supported electoral deals with the far right.[38]

Further research must be done on the French, Dutch, Swedish, and other cases to test the hypothesis that the reactions of other political parties and the media influence the success or failure of parties emerging from the extremes. If this hypothesis proves correct, it means that far-right parties need not be considered the inevitable "pathologies" of advanced industrial democracies, the by-products of immigration shocks, unemployment, or political alienation.

Public Debates and Ideational Change

This study suggests future avenues for research on the far right and on extremist political parties in general.[39] Yet its broader goal has been to develop and illustrate a theory of public debates in democracies. My central argument is that public debates transform the political environment in which they occur. I have focused on those periods when societies are locked in a struggle over the ideological foundations of politics, when political elites offer radically different ideas and values, and when the mass media transmit this debate to the general public. To be sure, contestation over basic values is constantly occurring in democratic societies. Much of the time, however, such debates over fundamental questions are muted. Perhaps the debate is limited to experts. Perhaps it is only small and marginal groups that are actively involved in contesting a particular issue. Perhaps policymakers can settle a debate before it has a chance to

---

[37] *Le Monde*, 2 May 1988.

[38] Marcus, *National Front*, 143.

[39] It also suggests an explanation for the variation in the success of postcommunist parties in Eastern Europe. As Anna Grzymala-Busse has shown, postcommunist parties have been integrated in some countries and marginalized in others. In the Czech Republic, for example, other political parties refused to cooperate with the Communist successor party and thereby weakened it further. Anna M. Grzymala-Busse, *Redeeming the Communist Past* (New York: Cambridge University Press, 2002), 238–241.

develop momentum. There are, in other words, any number of plausible reasons why ideational contestation may not reach beyond a small circle of specialists, activists, and policymakers. Yet, there are undeniably periods when public debates become high-volume affairs, when elites simply cannot ignore an issue but must articulate and defend their ideas.

I am skeptical that political scientists can predict either the occurrence of such public debates or their outcomes. They are highly contingent events, shaped by the complex interplay of agency, interests, the media landscape, and preexisting ideas and cultures. But the goal of this inquiry has been to specify the common mechanisms and processes of public debates that produce new ideas, change elite and mass ideas, and create alternative discourses – or paradigms – for thinking about political issues. In so doing, this study has woven connections between normative political theory, the literature on social movements, and empirical studies of political communication and public opinion. In particular, it has brought many concepts in the field of American politics to bear on areas, such as the legacy of the past and the formation of party systems, that normally fall within the purview of comparative politics. If this endeavor has been successful, it is because these two fields have more to say to one another than the current compartmentalization of the discipline suggests.

Finally, this study has offered another way of thinking about how ideas enter political life and how they affect it. It has borrowed from the historical-institutionalist paradigm in conceiving of political change as discontinuous and punctuated by episodes of breakdown and transformation. While scholars working in this school have focused on the creation of institutions and critical junctures, this study suggests a similar understanding of ideational change. Public debates represent critical moments in the process of ideational change, and the ideas they produce survive the circumstances of their creation and shape future political outcomes. To understand fully the ideas that structure politics, we need to explore those public debates that produced them.

Appendix A

Coding Scheme for Die Zeit *Content Analysis*

To measure the intensity of the Nazi past in political discourse, the total column inches of articles about the Nazi past in the politics (the front section) of the weekly *Die Zeit* were counted for each year between 1980 and 1999. Articles that counted toward the total contained at least one of the following words in their titles. Articles that contained one of these words but were not related to the Nazi past were not counted.

Anti-Semitismus

Auschwitz

Befreiung (liberation)

Bewältigung (mastering, often of the past)

Bitburg

Errinerung (memory, commemoration)

Fassbinder

Gedächtnis (memory, commemoration)

Gedenken (remembrance)

Gedenktag (day of remembrance)

Geschichte (history)

Goldhagen

Historikerstreit (Historians' Dispute)

Hitler

Holocaust

Kriegsende (end of the war)

Mahnmal (memorial)

Mai 8

National Socializmus

Niederlage (defeat)

Normalität (normality)

NS (abbreviation for National Socialism)

NS-Prozess (trials of former Nazis)

Revisionisten (revisionists)

Schlusstrich (a line under the past)

Vergangenheit (the past)

Vergessen (forgetting)

Versöhnung (reconciliation)

Vertriebene (the German expellees after World War II)

Waffen-SS

Walser

Wehrmachts

Wehrmachtausstellung

Appendix B

Breakdown of Interviews Conducted

TABLE B.I. *Interview Breakdown*

Germany: 107	Austria: 68
Politicians: 83	Politicians: 49
PDS (former Communists): 5	
GRÜ (Greens): 10	GRÜ (Greens): 14
SPD (Social Democrats): 17	SPÖ (Social Democrats): 16
FDP (Liberals): 14	
CDU/CSU (Christian Democrats): 29	ÖVP (Christian Democrats): 14
Republikaner (far right): 7	FPÖ (far right): 12
Intellectuals/civic activists: 19	Intellectuals/civic activists: 15
Journalists: 5	Journalists: 4

Appendix C

Coding Semistructured Interviews with German Politicians

I conducted seventy-five semistructured interviews with German politicians in which I asked the following five questions (in addition to many others):

1. How do you understand the term "mastering the past" (*Vergangenheitsbewältigung*)?
2. What is the proper designation for May 8, 1945?
3. Was the Holocaust singular or comparable to other atrocities?
4. Did you support or oppose the *Wehrmachtsausstellung*?
5. How do you understand the term "normality" (*Normalität*)?

I then coded each answer on a scale, from −2 to +2 using the following procedure:

Question 1

Respondents received a score of −2 if they offered a highly defensive answer, such as "You Americans should master your past first" or "I can't hear that word anymore." Respondents received a score of −1 if they offered a mildly defensive reaction to the term, such as "Mastering the past is fine as long as other parties do not use it for gain, as they are doing now" or "We must not create guilt among the younger generation." A score of 0 was given to neutral answers, examples of which include "examining the past" or "making sure that things don't happen again." Respondents received a score of +1 if they indicated that mastering the past was very important. Those who found the term "mastering the past" problematic because it implied forgetting, drawing a line under the past, or closing something received a score of +2.

Question 2

Respondents who described May 8th as a defeat received a score of −2. Those who described it as something besides a defeat or a liberation, such as "the end of the war" or "the day of the collapse," received −1 points. The answer "both a defeat and a liberation" was scored 0, while those who described it as a liberation received +1 points. Those who called May 8th a day of liberation before the question was asked received +2 points.

Question 3

Respondents who explicitly compared the Holocaust with other atrocities, such as the atomic bombing of Hiroshima, Stalinism, and slavery, received a score of −2. Those who argued that the Holocaust could happen elsewhere, and thus was not singular, received a score of −1. A score of zero was given for a "don't know" answer or for answers that didn't address the question ("The Holocaust was really terrible; I remember my mother telling me that..."). Respondents received a +1 for stating that the Holocaust was singular, and those who referred to the Holocaust as singular before the question was asked received a +2.

Question 4

Opponents of the exhibit received a score of −1, supporters a +1, and neutral or uninterested observers received a 0.

Question 5

Respondents who argued that there must be an end to the discussion of the Nazi past received a −2. Those who argued that Germans were normal received a −1. A 0 was given to those who did not understand the question or gave irrelevant answers. Respondents who stated that Germany, given the Nazi past, can never be normal received a +1. Those who answered that normality means remembering the victims of the Holocaust received a score of +2.

Given time constraints, anecdotes that the participant insisted on telling, and the sudden interruptions to which interviews with politicians are prone (phone calls, role-call votes, speeches, unplanned meetings, etc.), I was not always able to ask all five questions in each interview. When a question was not asked, the respondents received a score of 0.

Restricting my contrition composite to the five questions presented a problem. How could interviews with politicians who were very contrite, such as those who had spent years working for Holocaust education centers or researching slave labor in Eastern Europe, but did not answer all of the five questions, be scored? Conversely, how could interviews with highly uncontrite politicians be scored fairly if they answered only several of the five questions? To address this problem, I assigned positive and negative points for other statements that occurred during the course of the semistructured interview.

Positive Points

- Demonstration of personal involvement in remembrance of Nazi crimes, such as work in museums or Holocaust documentation centers or historical research
- The statement "We can never draw a line under the Nazi past"
- Statements to the effect that remembrance is a political responsibility
- Demonstration of political involvement for reparations or monuments
- Political sponsorship of historical examinations of the Nazi past
- Visit to Yad Vashem, the Holocaust Memorial Museum in Washington, D.C., or a concentration camp

Negative Points

- References to the misdeeds of others (the United States in Vietnam, the bombing of Dresden, etc.)
- Statements that the Wehrmacht behaved honorably in the Second World War
- Statement that confronting the past is masochistic
- Reference to political correctness preventing one from speaking truthfully
- Qualified defense of some aspect of the Third Reich (economic, political, social)

To calculate the final contrition score, I added the scores from questions 1–5 and any additional points from the rest of the interview. Total contrition scores ranged from −10 to +9.

This coding procedure has several obvious drawbacks, the most important of which is that I code missing data (when respondents gave irrelevant answers or did not have time to answer the questions) as a "medium" score (a 0). I considered this a better solution than imputing values to missing data. But given the limitations, I would urge the reader to consider the quantitative analysis of the interviews as just one aspect of the overall evidentiary base of this book. The interview data are consistent, I believe, with the myriad qualitative data I have marshaled in support of my central arguments.

Appendix D

Coding Semistructured Interviews with Austrian Politicians

I conducted fifty semistructured interviews with Austrian politicians. In these interviews, I asked questions 1–4 from the German interviews and replaced question 5 with the following: "Do you think that Austria was a victim or a perpetrator during the Second World War?"

The answers to question 5 were scored as follows: −2 points for answers that described Austria only as a victim, −1 for answers that stressed Austrian victimization over complicity, 0 for the answer "both," +1 for answers that stressed Austrian complicity over victimization, and +2 for answers that described Austria as a perpetrator.

The same procedure used for German interviews (see Appendix C) was used to assign positive and negative points to Austrian interviews. Composite contrition scores ranged from −9 (the least contrite) to +10 (the most contrite).

Appendix E

Question Set – Germany

1. The term "mastering the past" is often used in political discourse. How do you understand the meaning of this term?
2. Which debates about the Nazi past do you remember? Which did you find important and why? What positions did you take?
3. Do you see a difference in how the various political parties deal with the topic of the Nazi past?
4. On May 8, 1985, President Richard von Weizsäcker described May 8, 1945, as a "day of liberation." Others described it as a "day of defeat." How do you understand the meaning of May 8th?
5. In the middle of the 1980s, there occurred the so-called Historians' Debate. Do you know what this debate was about?
6. Was the Holocaust singular or can it be compared with other events in other countries?
7. The term "normality" is often used in political discourse. How do you understand the meaning of this term?
8. What does "constitutional patriotism" mean?
9. In March 2001 there was a debate about the topic of pride in Germany. Did you follow this debate? Did you take a position?
10. In September 2000 there was a debate about the "leading culture" of Germany. Did you follow this debate? Did you take a position?

Appendix F

Question Set – Austria

1. The term "mastering the past" is often used in political discourse. How do you understand the meaning of this term?
2. Which debates about the Nazi past do you remember? Which did you find important and why? What positions did you take?
3. Do you see a difference in how the various political parties deal with the topic of the Nazi past?
4. There was recently a debate in Austria about the meaning of May 8, 1945. Some described this date as a "day of liberation," while others referred to it as a "day of defeat." How do you understand the meaning of May 8th?
5. Was the Holocaust singular or can it be compared with other events in other countries?
6. Some consider that Austria was the first victim of Nazi aggression. Others argue that Austria was fully complicit in Nazism's crimes. What position do you take in this ongoing debate?
7. The exhibit "Crimes of the German Army" recently reopened in Vienna. How do you feel about this exhibit?
8. Are you proud to be an Austrian?

Bibliography

Primary Sources

Newspapers and Magazines

Berliner Morgenpost (Berlin)
Bild (Hamburg)
Die Furche (Vienna)
Die Presse (Vienna)
Der Spiegal (Hamburg)
Der Standard (Vienna)
Die Welt (Hamburg)
Die Zeit (Hamburg)
Focus (Vienna)
Format (Hamburg)
Frankfurter Allgemeine Zeitung (Frankfurt)
Frankfurter Rundschau (Frankfurt)
Kärtner Nachrichten (Klagenfurt)
Kleine Zeitung (Graz)
Kurier (Vienna)
Neue Kronen Zeitung (Vienna)
Oberösterreichischen Nachrichten (Linz)
Österreichische Monatshefte (Vienna)
Profil (Vienna)
Salzburger Nachrichten (Salzburg)
Stuttgarter Nachrichten (Stuttgart)
Süddeutsche Zeitung (Munich)
Südost Tagespost (Graz)
Tagespiegal (Berlin)
Tiroler Tageszeitung (Innsbruck)
Wiener Zeitung (Vienna)

Public Opinion Institutes

American Jewish Committee
IFD (Allensbach, Germany)
Eurobarometer (Brussels)
Gallup (Vienna)
IMAS (Vienna)

Index

combat strategy, 8, 11, 160–161
coming to terms with the past, 3–4,
  14, 15–20; cultural strategy, 19; as
  ideational contestation, 20;
  institutional strategy, 19; opposition
  to in Austria, 102, 113–115, 120,
  123–130; opposition to in Germany,
  55, 59–60, 64–65, 75–77
consociational democracy, 107
constitutional patriotism, 10, 76,
  92–94
contrition: in Austria, 130–132;
  culture of, 49, 51, 85–96, 97, 120,
  123; frame, 10, 20, 51, 65, 72, 77,
  79–81; index, 79, 98, 136; scores,
  79, 98, 136, 143
Cruz, Consuelo, 18

Dachau, 78
Day of Commemoration for Victims
  of National Socialism, 78
dealing with the past, *see* coming to
  terms with the past
Dechant, Josef, 128
Declaration of Independence,
  Austrian, 105
deliberative democracy, 14, 27
Denazification: in Austria, 109–110; in
  Germany, 53
Deutsche Demokratische Republik
  (DDR), *see* German Democratic
  Republic (GDR)
Deutsche Volksunion (DVU),
  200–201
Dichand, Hans, 119
Diepgen, Eberhard, 73, 87
discursive norms, 38
Dregger, Alfred, 60, 72

Eastern Germany, 43, 198–201
East Germany, *see* German
  Democratic Republic
easy issues, 3, 13, 41
Eichmann, Adolf, 43, 57
Eldredge, Nils, 29
elite(s), 2; consensus, 22, 35–37,
  79–82; debate, 24–27; definition of,

25; discourse, 26, 30, 35; and
  ideational change, 23–24; and mass
  attitudes, 2, 26, 29, 38; norms, 11,
  161, 168; opinion, 1, 35–38;
  polarization, 36–37, 136–138
Erhard, Ludwig, 54, 60
Eurobarometer, 5
extreme right parties, *see* right-wing
  populist parties

Falter, Jürgen, 156
far right parties, *see* right-wing
  populist parties
Figl, Leopold, 105, 106
Fischer, Heinz, 112
Fischer, Joschka, 59, 92
Fortuyn, Pim, 208–209
foundation myths, 17
FPÖ, *see* Austrian Freedom Party
frame(s), 1, 34–35; in Austria,
  120–125; contrition, 10, 20, 51, 65,
  72, 77, 79–81; in
  Germany, 64–77; new victim, 10,
  102, 120–125; normalization, 10,
  51, 65, 77; victim, 21, 22, 103–109,
  128–130, 135
framing, 30, 67, 124
Frankfurter Allgemeine Zeitung
  (FAZ), 44, 67, 71, 75–77, 91, 171
Frankfurter Rundschau, 67, 71–72
Frankfurt School, 58
Free Democratic Party (FDP), 47,
  171–174
Friedrich, Jörg, 203
Frischenschlager, Friedhelm, 178–181,
  182

Gauweiler, Peter, 90
Geissler, Heiner, 164, 173
generational change, 79; in Austria,
  143; in Germany, 97–98
Georgen, Fritz, 173
German Democratic Republic (GDR),
  11; narrative of Nazi past, 43, 198,
  199
German expellees, *see* die Vertriebenen
Givens, Terri, 151

For EU product safety concerns, contact us at Calle de José Abascal, 56–1°, 28003 Madrid, Spain or eugpsr@cambridge.org.

www.ingramcontent.com/pod-product-compliance
Ingram Content Group UK Ltd.
Pitfield, Milton Keynes, MK11 3LW, UK
UKHW010041140625
459647UK00012BA/1532